REBUILDING EXPERTISE

Rebuilding Expertise

Creating Effective and Trustworthy Regulation
in an Age of Doubt

William D. Araiza

NEW YORK UNIVERSITY PRESS
New York

NEW YORK UNIVERSITY PRESS
New York
www.nyupress.org

References to Internet websites (URLs) were accurate at the time of writing. Neither the author nor New York University Press is responsible for URLs that may have expired or changed since the manuscript was prepared.

Library of Congress Cataloging-in-Publication Data
Names: Araiza, William D., author.
Title: Rebuilding expertise : creating effective and trustworthy regulation
in an age of doubt / William D. Araiza.
Description: New York : New York University, [2022] |
Includes bibliographical references and index.
Identifiers: LCCN 2021039795 | ISBN 9781479812288 (hardback) |
ISBN 9781479812295 (ebook) | ISBN 9781479812318 (ebook other)
Subjects: LCSH: Administrative law—United States—Decision making. | Policy scientists—
Legal status, laws, etc.—United States | Expertise—Political aspects—United States. |
Public administration—United States—Public opinion.
Classification: LCC KF5402 .A889 2022 | DDC 342.73/06—dc23
LC record available at https://lccn.loc.gov/2021039795

New York University Press books are printed on acid-free paper, and their binding materials are chosen for strength and durability. We strive to use environmentally responsible suppliers and materials to the greatest extent possible in publishing our books.

Manufactured in the United States of America

10 9 8 7 6 5 4 3 2 1

Also available as an ebook

To Stephen

CONTENTS

List of Abbreviations   ix

Introduction: From the Sea of Tranquility to Desert One   1

PART I: YOU ARE HERE   19

  1. The Great Transition   21

  2. Political, Doctrinal, and Bureaucratic Changes   29

  3. Politicization Consolidated   48

PART II: A FRAMEWORK FOR EXPERTISE   71

  4. A Call to Congress   73

  5. Curbing Political Control   89

  6. Relationships within the Agency   116

  7. Judicial Review   136

PART III: INFORMATION, CAPACITY, AND ENGAGEMENT   163

  8. Protecting Informational Integrity   165

  9. Nurturing and Protecting the Bureaucracy   182

  10. Rebuilding Trust   207

  Conclusion: The Return of the Elephant   231

Acknowledgments   235

Notes   237

Bibliography   277

Index   293

About the Author   305

LIST OF ABBREVIATIONS

ACA: Affordable Care Act

ACUS: Administrative Conference of the United States

ANPR: Advance Notice of Proposed Rulemaking

APA: Administrative Procedure Act

CBA: Cost-Benefit Analysis

CFPB: Consumer Financial Protection Bureau

CRD: Civil Rights Division (Department of Justice)

DHS: Department of Homeland Security

DOI: Department of the Interior

DOJ: Department of Justice

DOT: Department of Transportation

EPA: Environmental Protection Agency

FCC: Federal Communications Commission

FDA: Food and Drug Administration

FEMA: Federal Emergency Management Agency

FNS: Food and Nutrition Service (Department of Agriculture)

FWS: Fish and Wildlife Service (Department of the Interior)

IG: Inspector General (Agency-Specific)

IRS: Internal Revenue Service

NASA: National Aeronautics and Space Administration

NOAA: National Oceanic and Atmospheric Administration (Department of Commerce)

NHTSA: National Highway Transportation Safety Administration

NLRB: National Labor Relations Board

NPR: Notice of Proposed Rulemaking

OIRA: Office of Information and Regulatory Affairs

OMB: Office of Management and Budget

OSHA: Occupational Safety and Health Administration

PATCO: Professional Air Traffic Controllers Organization

RARG: Regulatory Analysis Review Group

SEC: Securities and Exchange Commission

SES: Special Executive Service

SORNA: Sexual Offender Registration and Notification Act

USGS: United States Geological Survey

Introduction

From the Sea of Tranquility to Desert One

Two Snapshots—and the Bigger Picture

On July 20, 1969, Americans landed on the moon. An estimated worldwide audience of 650 million persons (20 percent of the planet's population at the time) watched the event on television. For those who witnessed it, it was an extraordinary spectacle watching humans step onto the moon's surface from the landing base in the Sea of Tranquility. Beyond the very idea of humans traveling to another heavenly body, anyone who paused to consider the planning and technology required to achieve that feat—let alone bring the astronauts home safely—could only wonder at America's scientific and technical prowess. The marvel of that technology also inspired confidence in other large-scale government-led initiatives.[1]

On April 24, 1980, eight US military helicopters set out from the USS *Nimitz*, steaming off the coast of Iran, for a staging area deep inside Iran code-named Desert One. The mission was a complex and audacious attempt to rescue the American hostages being held in Teheran by the revolutionary government. Three of those helicopters arrived at Desert One in a disabled condition and, in accordance with a previously agreed-to decision, the rescue mission was aborted. During an intricate refueling maneuver, one of the remaining helicopters collided with a transport aircraft on the ground, causing an explosion and fire. Eight servicemembers died, the evacuating remnant of the team failed to destroy the remaining helicopters and mission plans, and the United States suffered a humiliating blow to its prestige.

It is surely too simple to isolate these two events, which almost perfectly bracket the 1970s, as demarcating the deterioration of American expertise, the decline of Americans' trust in that expertise, or some combination thereof. On the date of the moon landing, the nation was more deeply entangled than ever in an ultimately lost war in Vietnam—a war initially prosecuted by "whiz kid" technocratic elites populating the highest reaches of the Kennedy and Johnson administrations.[2] In that same year, the nation was convulsed by the protests and violence of the late 1960s. For its part, the Iran rescue mission failed because of flaws specific to that plan, as well as simple, tragically bad luck on the ground.

Still, when one contextualizes those events, a broader narrative emerges. In 1971, President Nixon declared war on cancer, launching a scientific research program that promised to eradicate or at least blunt the impact of that feared disease. In the years bracketing 1971, he also signed far-reaching environmental laws that promised to clean the air and water, protect endangered species, and minimize government action that adversely affected the environment. None of these initiatives would have been viable a decade later.[3] Indeed, the same year as the hostage rescue attempt, a president was elected who insisted that government was not the solution to our problems, but rather, *was* the problem. Eight months before the moon landing, a Pew poll found that 62 percent of Americans trusted the government all or most of the time. One month before the hostage rescue attempt, that figure had inverted, to 26 percent.[4]

These two vignettes, and the developments that surrounded them and give them larger meaning, illuminate the issue this book will examine. As they suggest, that issue encompasses both the decline of expertise in American government and the public's perception of that decline. These ideas are, of course, related. Most notably, declines in actual expertise influence public perceptions of that expertise.[5] But the relationship can also run in the opposite direction: Declining public trust in the government can fuel calls to deemphasize or even abandon it, thus starving it of both resources and administrative autonomy and thereby setting the stage for actual failure. This book's diagnoses and prescriptions will engage both these phenomena. In support of that effort, the book begins by stating that it will consider the causes and consequences of *both* the actual decline of administrative expertise and the public's perception of that decline. As stated above, these two phenomena are related. Thus, repairing one requires repairing the other.

The Scope of the Problem

Before grabbing our diagnostic and repair tools, we should first make sure we have a problem. Indeed, one perspective insists that the problem, if it does exist, is exaggerated. First, the reality: Some evidence suggests that the expertise of the federal government remains as vibrant as ever. When armed with the tools the Clean Air Act and the Clean Water Act provided it, the federal government has accomplished an extraordinary feat: It has actually made major progress in cleaning the nation's air and water.[6] Airplane accidents have declined precipitously. Consumer products are safer. Life expectancy has risen. Concede that private innovation played a significant role in these advances; nevertheless, so did government regulation. Across a broad range of regulatory areas, America's bureaucrats have succeeded. Not always and everywhere (of course). But not never, either—not by a long shot. Even the government's otherwise highly problematic response to the COVID-19 pandemic had its bright spots: With the help of generous federal financing and fast-tracked approval procedures, highly effective vaccines were developed in record time and by the spring of 2021 were being quickly and widely distributed.

But what about perceptions? That question requires some untangling. It's hard to deny that surveys reflect a deep distrust in government. Nevertheless, one should be careful to distinguish between trust in political institutions and trust in regulatory ones. When Americans think of "the federal government," they usually think of the former. In our politically polarized era, it may be unsurprising that Americans' trust in "the federal government" is not particularly high, since it is likely that approximately half of the nation will dislike the political leaders that represent, in their minds, "the federal government." But polarization is only part of the story. That phenomenon was not particularly salient in the 1970s, yet, as noted earlier, trust in the federal government plummeted during that period. Chapter 1 will explore the reasons, but anyone familiar with that decade will intuit some of them—Vietnam, Watergate, and economic stagflation.

How about administrative agencies? Scholars have suggested that low levels of public knowledge about agencies might cause them to suffer declines in trust when the public comes to distrust government institutions more generally, as a halo effect, or more colloquially, a case of guilt by association.[7] On the other hand, Paul Verkuil, a prominent scholar of the bureaucracy, has written that the public is "remarkably discerning in evaluating agency performance."[8] He cites a 2015 Pew survey of public attitudes toward seventeen federal agencies that found the Postal Service and the National Park Service to have the highest favorability ratings. He attributes those high ratings to Americans' familiarity with them. On the other hand, the lowest scores were earned by two agencies with whom many Americans are also familiar—the IRS and the Department of Veterans Affairs. Perhaps we can enrich his hypothesis about familiarity to account for the circumstances of such familiarity—positive (as with the Park Service) or negative (as with the IRS).

But what about all the agencies in the middle—the ones with which Americans do not normally have personal contact? That question suggests a different way to think about the trust issue: To what extent do we place our lives and our welfare in the hands of federal agencies? Quite a lot, it turns out. We get on airplanes. We drink tap water—even after incidents such as the one in Flint, Michigan, although such incidents may well cause lower trust in particular communities.[9] We buy stocks.

To be sure, some of this trust may flow from trust in other sources (airplane manufacturers, local water authorities, or our own self-confidence in our stock picking). But if we really thought that the airplane parked at the gate might well fall from the sky, or that our tap water might poison us, or that the stock we are trading is a worthless icon on a day trader's computer screen, we presumably wouldn't engage in those activities so readily. Indeed, by early 2021, even with all the missteps that attended the federal government's COVID-19 response, increasing majorities of Americans were expressing confidence in the vaccines' safety.[10] Americans seem to put their lives, health, and fortunes in the federal government's care, and to do so without a lot of worry.

Despite these encouraging signals, it is hard to deny that the problem of distrust in government is real. Regulatory challenges, from climate change to Internet governance to opioid abuse and income inequality, continue to pile up. Front pages report regulatory failures—indeed, in areas that had been bright spots, such as airplane and drinking water safety (remember, respectively, the Boeing 737-MAX and Flint). With these issues come the inevitable challenges to public trust in the bureaucracy: Whatever one thinks about the public's perceived connection between regulators and political leaders, one would be hard-pressed to conclude that, over the last twenty years, public attitudes toward the former have improved. And who could blame them, when one considers the events of those years: the 9/11 attacks, the 2008 financial meltdown, the increasing (and increasingly obvious) severity of both the climate crisis and rising income inequality, the COVID-19 pandemic, and, at the local level, well-publicized police misconduct?

Obviously, it is unfair to lay these failures and challenges solely at the feet of the bureaucratic apparatus. Political leaders control that apparatus: If they act incompetently, selfishly, or even maliciously, one can understand how the effects would trickle down to the bureaucracy's performance and, ultimately, to the public's perception of the bureaucracy. (Indeed, those political leaders might aim directly at the public's perception of the bureaucracy, as various Trump administration officials did when attacking what they called "the deep state.") But this observation just reinforces the point that, when diagnosing and prescribing fixes for the decline of regulatory expertise, we must cast our gaze beyond the bureaucracy itself.

What Is Expertise?

Before casting that gaze, though, we need to clarify our terms, starting with "expertise." We might think we know what that means. Indeed, the story this introduction has told, of a decline in the reality and perception of government expertise since the 1960s, might seem a well-understood tale, which implies that the phenomenon—expertise—is similarly well-understood. But expertise is a concept that requires some unpacking.

Start with a basic object of expertise: science. This book will talk a lot about "science," "scientists," and "scientific (or technical) expertise." Before we talk about expertise, it is important to recognize that this book defines "science" broadly, to go beyond what we might normally envision when we think about that term—white coats and microscopes and laboratories. It includes that, but also much more. Consider the Environmental Protection Agency's Scientific Integrity Policy—the agency's statement of its norms and standards for protecting the integrity of the "science" it conducts. It states that:

> "science" and "scientific" are expansive terms that refer to the full spectrum of scientific endeavors, e.g., basic science, applied science, engineering, technology, economics, social sciences, and statistics. The term "scientist" refers to anyone who collects, generates, uses, or evaluates scientific data, analyses, or products.[11]

This definition helps sharpen our focus on the scientific process and the expertise it generates. Consider it again. It states that "science . . . refer[s] to the full spectrum of scientific endeavors, e.g., basic science, applied science, engineering, technology, economics, social sciences, and statistics." Thus, when this book speaks of "science," it includes the person wearing the white coat looking through a microscope in the laboratory. But it also includes the economist at the Securities and Exchange Commission who studies capital markets and the engineer at the National Highway Transportation Safety Administration who studies how crash test dummies respond to different types of automobile collisions. It's a broad definition, especially given the myriad ways scientific knowledge interacts with agencies' missions. For example, the National Oceanic and Atmospheric Administration (NOAA) uses social scientists to determine what types of severe weather warnings will resonate and convince persons to seek shelter. Behavioral psychology is now part of NOAA science.[12]

Now consider the "expertise" that arises from that "science." Think of expertise and, logically enough, one likely thinks of experts—probably scientists, now broadly defined as explained immediately above. Think of *government* expertise, and one likely expands one's vision to include both scientists and bureaucrats. Why? Probably, you say, because experts know how to get things done and bureaucrats are also supposed to know how to get things done. Much wisdom resides in that answer—but ambiguity, also.

The first piece of wisdom is that expertise reflects the ability to *do* things—to build the Hubble Telescope or a predictive model for the climate. It does not simply reflect knowledge of astronomy or meteorology. Sociologists who study expertise call this practical type of expertise "contributory expertise." Two sociologists, Harry Collins and Robert Evans, in turn coined the term "interactional expertise" to connote knowledge about those topics sufficient to engage in a meaningful dialogue with those who have contributory expertise.[13] One can have such interactional expertise even if one doesn't have contributory expertise— think of a sophisticated science journalist, who may not know how to build a telescope or climate model but can intelligently talk astronomy or meteorology with persons who do. But contributory expertise does presuppose interactional expertise—one cannot build a telescope or a climate model unless one is able to engage in conversation about astronomy or meteorology.[14]

This distinction between contributory and interactional expertise suggests that expertise in the actual act of regulating requires more than "book knowledge," or what Collins and Evans call interactional expertise. After all, regulating is an activity, just like building a telescope or a scientific model. It thus requires more than theoretical knowledge about either the subject matter of the regulation or the regulatory process itself. Instead, one gains such practical—contributory—expertise by experience: For example, one becomes an expert in regulating by actually performing regulatory activities. For that reason, such expertise, especially in skills such as regulating, becomes quasi-instinctual.

Here are two examples of such quasi-instinctual expertise. First, consider Hubert and Stuart Dreyfuses' explication of a five-stage process of gaining expertise in driving a car with a manual transmission. Early stages, reflecting book- (or instructor-) learned rules (for example, "shift from second to third gear at 20 miles per hour"), yield a jerky ride with the driver rigidly following absolute rules about when to shift gears and how to work the clutch. (Anyone who learned how to drive a stick shift will get the idea.) By contrast, the final stage, called expertise, is a situation where:

> complete contexts are unselfconsciously recognized and performance is related to them in a fluid way using cues that it is impossible to articulate and that if articulated would usually not correspond, or might even contradict, the rules explained to novices.[15]

That may be a bit abstract, so consider how another scholar, Gil Eyal, describes the most advanced-stage expertise of a plumber, called to investigate a water leak, who tells the homeowner that the problem is a cracked pipe:

When I ask the plumber how he knows that the pipe needs to be replaced, he mutters something about how in three out of four cases it is always the pipe that needs to be replaced, and how the pipe "sounds" cracked. He invites me to listen. I hear nothing, but he gives me a look that plainly says, "keep to what you know best, Professor, and leave the pipes to me."[16]

Map these insights onto the subject of this book. With regard to regulation, the relevant expertise is contributory, not merely interactional, since this book's subject is how bureaucrats actually perform the task of regulating. Interactional expertise is necessary: As noted above, one cannot have contributory expertise—the ability to perform a task—without also having interactional expertise—the ability to talk about the task intelligently. But performing regulation requires more than simply knowing about it. Like Eyal's plumber who "just knows" that the pipe "sounds" cracked, or the Dreyfuses' expert driver who "just knows" when the transmission is ready to be upshifted, regulators "just know" how to regulate.

But what does it mean to "just know" how to regulate? Or, to restate the question, what does it mean to *perform* regulation with the requisite (contributory) expertise? Using the insights above, it should be clear that the task requires more than theoretical knowledge—either of the agency's subject matter (space exploration, the environment, or capital markets) or of regulation as its own science (as one might learn, for example, in a public policy graduate program). Such knowledge is indispensable, but insufficient.

Sidney Shapiro, a scholar of administrative law, has written with great insight on this issue. He explains the type of expertise regulatory professionals develop:

[A]gency professionals (and some nonprofessionals) develop expertise in reconciling and accounting for conflicting evidence and arguments, disciplinary perspectives, political demands, and legal commands. This expertise is a "craft" form of expertise because it is learned more from experience than from formal knowledge and because it is beyond the disciplinary training of individual professionals. This decision-making expertise is the institutional expertise of agencies; it is the unique wisdom of a regulatory agency.[17]

Thus, regulation—of the environment or capital markets or anything else—involves more than simply applying book knowledge to a regulatory problem. Indeed, it involves more than simply applying what one might very roughly call "book knowledge" *about regulating*. We can analogize such book knowledge to what another administrative law scholar, Thomas McGarity, calls "comprehensive analytical rationality." Such rationality provides a rule book for how to respond to a regulatory problem. He explains the components of this type of rationality:

> The term "comprehensive" suggests that this kind of thinking ideally explores all possible routes to the solution of a problem. The term "analytical" implies that it attempts to sort out, break down, and analyze (quantitatively, if possible) all of the relevant components of a problem and its possible solutions. The term "rationality" captures the pride that its proponents take in its objectivity and . . . dispassion.[18]

By contrast, the sort of expertise Shapiro (and McGarity) extol involves practical wisdom, which encompasses "reconciling and accounting for conflicting evidence and arguments, disciplinary perspectives, political demands, and legal commands."[19] To be sure, performing those functions requires that regulators understand the various specialties whose insights go into that reconciliation process. For example, an EPA regulator may not be able to build a meteorological model, but if she is drafting an air pollution regulation she must be able to converse with meteorologists—that is, she must have interactional expertise about meteorology. But her expertise must go beyond that, to encompass expertise—both interactional and contributory—about the actual craft of regulating.[20]

Because that latter "regulatory expertise" is practical, and is based on actually performing regulation rather than theorizing about it, it recognizes the necessity of compromising and satisficing rather than maximizing. As McGarity describes it, this sort of regulatory rationality

> is a rationality built on a unique understanding of the regulatory universe that is born out of frustrating hands-on experience with unanswerable questions of extraordinary complexity. It is, in a sense, a "second best" rationality that recognizes the limitations that inadequate data, unquan-

tifiable values, mixed societal goals, and political realities place on the capacity of structured rational thinking, and it does the best that it can with what it has.[21]

One can perceive the connections between McGarity's description, with its emphasis on experience, second-best compromises, and awareness of the reality of limited resources, and Shapiro's focus on reconciling conflicting imperatives based on the regulator's experience.

Let's take stock and consider how far we've gone from our initial insight, at the start of this section, that "experts know how to get things done." What we've done since stating that seemingly simple phrase is flesh out what those "things" are (they're regulatory outputs, not simply new learning about astronomy or climate or anything else), and how those things (outputs) are "done" or accomplished (through the use of the craft know-how also described as contributory expertise). We have also made clear that that act of "doing"—that is, the act of regulating—is quasi-instinctive rather than formally rule-bound. It's the difference between an expert (the correct word) driver who knows from the feel of the car when it's time to shift from second to third gear and an amateur who mechanically shifts the transmission exactly when the car reaches 20 miles per hour.

This is the sort of expertise that this book calls "regulatory expertise," the rebuilding of which constitutes this book's project. The character of that expertise—its "craft" or contributory nature, as this section has described it—will be crucial to our analysis of how it declined and what it will take to rebuild it.

What Agencies Do—and What This Book Will Examine

This book will examine the process of agency regulation to uncover its relationship to the expertise the previous section described. But the concept of "regulation" itself requires a brief mention. One might think that that concept is more or less self-defining; quite literally, regulation is what agencies do. That's correct, but that definition requires a caveat, at least for this book's purposes.

Agencies do indeed "do" regulation. But they "do" it in many different ways. They promulgate rules of conduct (literal "regulations") and enforce them in courts, which can themselves be agency entities or traditional federal courts. In the course of performing this work, they also perform a wide variety of other tasks—everything from monitoring compliance, to studying issues, communicating with stakeholder groups, and much more. This book studies only one sliver of these "regulatory" activities—the act of promulgating regulations.

Why limit the book in this way? Simply put, space. Agency actions are too variegated and, within each area, too intricate to study without turning this book into a treatise. Still, this coverage decision is consciously made. Decisions to promulgate regulations tend to be an agency's most important and prominent decisions. This is not always the case: For example, an SEC prosecution of a Wall Street financier for stock manipulation can be front-page news. But as a general matter, that statement holds up. More important, the process by which agencies promulgate regulations illustrates very well the themes of expertise and trust running through the book. For similar reasons, this book limits itself to federal, not state, regulation, although it occasionally references state government examples.

Does this focus distort the book's analysis? Somewhat. But not too much: Basic questions of regulatory expertise, and public trust in that expertise, apply to all arenas in which agencies act. But when diagnosing those issues, a deeper look at one thing agencies do (promulgating regulations) allows readers to learn more about what agencies do more generally ("regulate"), especially when that one thing illustrates those general themes so well. Regardless, as you work your way through this book, keep in mind that, for the most part, it will focus on that one sliver of agency conduct. It's not quite just the tip of the iceberg—it's a big part of it, even if not all of it. However, the hope is that this limited focus will assist the reader in learning about the qualities of the ice more generally.

Expertise and Politics

One further point needs mentioning before we plot our plan of attack. The task of rebuilding administrative expertise assumes that expertise has played too small a role in regulation in recent years. That assumption is correct; expertise *has* played too small a role. But this book's goal is not to elevate expertise to a dominant position in regulation. The work of regulating is the work of government. Government, in turn, requires a popular mandate for it to be legitimate. (At least it does in a democracy.) Thus, regulation requires a democratic mandate.

That mandate cannot come only from unelected experts. Chapter 10, the last chapter, will suggest that experts and expertise can in fact promote democratic legitimacy, but even that chapter concedes that they can't do the entire job. Indeed, two scholars have noted what they described as "the tendency among watchdogs to overemphasize the role that science should play in the federal policymaking process."[22] That overemphasis is a risk because regulatory decisions are, at base, political decisions. In addition to science, political values also matter. In December 2020, *New York Times* columnist Ross Douthat, in a column arguing that we can't always just "trust the science," observed that moral, legal, and political assumptions lurk in even technocratic-sounding questions such as the timeline for making COVID-19 vaccines available.[23] This book shorthands those assumptions as "political" (because they reflect values).

A foundational assumption of this book is that politics and expertise both have a role to play in effective regulation. Finding the right roles for each, and balancing the one against the other, pose tricky questions. Answering those questions is this book's aspiration.

The Plan of the Book

This book proceeds in three parts. Part I, "You Are Here," examines how we got to our current place—a place marked by significant concerns about the reality and public perception of bureaucratic expertise. Chapter 1 sets the historical context by explaining how changes in American society in the 1970s created the conditions for both the public and political actors to question that expertise. Those conditions did not arise from a sudden collapse in government competence. Nevertheless, the fallout from mistakes the government made and new challenges the nation faced created an atmosphere that President Carter in 1979 described as a national "crisis of confidence." Chapter 1 sets the stage for our story by explaining what made Americans feel like something was wrong with their government.

Chapter 2 explains how the political leaders who came to power in 1980 responded. 1980 witnessed the landslide election of Ronald Reagan, reprised even more emphatically four years later. Reagan was more than a successful candidate; he was a transformational president, the first since Franklin Roosevelt to question foundational aspects of the New Deal. Domestically, he blamed the malaise afflicting the nation on over-burdensome regulation, and he promised to recreate a vibrant economy by unharnessing American business.

To achieve that goal, Reagan and his advisors were convinced that they had to seize hold of the bureaucracy. One of his most lasting innovations was an executive order mandating that important administrative regulations be submitted to a White House office for review to ensure that they satisfied cost-benefit criteria. The impact of White House regulatory review has been widely debated, but one consequence is clear: Federal regulation became more closely associated with the incumbent presidential administration than at any time since perhaps the New Deal. That development was assisted by both careful vetting of presidential appointments to high-ranking agency positions and evolving judicial doctrine that extolled presidential control of the administrative apparatus. Chapter 2 tells the story of how the bureaucracy became politicized.

Chapter 3 continues the narrative into the 1990s and beyond. Bill Clinton, the first Democratic president in a dozen years, reversed many Reagan-era policies. But he continued the practice of regulatory review. He also accelerated another Reagan-era trend, toward outsourcing regulatory functions to private contractors. Moreover, he went beyond his Republican predecessors by associating himself publicly with particular regulatory initiatives to a degree previously unseen. Subsequently labeled "presidential administration," this phenomenon further politicized regulation and regulators.[24]

Chapter 3 will also explain how the George W. Bush and Obama administrations built on the Clinton example and those of its Republican predecessors. But with Clinton, the pattern had been set: Given their embrace by a Democratic administration, the Reagan era's deregulatory orientation, politicization of regulation, and deemphasis on civil service expertise had all been consolidated. As chapter 3 explains, judicial doctrine also continued to evolve in directions more favorable to presidential assertions of control over the bureaucracy.

And then there was Trump. Donald Trump was the first successful candidate in at least a century, and probably longer, to ascend to the presidency while lacking both deep connections to his party's establishment and experience governing. The results were (unsurprisingly) bad, at least from the perspective of expert federal regulation of serious national issues. Perhaps most notably, both the administration's rhetoric and its results exacerbated the preexisting phenomena that were already causing deterioration in the reality and public perception of administrative expertise.

Chapter 3 concludes by turning the lens toward Americans' attitudes toward expertise. It examines communication and broader social trends over the last generation—everything from talk radio and social media to a culture in which every person considers himself an expert—that cumulatively further created conditions for a decline in trust in bureaucratic expertise.

The upshot of this wide-ranging chapter is that our current situation is marked by skepticism about regulation and the civil service that would normally implement it, a presidentialist mode of governing that deemphasizes the role of an autonomous expert bureaucracy, and judicial doctrine that is generally favorable to claims of such presidential power. It's not a good prognosis for the rebirth of expert regulation, embraced as legitimate by the American people.

Part II, "A Framework for Expertise," begins to consider the appropriate treatment, by examining the proper relationship between federal agencies and the federal government's other major institutional players. It begins, in chapter 4, by considering an intuitive solution to the picture chapter 3 presented, of politicized regulation powered by aggressive White House interference in the regulatory process. That solution entails making Congress responsible for making the fundamental value judgments that accompany any regulatory program. The idea is that such a mandate to Congress—whether accomplished via constitutional analysis or statutory interpretation—would depoliticize regulation by ensuring that Congress, not agencies, make the value choices that underlie regulation. After evaluating both the constitutional and statutory paths to such a result, however, chapter 4 concludes that, for better or worse, they are simply not viable. We will need to look somewhere else to revive bureaucratic expertise and the public's trust in it.

Chapter 5 looks at the other source of regulatory politicization—the rise, since at least Reagan, of White House control of agency action. Chapter 5 considers both Reagan-style regulatory review and Clinton-style personal involvement in regulation, and finds them both problematic. That's not because the president has no legitimate role in overseeing the bureaucracy—he does. But chapter 5 concludes that increased presidential influence over the last generation has unsettled the balance between, on the one hand, the imperative that a democratically accountable president enjoy some influence over regulatory outputs and, on the other hand, the need to preserve space for autonomous agency expertise. Chapter 5 concludes by noting, and critiquing, yet another vehicle for presidential control that has become more prominent in recent decades—the explosion in the number of political appointees presidents can place inside agencies.

Chapter 5's takeaway is simple. Presidential influence over the bureaucracy is legitimate and, indeed, necessary. But far more of such influence exists than is necessary for democratic accountability or healthy for any robust conception of bureaucratic expertise.

Chapter 6 shifts the focus from 1600 Pennsylvania Avenue to the agencies' headquarters buildings. It examines—from a bird's eye view, to be sure—agencies' internal processes for developing regulations. It performs that examination with the same goal as chapter 5's exploration of White House review: to determine the appropriate balance between presidential control (now, via his political appointees within agencies) and career agency bureaucracies. Chapter 6 concludes that that balance requires that career experts both enjoy relative freedom to develop relevant scientific information and be included in all stages of the agency's subsequent process of deliberating on that information to make regulatory choices. But it also concludes that, at the end of that process, the agency's political leadership must have the discretion to make the final regulatory decision, even if that means the decision ends up heavily influenced by political considerations. Chapter 6 ends by considering legal and structural protections for the sort of autonomy and participation rights this chapter urges career agency experts be given.

Chapter 7 turns to the courts, to consider the appropriate review they should accord agency action when a plaintiff challenges it. It recommends that courts focus their scrutiny so as to incentivize agencies to institute and implement the sorts of decisional structures chapter 6 set forth. In other words, it argues that courts should attempt to guarantee that agencies make the structural changes chapter 6 suggested. Chapter 7 has good news and bad news for this argument. The good news is that, while it requires some recalibration of current approaches to judicial review of agency action, the changes are not major. The bad news is that this proposed approach to judicial review will not magically solve the problem. Other fronts will need to be opened to win the war for expertise.

Part III, "Information, Capacity, and Engagement," ends the book by reconsidering the work of agencies. Its three chapters reflect the three concepts in its title. Chapter 8 considers one of those additional fronts in the war for expertise: information. As one might guess, information, as well as the ability to generate it and disseminate it without distortion, is critical to regulatory expertise. Chapter 8 considers the proper roles of career experts and political leaders in managing scientific information. It argues that those experts should enjoy wide autonomy to generate information, recognizing that political leaders' decisions to embark on particular regulatory projects will necessarily frame the information-gathering experts should then be free to perform. Chapter 8 also insists that those political leaders should have no authority to distort or edit the information thus generated. It concludes by acknowledging, as chapter 6 did, a role—albeit a limited one—for those leaders' discretion, in this case, discretion to restrict dissemination of that information.

Chapter 9 considers—finally—the actual experts we're talking about. If judicial review is insufficient to ensure that political leaders create structures that appropriately respect agency expertise, much of the gap must be filled by a robust and empowered bureaucracy itself. Chapter 9 considers the state of that bureaucracy. After briefly recounting the historical rise of an expert, apolitical federal bureaucracy, it then traces its deterioration. The story of that deterioration focuses heavily on the practice of outsourcing bureaucratic work. As chapter 9 explains, such outsourcing, while it has its place, has been seriously overused, causing the withering of career civil service expertise. Chapter 9 offers a prescription for distinguishing between functions that may and should not be outsourced. It concludes by considering the bureaucracy's material circumstances—its numbers, compensation, and working conditions—that must be addressed if the nation is to rebuild a robust and capable expert bureaucracy.

Chapter 10, the book's last substantive chapter, returns to the topic that animated chapter 1, and, really, this entire book—the public's trust in the bureaucracy. All of this book's prescriptions will be futile if the American public remains skeptical of its bureaucracy. To be sure, the improved performance those earlier chapters aim to encourage will help rebuild public trust. But chapter 10 focuses on how agencies can directly improve the picture by engaging with the American people. The suggestions it offers are more than public relations exercises. Because regulation affects Americans, they have their *own* unique expertise about regulatory choices. If agencies meaningfully engage with the citizenry, they will not only improve their standing with them, but will also gain knowledge and perspectives that will improve the substance of their regulatory outputs. That result—better regulation—would be beneficial in itself. But it would also create a virtuous circle, in which better substantive performance encourages more public engagement, which further improves that performance and, with luck, increases public support for augmenting regulatory capacity that improves that performance even more.

The book ends by reflecting not just on the difficulty of improving the reality and perception of regulatory expertise, but on the importance of that effort. This is not just a task for bureaucrats. In creating the bureaucracy we need and deserve, we ourselves are the regulators. We should develop some expertise about that task. This book aims to help.

The Elephant in the Room

One more thing before beginning. This book was written during the spring of 2021. During the writing process, the COVID-19 pandemic turned one year old and claimed its 500,000th American life; as it was being edited, that number rose to above 700,000. A reader might well expect a book about administrative expertise to be about—*all about*—the Trump administration's handling of that horror. And indeed, it will come up, several times.

But this book is not only about what happened in 2020. As awful as the administration's handling of the pandemic was—and it *was* awful, although fairness requires recognizing the truly impressive speed with which vaccines were developed—the topic of regulatory expertise is bigger than one administration and one tragedy, even one as crushing as the pandemic. The sad fact is that the deterioration of both the reality and perception of bureaucratic expertise has been a long time in the making. No one administration and no one party owns all of it. As chapter 1 makes clear, this book dates the start of that decline to the 1970s. The exact starting date is unimportant.[25] The critical point is that the phenomenon this book sets out to diagnose, and for which it offers tentative solutions, is a long-term one. One change in presidential administrations will not fix it. But this book is written in the hope that that change can be a start.

PART I

You Are Here

The first three chapters of this book recount the developments that have brought us to our current location—one marked by the over-politicization of regulation and the deemphasis of expertise-based regulation performed by appropriately autonomous, well-resourced administrative agencies. Chapter 1 starts the story by recounting the developments before 1980 that set the stage for what came after. Chapter 2 considers the Reagan administration's actions that accelerated the nation's course toward three closely related phenomena: deregulation, White House control over agencies and the regulations they promulgate, and the outsourcing of regulatory work. Chapter 3 examines how the Clinton administration consolidated, and in some ways extended, those changes and thus set the template for both Democratic and Republican presidents since 2000. That chapter also considers how social, political, and technological changes have increased Americans' distrust of regulatory expertise. Both chapters 2 and 3 consider how, over time, courts began to embrace the sort of regulatory politicization presidents of that era promoted.

Part I thus explains how we have arrived at the predicament for which the rest of the book seeks solutions.

1

The Great Transition

In December 1958, 73 percent of Americans polled stated that they could always or usually trust the federal government to do the right thing. Almost six years later, in October 1964, that number had climbed to 77 percent. Four years later it had fallen to 62 percent, and two years after that, in December 1970, it had fallen again, to 54 percent. While that latter trend certainly reflected a decline, at the start of the 1970s more than half of Americans still expressed the basic level of trust that polling question queried. Almost exactly ten years later, in October 1980, that number had plummeted to 25 percent.[1] Public opinion poll results do not tell the whole story of Americans' attitudes toward the federal government, let alone provide the root causes, and trust in "government" is not the same as trust in "the bureaucracy." Nevertheless, the numbers are remarkable. They compel us to begin our analysis of the decline in the public's trust of federal bureaucratic expertise by asking, simply, "what went wrong?"

The growth in the public's distrust of government, and in turn the successful political attack on the bureaucracy that triggered its subsequent defunding, restricting, and privatizing, arose from a set of independent phenomena and the reactions to them. Those phenomena became particularly prominent in the 1970s, but their groundwork was laid years before.

The Antecedents

The 1960s dawned as the decade of expertise. John F. Kennedy won the presidency with a call to explore a new frontier. He challenged the nation to go to the moon, and he sent the Peace Corps into the developing world. He read Mao and Che Guevara and helped shape the Green Berets into a counter-insurgency force, armed with studies from the Rand Corporation. And he brought the best and the brightest to Washington.

His successor, Lyndon Johnson, continued these initiatives and retained many of the "best and the brightest" President Kennedy had recruited. But he also put his own stamp on the decade by declaring war on poverty and promising, in his 1965 inaugural address, to build what he called a Great Society. These initiatives all emanated from the federal government, which, as the earlier poll reflected, during the early 1960s enjoyed the overwhelming trust of the American people. And why wouldn't it? It had defeated fascism and transitioned Franklin Roosevelt's New Deal into what seemed a limitless future of prosperity based on a rock-solid middle class open, it appeared, to anyone willing to work. What was not to trust?

During this time, anti-regulatory forces were largely muted. By the 1950s the Republican Party, the natural opponent of increased federal regulatory power,[2] had been captured by moderates; their leader for most of that decade, Dwight Eisenhower, stood for a watered-down but still recognizable New Deal. Small government, anti-regulation, anti-federal power forces took control of the party in 1964, nominating Arizona senator Barry Goldwater, but they suffered a crushing defeat.

Nevertheless, even as President Johnson was promising a Great Society and a war on poverty, forces were in motion that would allow anti-regulatory forces eventually to gain ascendancy. The nation became more and more mired in the Vietnam War, generating increasing cynicism about the administration's insistence that it could perceive light at the end of the tunnel. Urban unrest increased the public's anxiety and bolstered arguments that centralized regulation of social life did not necessarily create a better, let alone a great, society. These and other developments led to Republican congressional gains in 1966 and a presidential victory in 1968. Beyond the Democrats' electoral loss, the chaos of the anti-war demonstrations at their Chicago convention and George Wallace's defection as an anti–civil rights candidate illustrated the final collapse of Roosevelt's New Deal coalition. That collapse created opportunities.

Shocks to the System

Still, from the standpoint of the early 1970s, the idea of a sustained attack on federal regulation seemed far-fetched. President Nixon disappointed his more strident supporters when, largely for electoral reasons, he supported the enactment of sweeping environmental laws at the start of the decade. Government programs, such as the space program and health research, did not appear to be at serious risk. Even social welfare programs remained relatively robust, at least until the latter part of the Nixon presidency, by which time his weakened political position made any serious cutbacks unlikely.[3]

Nevertheless, new external shocks added to the stress on the postwar regulatory consensus. The 1973 Arab Oil Embargo and the 1979 Second Oil Shock severely curtailed American economic growth, first by (literally) depriving the economy of fuel and, second, even after the oil began flowing again, by raising energy prices at a fast clip. An ultimately more significant development, the increase in foreign competition arising from the full recovery of European and Asian economies from World War II, also challenged American industries which, until then, had enjoyed a quarter-century of unquestioned global dominance. These phenomena sometimes interacted: It is no coincidence that the 1970s saw the first real threat to the American automobile industry's dominance of the domestic market, as public tastes shifted to fuel-efficient foreign economy cars. Throughout the 1970s, both Republican and Democratic administrations struggled to improve the economy, with at best mixed success.

Phenomena left over from the 1960s also continued to damage Americans' confidence in their nation's institutions. The Vietnam War ended in a humiliating defeat in 1975. That defeat, and the nation's subsequent hesitation about foreign military involvements, appeared to usher in a period of Soviet expansionism in the developing world. The injury to American prestige also coincided with the rise of Communist parties in western European politics; for a time, it appeared that the Italian Communist Party was poised to take a turn leading that nation's government. Domestically, American cities continued to reel from the effects of the mid-decade economic downturn and the white flight that accelerated after the urban unrest of the late 1960s. These developments sometimes arose in close temporal proximity: six months to the day after US helicopters evacuated the nation's embassy in Saigon, President Ford was seen as leading yet another evacuation when he refused federal assistance for New York City's desperate attempt to avoid bankruptcy. The next day, the *Daily News* ran its now-famous headline: "Ford to City: Drop Dead."

Of course, the Watergate scandal also shook Americans' trust in the federal government. That trust had already taken a blow from the government's deceptions during the Vietnam War, especially after the Pentagon Papers were published in 1971. The Watergate revelations in 1973 and 1974, culminating in President Nixon's resignation in August 1974, further damaged the government's credibility; between October 1972 and December 1974, the percentage of Americans who trusted the federal government to do the right thing all or most of the time fell to less than 50 percent. No major poll monitored by the Pew Research Center would again register majority support for that level of trust until immediately after the attacks of September 11, 2001.[4]

Thus, by the middle of the decade the government had suffered blows to both its perceived competence and its good faith, while persistent economic and national pride anxieties plagued the nation. Given that atmosphere, it is not surprising that Americans' opinions of their government institutions suffered.

The Rise of the Anti-Regulation Movement

These developments coincided with attacks on those institutions' regulatory programs. After the 1964 Goldwater debacle, conservative intellectuals and politicians regrouped. By the end of the decade, conservative donors had begun funding think tanks and other centers of intellectual thought that promoted alternatives to New Deal/Great Society orthodoxy. Those answers ranged from flat-out libertarianism to more moderate, incrementalist arguments favoring market-based regulatory approaches.[5] In 1971, a year before his ascension to the US Supreme Court, Lewis Powell wrote a famous memorandum for the US Chamber of Commerce, urging businesses to speak out more forcefully against regulations that he argued were slowly destroying the free enterprise system. He recommended that that campaign include lobbying, founding and funding conservative public interest legal institutions, and insisting that universities present conservative views alongside liberal ones.

Scholars disagree about the impact of the Powell memo.[6] But whatever the impetus, by the mid-1970s conservatives had found their voice.

Think tanks and journals espousing anti-regulatory ideas appeared, and businesses had begun to assert their interests more aggressively, through both lobbying and advertisements directly aimed at the American people.[7] Conservative ideas were beginning to capture the public's attention. Illustrating this trend, in 1980 the Public Broadcasting Service aired *Free to Choose*, a series of discussions of economic issues in which conservative economist Milton Friedman discussed and debated his libertarian views. Tellingly, *Free to Choose* was a response to *The Age of Uncertainty*, an analogous series hosted by a liberal economist, John Kenneth Galbraith. Once again, conservative voices had arisen to challenge liberal ones.

The Political Impact

Those conservative voices influenced political opinion and ultimately government policy. While many regulatory initiatives remained popular,[8] conservative ideas also seemed to grow in popularity. In the West, the first Sagebrush Rebellion attacked federal ownership and control of broad swaths of land.[9] Farther west, in California, anti-tax crusaders succeeded in 1978 in enacting Proposition 13, a landmark limitation on property taxes. In 1976, Ronald Reagan, running for president on an anti-federal regulation, tax-cutting platform, came within a hair of denying an incumbent his party's nomination. The Democratic candidate, Jimmy Carter, accepted his party's 1976 presidential nomination with a speech that sounded anti-regulatory themes.[10] By the end of its term, his administration was embarking on large-scale deregulation of industries, such as trucking and commercial air travel, that had long been subject to federal rate regulation.

The forces calling for these changes crafted a compelling narrative of regulation that was too strict, too onerous, and too destructive of private initiative. One strand of this critique called for replacement of traditional command-and-control environmental regulation[11] with market-based regulation that set a price for pollution and allowed market forces to sort out how polluters responded.[12] A related but potentially more fundamental critique insisted that many regulations, including but not only environmental ones, imposed costs that were not justified by the benefits they bestowed.[13] To be sure, the movement was not all in an anti-regulation direction; for example, Congress enacted major amendments to the Clean Air Act in 1977 and a massive toxic waste site cleanup bill in 1980. In 1974, President Carter's predecessor, Gerald Ford, signed into law a major program regulating corporate pensions.

Nevertheless, anti-regulation critiques were now demanding attention. Conservative politicians and opinion shapers created a narrative in which over-reaching bureaucrats destroyed American industry by imposing stringent regulations that were either unnecessary or, at best, imposed unjustified costs.[14] At their most aggressive, these arguments called for rejecting such regulations. At their more modest or procedural, they called for White House oversight of agency action, to ensure that mission-oriented bureaucrats were not over-regulating. These arguments soon found receptive voices—in a Democratic White House.

The Results before Reagan

By the late 1970s, external economic shocks generated calls for less regulation while conservative intellectual ferment had found success in promoting the idea that regulations ought to be cost-effective. These developments led the Carter administration to deemphasize stringent enforcement of regulatory statutes, especially toward the end of the decade when energy and economic concerns became more urgent.[15] Instead, he emphasized the importance of regulatory cost-benefit analysis. To promote that goal, President Carter issued an executive order requiring agencies to conduct cost-benefit analyses of their proposed regulations.[16] He also created a White House entity, the Regulatory Analysis Review Group (RARG), and tasked it with implementing that order.

Previous presidents going back to at least Nixon had sought to assert some sort of White House–based control over the output of administrative agencies. President Nixon required agencies to submit "significant" proposed regulations to a White House "Quality of Life" Council that then routed them to other agencies for comment on the regulation's economic impact. In addition to continuing that process, President Ford also required agencies to submit "Inflation Impact Statements" as part of their rulemaking process, and convened a separate White House group to analyze those statements and comment on them as part of the regulation's public rulemaking process.[17]

Carter's executive order took a step beyond these previous initiatives, by requiring agencies to generate, for any regulation having an overall impact exceeding $100 million, an analysis of the economic impact of the regulation and any regulatory alternatives. It also required the RARG to select ten to twenty regulations per year during their proposal stage and place them under intensive economic scrutiny, the results of which would be transmitted to the agency and placed on the proposed regulation's rulemaking record. President Carter also proposed a new law, entitled the Reform of Regulation Act, which would have authorized agencies to suspend regulations and engage in regulatory experiments, such as employing economic incentives to reach regulatory goals.[18]

In addition to their practical impact, these moves reflected a rhetorical commitment to smaller government. As President Carter said in 1978, in his second annual report to Congress, "Government cannot solve our problems."[19] Considering the front-page failures of government competence and integrity that dominated the 1970s, it is hardly surprising that the political mood was such that even a Democratic president would express these sentiments.[20] But it wasn't enough. Even though his caution about aggressive federal regulation dated back to his 1976 campaign, his opponent in 1980, Ronald Reagan, nevertheless cast the election in part as a referendum on big government and over-regulation led by an out-of-touch bureaucracy. In mounting those attacks, Reagan used his impressive communication talents, including a willingness to tell out-and-out falsehoods that nevertheless resonated with listeners. For example, Reagan often told a story (apparently not based in fact) about how the Occupational Safety and Health Administration had 144 regulations governing how to climb a ladder.[21]

Thus, by the time Reagan won his overwhelming 1980 victory, the building blocks were in place for an attack on the bureaucracy. Domestic and foreign setbacks shook Americans' faith in government's basic competence and honesty, while growing economic anxieties had eroded Americans' willingness to authorize broad and deep regulation of industry. Conservative intellectuals had developed proposals for introducing cost-benefit analysis into regulatory decision-making, and conservative

opinion leaders broadcast those ideas. In response, the Carter administration had attempted to balance traditional Democratic commitments
to social welfare and environmental protection with concerns about eas-
ing regulatory burdens and ensuring cost-effective regulation. He had
also built on his predecessors' work in institutionalizing White House
review of regulations in pursuit of that goal.

President Reagan would take these moves to the next level.[22]

2

Political, Doctrinal, and Bureaucratic Changes

The 1980s witnessed important changes in federal regulatory policy, the relationship between the White House and federal agencies, judicial doctrine governing administrative law, and the very character of the federal bureaucracy. These changes were closely interrelated. They all impacted both the reality and perception of bureaucratic expertise. While the foundations of these changes were laid in the previous decade and even earlier, the 1980s nevertheless was a decade of significant change.

The 1980 Election

The 1980 election was a watershed. All post-1945 Republican nominees, with the notable (and unsuccessful) exception of Barry Goldwater in 1964, accepted the basics of the New Deal: significant federal regulation of the economy and the provision of a meaningful social safety net. (Indeed, in 1974 President Nixon proposed a health insurance program that partially resembled the Affordable Care Act.) A political manifesto supporting Barry Goldwater's 1964 campaign reflected, if despairingly, this postwar consensus, urging the Republican Party to present Americans with what it called "A Choice Not an Echo."[1] With the exception of that year, however, conservative Republicans could fairly complain that, indeed, all the GOP offered was a faint echo of the New Deal.

In 1980, Ronald Reagan offered a choice. As a governor, public figure, and then presidential candidate, he unapologetically attacked social welfare programs and government regulation of the economy, two of the pillars of the New Deal and the Democratic Party's follow-up programs, especially Lyndon Johnson's Great Society. His attack on government regulation took the form of a philosophical critique of regulation but also an indictment of what he considered bureaucratic overreach in implementing regulatory statutes. Many of his factual claims were shaky: Recall from chapter 1 Reagan's (apparently baseless) claim that the Occupational Safety and Health Administration had promulgated more than one hundred regulations addressing how to climb a ladder.[2] But no matter. His overwhelming victory over Jimmy Carter in the 1980 election and reelection in 1984 ensured that his vision—the "choice" he offered the American people—would dominate federal policy throughout the 1980s. For the bureaucracy, that choice was a fateful one.

Deregulation

Begin with regulatory policy. One pillar of the Reagan administration's domestic policy was economic deregulation. Regulation of economic activity has been a hallmark of American government since colonial times,[3] with the federal government coming to play a more important role in that regulation starting in the late nineteenth century, accelerating during the New Deal era of the 1930s, and continuing in later decades. But by the mid-1970s, energy shocks and increased foreign competition combined to impose significant strains on the US economy, just as Congress had enacted new environmental and safety laws that business interests criticized as drags on economic growth. As chapter 1 recounted, calls grew for deregulation and, if regulation was required, for a greater emphasis on market forces to achieve regulatory goals. Chapter 1 also noted how the Carter administration initiated such moves, for example, by deregulating transportation industries.

The Reagan administration stepped up those initiatives. Regulations were rescinded, others were left under-enforced, and regulatory choices were made with a thumb on the scale of promoting market-based solutions and increasing compliance flexibility for industry.

The ultimate success or failure of this deregulatory program is not directly relevant to this book. What *is* relevant, however, is that program's necessary implications for the administration's relationship to the bureaucracy. Administrative agencies regulate—that's what they do. While an agency can certainly oversee a program of deregulation or market-based regulation, such projects stand in at least some tension with an agency's underlying mission. The tension is especially great when the statutes an agency is charged with implementing implicitly reflect command-and-control regulatory philosophies, mandates to achieve a certain good, such as clean air or safe workplaces—regardless of the cost, or even mandates to regulate up to the point of economic or technical feasibility.[4] (Even more intractable conflicts arise if a statute *explicitly* requires such regulation.) Thus, the fundamentally deregulatory philosophy embraced by the Reagan administration placed it in tension, if not actual conflict, with the orientation of the protective mission-focused career civil servants within the agency.[5]

Such deregulatory moves and the tension they created with the bureaucracy could conceivably have triggered bureaucratic resistance and even attempts to undermine those policies. Interestingly, Professor Marissa Golden's careful study of bureaucrats' attitudes during the 1980s suggests that neither open warfare nor guerilla resistance inevitably marked the civil service's reaction to the Reagan program.[6] Still, deregulatory rhetoric did imply a devaluation of bureaucracy, as the vehicle of a now-disfavored approach to governance. Favoring market-based governance—either by deregulating entirely or shifting to market-based regulatory approaches—inevitably compares bureaucrats unfavorably with market forces. But observers did not have to guess President Reagan's attitude about the bureaucracy. He made it clear in his public statements, ranging from his complaint as a candidate about (non-existent) OSHA ladder regulations to his statement during his first inaugural address that government, rather than being the solution to our problems, *is* our problem.[7] One scholar of the civil service, commenting on the Reagan era, remarked on its "strident antibureaucratic rhetoric that had come to be known as 'bureaucrat bashing.'"[8]

Beyond the rhetoric, this tension made the administration, and many of its political leaders in the agencies, highly suspicious of the career bureaucracy. That suspicion—that federal bureaucrats fundamentally could not be trusted—made it more tempting for the administration to assert increased control over both bureaucrats' work product and bureaucrats themselves. It also led it to search for other people to perform regulation. This chapter now turns to those initiatives.

Regulatory Review

The Reagan administration's most lasting regulatory innovation was its institution of direct White House review of agencies' regulatory output. As chapter 1 recounted, such review had existed to some degree before

1981.[9] But the Reagan administration expanded and institutionalized such review. The resulting increase in presidential control was so attractive to future presidents that, when party control of the White House shifted in 1993, President Clinton surprised many observers by continuing its basics.

The Reagan administration instituted this review primarily by means of Executive Order 12,291, issued less than a month into Reagan's first term.[10] That order required agencies to ensure that their important regulatory actions complied with a set of cost-benefit criteria. While it conceded that such requirements applied only "to the extent permitted by law," the order furnished the basis for several heated disagreements between the White House office charged with performing that review (the Office of Information and Regulatory Affairs, OIRA, housed within the Office of Management and Budget, OMB) and the agencies that had the actual congressional authorization to promulgate the relevant regulations. For example, when reviewing an EPA rule designed to reduce acid rain, OIRA apparently ordered EPA to consider options for requiring smokestacks to be of a certain height even after a court had declared those options unlawful in that very same rulemaking.[11]

Beyond risking such collisions, OIRA regulatory review also raises fundamental questions about the constitutional separation of powers. On the one hand, Article II of the Constitution grants "the executive power" to the president; similarly, it empowers (or admonishes) him to "take Care that the Laws be faithfully executed."[12] Some scholars embrace the "unitary executive" theory, under which those grants of power authorize the president to direct all actions of the bureaucracy's law-enforcing apparatus.[13] Those scholars insist that the president thus enjoys the power, which he can exercise via OIRA if he wishes, to review and, if necessary, alter or rescind regulatory actions taken by administrative agencies (or at least those that are not considered so-called independent agencies).[14] On the other hand, the agencies subject to OIRA review have been created by Congress, and gain their powers to regulate from congressional legislation. Thus, on one theory, those agencies are, literally, agents of Congress, created by it and empowered by it to regulate in particular ways, independent of White House influence.

For now, leave aside this constitutional issue, as difficult and important as it is. (It will reappear later in this chapter and in more detail in chapter 5.) Regulatory review via OIRA has become an ingrained part of the federal administrative landscape, with every administration since Reagan's adopting some form of it.[15] Short of a legal or political revolution, some type of White House regulatory review or coordination appears here to stay. Focus instead on the implications for the federal administrative system of the Reagan order's requirement that agency action satisfy cost-benefit criteria.

Cost-benefit analysis (CBA) is a highly value-laden enterprise. Far from a technocratic exercise of objectively quantifying regulatory costs and benefits and plugging them into an equation, CBA requires fraught value choices. How does one identify a figure for costs and benefits that will not manifest for many years? Does one factor in the likelihood that far-off costs will be mitigated by future inventions or social improvements? More fundamentally, how much should we value future costs and benefits? Do we owe our posterity nothing? Everything?

These questions relate broadly to what is called the discount rate— that is, the rate at which we discount costs or benefits that do not manifest until the future. Selecting that rate is a difficult enterprise—and, more important, involves the sorts of value choices implicit in the above questions. But it is a critical choice. Consider an example. An OSHA draft analysis of the benefits of a workplace safety rule calculated costs from particular types of injuries and losses that were nearly ten times greater than the number that appeared in the final report's analysis. The massive disparity was caused simply by the draft report's failure to use the White House–mandated discount rate. Small wonder that two academics concluded that "[e]xperience has shown that cost-benefit results are generally quite sensitive to the discount rate."[16]

But consider other, equally fraught issues. How can we value goods that are not easily monetizable? What is the value of clean air? The lost productivity of workers who develop respiratory diseases? Their suffering? The suffering of children who are not yet working? The loss of a magnificent view? Do distributional effects count, or do we just assume that, somehow, the political process will redistribute costs and benefits in an equitable fashion, whatever that might mean?

Very quickly, one gets the idea. These are real issues, though. Seemingly reasonable ways of resolving them quickly reveal themselves as problematic. For example, one might think that asking people about their willingness to accept money to run a particular risk is a good way of quantifying that risk. But then consider that the Obama administration, attempting to implement a prison rape prevention law that sought, perhaps bizarrely, to prevent the imposition of "substantial costs" on prisons, tried to square that regulatory circle by monetizing the value of a prevented rape by surveying people's willingness to pay to avoid a sexual assault.[17] Similarly, one would logically think that so-called willingness to pay does not adequately account for losses such as the extinction of a plant or animal species. But is there any better method?[18]

Indeed, the decision to embrace CBA is itself political. It is perfectly legitimate for a legislature to decide that a particular problem is so important that, literally, money is no object when solving it,[19] or that regulation should stretch to the limits of technical or economic feasibility. Much environmental law is cast in these latter terms.[20] Such policies may or may not be smart: Presumably, in deciding that question, one would want information about issues such as the seriousness of the harm in question, the magnitude of the risk of it occurring, the identity of the groups most likely to bear the cost of not eliminating it, the likely cost of bringing the risk down to zero, and the amount of wealth available to throw at the problem. But applying those factors itself involves value choices. CBA simply assumes the appropriateness of the approach it mandates.

None of this suggests that CBA is inherently a sham or, even if pursued in good faith, is incapable of reflecting objectively grounded expertise. For example, EPA and White House staffers during the Reagan administration used CBA to convince their political bosses of the wisdom of eliminating lead in gasoline, a stupendously beneficial public health decision. Nevertheless, two facts remain. First, the performance of CBA requires value choices. Second, the decision to perform CBA itself reflects a value choice.

Given the inevitably political nature of any application of CBA, let alone any decision to even embark on it, the Reagan White House's directive that administrative regulations satisfy cost-benefit criteria inevitably injected a note of politics into regulation. That injection was not necessarily illegitimate: One does not have to embrace the unitary executive theory to believe that presidents have a legitimate interest in at least nudging regulation in the direction the incumbent administration favors. Nevertheless, increased White House involvement in the regulatory process, as reflected in initiatives like Executive Order 12,291, necessarily detracts from a vision of administration in which apolitical career civil servants simply apply statutory mandates to the best of their expert ability.

Of course, that vision never fully corresponded to reality. Regulation always involves political choices, of either the profound sort (whose interests will a regulation favor?) or the more quotidian but still consequential type (how does one quantify costs and benefits when doing so requires making assumptions about discount rates or the magnitude of a risk?). But formal White House review of regulatory action—making the White House the official final stop before a regulation can be promulgated—changed the reality and the perception of administrative action as fundamentally and primarily grounded in expertise. How could it be so grounded, if it had to survive a final examination at 1600 Pennsylvania Avenue, and if that review involved White House evaluation of how the agency performed a task as inherently political as cost-benefit analysis? That perception was only strengthened by the constant deregulatory rhetoric emanating from that same address. In the 1980s, nobody thought that White House review aimed at prodding agencies to *increase* regulation when such an increase was cost-benefit justified. Instead, it was seen—accurately—as another tool in the deregulation toolbox.[21]

Political Vetting

Beyond their rhetoric, probably the bluntest steps Reagan administration officials took to accomplish their deregulatory goals involved emphasizing political loyalty when selecting high-ranking agency officials. Presidents always selected cabinet heads for political reasons. Still, we have come a long way from the Coolidge administration, whose vice president called agency heads "the natural enemies of the President."[22]

Despite that distance, up to the Reagan administration, political criteria were tempered with concern for finding persons who would be both competent managers and independent voices that could advise the president.[23] For example, when Richard Nixon introduced his cabinet to the nation in December 1968, he insisted that he did not want a cabinet of "yes-men," and described each of them as "an independent thinker."[24] While this language might sound like boilerplate, before Reagan, cabinet secretaries were indeed often understood as advocates for the social groups interested in that agency's regulation.[25] For example, Nixon followed this strategy—one that would naturally suggest at least some degree of independence from the president's own political program.[26]

Reagan altered this practice. His appointments to lead domestic regulatory agencies, such as EPA and the Department of the Interior (DOI), strongly reflected his deregulatory goals. Perhaps even more notably, the vetting for sub-cabinet political appointments within agencies focused on similar policy loyalty criteria. A scholar generally favorable to what he called "the administrative presidency" has commented on the importance of such selection criteria to presidential control of the bureaucracy, as well as on the single-mindedness with which Reagan applied them.[27] Since then, such political criteria have played significant roles in each president's selection of his cabinet.

The Reagan administration also increased the sheer number of political appointees below the agency head level. Such appointees had always existed, and during the Eisenhower administration a particular class of political appointees, called "Schedule C," was created to allow the president to install persons of his choosing in key parts of the bureaucracy. While President Carter increased the number of such appointees, a significant expansion came with Reagan, who greatly increased their number in some agencies. Again, the Reagan administration took special care to vet those political appointments for ideological compatibility.[28]

One can understand a president's desire to place politically sympathetic persons in key bureaucratic positions. (Or, at least today, that preference has become second nature in our thinking about how a president selects political appointees.) A crasser and more troubling innovation of the Reagan administration was the attempt to extend that political vetting to holders of positions previously selected for their competence and expertise. For example, early in his presidency, a "hit list" of EPA staffers was created, based on their perceived political leanings. Similar criteria governed the staffing of advisory panels at DOI, the Food and Drug Administration, and the Agriculture Department. In one instance, the Secretary of the Interior sent a list of proposed members of one such panel to the Republican National Committee, with the secretary's selections resting on the RNC's political approval.[29]

To be sure, administrations before Reagan's interfered with bureaucratic decisions and staffing. In one notable example, President Nixon abolished the President's Science Advisory Committee when its members came out against a technology project he championed.[30] But Reagan's systematic and comprehensive political loyalty vetting reflected a newly prominent attempt to undermine apolitical regulatory expertise in support of a political agenda.

Privatization/Outsourcing

So far, this chapter has considered the Reagan administration's deregulation agenda, its imposition of deregulatory pressure on agencies via Executive Order 12,291's cost-benefit mandate, and its seeding of agencies with political appointees committed to that agenda. It has thus moved down from overall policy to pressure on agencies to act in ways consistent with that policy, and, in the last section, infiltration of agency ranks with political appointees committed to that policy. Consider now the administration's influence on the career bureaucracy itself.

Another important legacy of the Reagan administration was its acceptance, as a legitimate tool, of privatization of the functions performed by the federal government. Before considering this idea, we need to be clear about terminology. "Privatization" may mean many things. It may mean selling off state-owned commercial assets, as occurred in the 1980s in the United Kingdom and the 1990s in the former Soviet Union. This sort of privatization was not a major phenomenon in the United States for the simple reason that the US government never nationalized or otherwise came to own significant productive assets. The UK may have nationalized its steel industry (twice, in fact); United States Steel, despite its name, always remained in private hands. Privatization can also entail government providing grants to private entities to provide goods and services, such as subsidized housing and counseling services, that government would otherwise provide.[31] Indeed, it can also entail direct government distribution of vouchers that program beneficiaries could then spend on those goods and services.

Privatization can also mean using private contractors for goods and services necessary or helpful to the government's own functioning. The federal government had long used private contractors for such purposes—think of government purchases of food or office supplies or janitorial services for a federal workplace. But as used here, privatization refers to another part of government's internal functioning. It refers to the privatization of what one might call regulatory services—the services that develop and implement regulatory policy. For clarity, this book refers to this variant of privatization as outsourcing.

Perhaps surprisingly, given its suspicion of the bureaucracy, the Reagan administration did not immediately and aggressively embrace outsourcing. Administrative law scholar Jon Michaels explains this in part as the result of the administration's initial attempts to cut federal regulatory and social programs, without reference to who performed the residual regulation it was content to retain. He argues that only when those attempts collided with Americans' continued attachment to those programs did it turn to outsourcing the regulatory bureaucracy, and even then only tentatively.[32]

Still, something appears to have happened, as another prominent scholar, Paul Verkuil, has stated that "[t]he use of contractors grew significantly during the Reagan Administration."[33] Yet a third scholar concluded that federal spending on outside contractors nearly doubled between 1980 and 1990, with most of that increase occurring by 1986.[34] An interesting contemporaneous nugget is a 1982 Comptroller General report on federal hiring freezes instituted by Presidents Carter and Reagan. That report, and another one it cited, both concluded that at least some agencies coped with those freezes by increasing their use of contractors.[35]

Regardless of the degree to which he actually implemented outsourcing, Reagan laid both the rhetorical and the intellectual ground for it. His deregulatory instincts, emphasis on market solutions to social problems, and criticism of the bureaucracy in particular and "big government" in general, combined to make the outsourcing of regulatory services a viable option for future administrations. Perhaps surprisingly, as chapter 3 explains, that option would be first widely exercised by a Democratic president.

Legal and Judicial Doctrine

The 1980s witnessed a final phenomenon relevant to administrative expertise. Beyond the promotion of deregulatory policy, the increasing intensity of White House oversight of agencies' regulatory output and the displacement of professional bureaucratic staffs by political appointees and (eventually) contractors, the Reagan era also witnessed changes in judicial philosophy and doctrine.[36] Those changes reinforced the legitimacy of presidential claims to control the administrative apparatus. As such, they assisted in politicizing the bureaucracy and deemphasizing expertise.

As alluded to earlier, presidential control of the bureaucracy—and the attendant prominence it gives the president's political preferences in the regulatory process—flows from ideas about the Constitution's allocation of powers. A prominent theory that supports presidential control claims is the so-called unitary executive theory. Also as noted earlier, this theory maintains that Article II of the Constitution, in particular its conferral of "the executive power" on the president and its admonition that he "take Care that the Laws be faithfully executed"[37] gives the president complete or near-complete control over the federal government's law-executing apparatus—that is, the bureaucracy that translates statutory mandates into specific regulations, adjudicates (at least in the first instance) violations of such statutes and regulations, and manages regulatory programs more generally.[38]

The unitary executive theory is potentially far-reaching; taken to its extreme, it would allow presidential control of every decision made by every administrative agency. No White House has ever staked such an aggressive claim. For example, the Reagan administration's regulatory review executive order exempted administrative adjudications, possibly because those decisions are subject to the procedural guarantees of the Fifth Amendment's Due Process Clause—guarantees that would likely be violated by ex parte White House interference. It also exempted rulemakings conducted pursuant to statutorily required formal procedures—perhaps because the Administrative Procedure Act prohibits such ex parte contacts in those procedures.[39] Most important, the Reagan order also exempted rulemakings emanating from so-called independent agencies—agencies whose leaders Congress has immunized from at-will presidential removal.

Thus, Executive Order 12,291 shrank back from the most expansive assertions of unitary presidential authority. Nevertheless, the White House Office of Legal Counsel's opinion affirming the legality of what that order *did* mandate focused heavily on unitary executive-style reasoning.[40] More generally, such reasoning permeated the Reagan Justice Department's legal argumentation in important separation of powers cases in which the president sought to assert control over administrative functions.[41]

The unitary executive theory has major implications for presidential control over the bureaucracy. As implied by the White House lawyers who relied on it when affirming the legality of Executive Order 12,291, that theory justifies presidential control over much of what administrative agencies do, if perhaps not all of it. But even in its more limited form, its implications are startling. Indeed, as one scholar observes, Congress's normal practice of delegating power to an agency, rather than to the president himself, becomes merely advisory if the president has the constitutional authority to direct how that agency implements that delegated power.[42] Just as important, accepting the unitary executive theory calls into question the constitutionality of so-called independent agencies, such as the Federal Reserve Board and the Federal Communications Commission, whose heads Congress has chosen to immunize from at-will presidential dismissal. When one realizes that Congress made that choice largely because it hoped that such independence from political control would allow them to make full use of their expertise, we can understand how adoption or rejection of the unitary executive idea matters for this book's concern about expertise.[43]

Ideas analogous to those animating the unitary executive theory influenced other, sub-constitutional issues also relevant to expertise. Consider *Chevron*. In 1984, in *Chevron USA v. Natural Resources Defense Council*,[44] the Supreme Court attempted to clarify the law regarding the deference, if any, that was owed an agency when it interpreted a statute it was charged with implementing.[45] It concluded that the agency merited no deference when the statutory interpretation issue was clear: That is, when the statute clearly answered the relevant question, a court must simply apply that clear meaning.

More important—and controversial—was what came next. The Court continued that, if the statute does not clearly answer the relevant interpretive question, a court must defer to any reasonable agency interpretation, even if the court would not have selected that interpretation itself. Ever since *Chevron* was decided in 1984, scholars have debated the optimal theoretical foundation for this deference.[46] For our current purposes, what is noteworthy is that "*Chevron* deference" fits neatly with the idea, similar to the one animating the unitary executive theory, that agency action is legitimated by its connection with the president—the only politically accountable figure directly involved in the administrative process. As Justice John Paul Stevens wrote for a unanimous Court in *Chevron*, justifying this deference:

> Judges are not experts in the field, and are not part of either political branch of the Government. Courts must, in some cases, reconcile competing political interests, but not on the basis of the judges' personal policy preferences. In contrast, an agency to which Congress has delegated policy-making responsibilities may, within the limits of that delegation, properly rely upon the incumbent administration's views of wise policy to inform its judgments. While agencies are not directly accountable to the people, the Chief Executive is, and it is entirely appropriate for this political branch of the Government to make such policy choices—resolving the competing interests which Congress itself either inadvertently did not resolve, or intentionally left to be resolved by the agency charged with the administration of the statute in light of everyday realities.[47]

Several justifications for judicial deference surface in this paragraph, including expertise and congressional delegation of the interpretive issue to the agency. Most relevantly for current purposes, the Court also legitimated agencies' choices about how to interpret vague statutes on the ground that the president, who is presumed ultimately to control executive agencies, is politically accountable.[48]

Indeed, this latter, political accountability justification arguably predominated in *Chevron* itself. The interpretive question in *Chevron* was whether a "stationary source" of air pollution meant a particular piece of machinery, such as a smokestack, or an integrated industrial facility, such as a refinery consisting of many smokestacks. That issue was one on which the EPA had flip-flopped over the years, largely (though not completely) in response to changes in presidential administrations. Yet the *Chevron* Court did not criticize the agency for that politically grounded inconsistency—something it might have reasonably done had the judicial deference it called for rested more heavily on notions of expertise.[49] In addition, it is worth noting that *Chevron*'s greatest proponent on the Court—Justice Antonin Scalia—was also a leading proponent of the unitary executive theory.

Chevron's (partial) grounding in the president's political accountability furnishes yet another mechanism by which the president can place his own political stamp on regulations. If "*Chevron* deference" partially rests on the president's political legitimacy to select one regulatory policy over another, then the intellectual/doctrinal path was clear for presidents to assert even greater control over agency action more generally, on the same political accountability ground. Far from a vision in which technical experts housed within largely autonomous agencies enjoyed broad latitude to use their expertise to select appropriate regulations, by the 1980s the nation's political and judicial leaders were beginning a tentative embrace of a vision in which agency action was subject to close presidential oversight that was exercised in order to further the president's political preferences.

In other words, regulation was becoming politicized.

The Dam Holds—Temporarily

To be sure, that last statement is incomplete and partially misleading. In particular, three features of the 1980s legal landscape still pushed back against this politicization, in favor of a more expertise-based approach to regulation. First, despite litigation pressure from the Reagan administration, the Court during this era refused to question the constitutionality of independent agencies—as noted earlier, agencies whose heads Congress has chosen to immunize from unrestricted presidential removal power. In other words, while the president may fire the Secretary of State for a good reason, a bad reason, or no reason at all, he may not fire a leader of an independent agency such as the FCC unless he finds that Congress's condition for such a termination (usually, some form of "good cause") is satisfied.

As one might intuit, independent agencies contradict the strongest versions of the unitary executive theory. For our purposes, the more important point is that their independence limits—although it does not remove entirely—the president's power to control what those agencies do. Independent agencies were especially popular from the late nineteenth century into the fourth decade of the twentieth century. Consistent with its more general faith in the natural and social sciences, that era possessed great faith in technical expertise—to oversimplify, the idea that if smart people were given adequate tools and then left alone, they could solve most any social problem. The unstated assumption, of course, was that social problems were technocratic rather than political in nature.

One can quickly perceive that such faith would lead congressional architects of an agency to insulate its leaders from the political branches, so it could use its expertise free from political interference.[50] And during that early period Congress did just that, creating many independent agencies that have survived into the modern day. Throughout the 1980s, the Reagan Justice Department attempted to limit the constitutional space for such entities, arguing that Article II required the president to have unqualified power to fire their leaders. That effort largely failed at the Supreme Court, most notably in the 1988 case *Morrison v. Olson*, where a seven-to-one majority upheld a statutory limitation on the president's power to fire independent counsels established to investigate White House wrongdoing.[51] Chapter 3 will describe how, in recent years, the drive to limit agency independence has shown signs of succeeding. But during the 1980s, that part of the expertise dam held.

So did another part—one dealing with the breadth of statutory authority Congress could grant agencies. Consider again our congressional architects of a new administrative agency. If they believed in administrative expertise, one would expect them not only to make those agencies independent but also to give them extremely broad mandates. Recall the assumption, widely held during the late nineteenth and early twentieth centuries, that regulatory issues, such as those arising from the new technology of radio broadcasting, posed primarily technocratic rather than political issues. Consider just one such issue: What was the best way to ensure that a community enjoyed maximum diversity of views and formats on radio programs? If one believed that a question like that was primarily technocratic, rather than value-based, then one would expect the architects of the federal radio statute to give the agency a broad regulatory mandate, letting it discover and implement the "best" policies to promote that goal, rather than specifying the details of either those policies or the agency's power to implement them.

Such broad regulatory mandates raised concerns that Congress was not really legislating, in the sense of selecting and enacting meaningful federal policy, but instead was delegating that legislative power to agencies. Throughout American history, claims had arisen that particularly broad federal grants of power to agencies amounted to unconstitutional shunting off, or delegation, of Congress's legislative power to the executive branch. In 1935, for the first (and possibly the only) time,[52] the Court found parts of a federal statute to violate the "non-delegation doctrine." But since then, the Court has given Congress extraordinary leeway to delegate "quasi-legislative" (that is, rulemaking) power to administrative agencies. Subject to other constraints, that leeway allowed agencies to select the policies that they thought best, based on their expert judgment.[53] By the end of the 1980s, the Court had shown only faint signs of restricting Congress's leeway to delegate such broad power to agencies. That part of the expertise dam also held.

But that leeway came at a price for agencies. Once it became clear to judges, scholars, and lawyers that regulation was not solely a matter of applying apolitical expertise, but instead involved value choices, agencies became seen as the venue in which those value choices were made. Ironically, the faith in expertise that justified both those broad delegations during the early part of the century and the Court's unwillingness to strike them down on non-delegation grounds placed agencies in the position of having to make decisions now understood as political. Indeed, recall that *Chevron* recognized that agencies should enjoy significant latitude to interpret vague statutes in part exactly because those interpretive decisions rested partially on policy, and thus were better made by a democratically accountable president, as controller of the agency, than by unelected judges. The recognition that part of what agencies do is make political choices naturally led to calls to allow politicians—most notably, the president himself—to exert greater control over agency action. Chapter 5 will explore the tensions caused by those assertions of presidential control.

That tension appeared in a third and final caveat to the earlier statement that the 1980s witnessed a jurisprudential turn toward increased politicization of the bureaucracy. Beyond the great constitutional questions posed by independent agencies and the non-delegation doctrine, and beyond the question of judicial deference to agency statutory interpretations (a question that carries its own constitutional overtones),[54] lay a seemingly straightforward requirement that agency action be reasonable. The Court's foundational modern statement about that requirement, handed down in 1983, also sent mixed signals about the tension between administrative expertise and political control.

The issue in *Motor Vehicle Manufacturers Association v. State Farm Mutual Insurance Company*[55] was the Reagan-era decision by the automobile safety agency, NHTSA, to rescind a Carter-era regulation mandating the installation of either airbags or passive seat belts in all new cars. The Court observed that the Administrative Procedure Act (APA) imposed a basic requirement that regulatory decisions not be "arbitrary or capricious." It explained that requirement in terms that would not seem exceptionally hard for agencies to satisfy. Essentially, the agency would have to explain its reasoning and the relationship it discerned between the facts that it found, the statutory factors it was supposed to consider, and the regulatory result it reached. Beyond that explanation requirement, the agency was also required to have actually considered those relevant factors and to have not committed "a clear error of judgment."[56] In essence, the agency had to use its expertise to explain how it connected the dots between the facts, the governing law, and the resulting regulatory decision. And it had to connect those dots in, well, a non-arbitrary way.

In a part of the Court's decision that was unanimous, the Court found the agency to have acted arbitrarily and capriciously in rescinding the regulation without even considering whether to promulgate a more limited regulation that would have addressed the agency's justification for rescinding the entire rule. Chapter 7 will address that part of the opinion. For our current purposes what matters is the other part of the opinion. In that latter part, a bare five-justice majority further faulted the agency for allegedly misinterpreting technical data and for justifying its rescission of the regulation on what the Court considered spurious explanations about public resistance to passive restraints.

Four justices dissented from that latter holding and would have up-held that part of the agency's analysis. The dissenters conceded that that part of the agency's reasoning was "by no means a model," yet they concluded that nevertheless it was "adequate."[57] Translated, one can understand those statements as expressing the sentiment that the agency made less than optimal use of its expertise, but used it enough—maybe just barely enough. Was something else going on that helped drag the agency's reasoning over the finish line? Yes, according to the dissenters: politics. As Justice Rehnquist, speaking for those four justices, wrote:

> The agency's changed view of the [regulation] seems to be related to the election of a new President of a different political party. It is read-ily apparent that the responsible members of one administration may consider public resistance and uncertainties to be more important than do their counterparts in a previous administration. A change in admin-istration brought about by the people casting their votes is a perfectly reasonable basis for an executive agency's reappraisal of the costs and benefits of its programs and regulations. As long as the agency remains within the bounds established by Congress, it is entitled to assess admin-istrative records and evaluate priorities in light of the philosophy of the administration.[58]

Thus, in *State Farm*, four justices recognized that the political philos-ophy and preferences of the incumbent administration are legitimate reasons to make a particular policy choice. Even though *State Farm* has been understood as making "arbitrary and capricious" review an oner-ous requirement for agencies, forcing them to spend significant time and money justifying the expertness of their regulations, the dissenters' recognition of a role for politics in regulation has persisted. Thus, just as with the non-delegation doctrine, an expertise-promoting doctrine trig-gered a responsive echo sounding in politics. As chapter 3 will explain, those echoes grew louder in later years and gave presidents room to further expand their politically motivated control over agency action otherwise justified as grounded in expertise.

These last two sections have provided a lot of details, but can be summed up relatively simply. Constitutional law, often but not always expressed in court opinions, started to evolve in the 1980s in ways that impacted bureaucratic expertise. Outside the courtroom, the unitary executive theory found a warm welcome in the Reagan administration, which deployed it to justify both its executive order on regulatory review and its more general claims to broad presidential control over the administrative process. Inside the courtroom, the Court accorded a mixed reception to presidential claims for increased room for politics in administration. But for the most part, the expertise dam held.[59]

Nevertheless, the groundwork had been laid to question those pro-expertise principles. As chapter 3 will explain, in recent years the unitary executive theory has continued to gain ground in the courts. This development casts into new doubt the constitutionality of agencies whose leaders—and thus regulatory output—Congress attempted to at least partially immunize from presidential politicization.[60] In very recent years even the non-delegation doctrine has shown signs of life. Outside the courtroom, presidential attempts to control bureaucratic output have continued apace.

Taken together, what happened (and what started to happen) in the 1980s called into question the New Deal ideal type of an agency: one staffed by experts, its leadership (and output) immunized from direct presidential control, operating under a very broad statute, and making decisions justified as expressions of apolitical expertise. Many of those changes—the completed ones and the portended ones—emanated from the Supreme Court. Chapter 3 will tell the story of these developments. But first, that chapter will begin by focusing not on the courts, but on the president. Far from being outlier phenomena reflecting a uniquely pro-presidential power and pro-privatization philosophy, the regulatory innovations begun by the Reagan administration continued to flourish when the Democrats retook control of the White House.

3

Politicization Consolidated

In retrospect, the 1980s was a decade that fundamentally changed our understanding of the administrative state. The Reagan administration ushered in a period of deregulation and reliance on market ordering that halted, even if it did not reverse, the course of economic and social regulation since the New Deal. In so doing, it gave greater credence to the concept of privatizing the delivery of social services and, ultimately, the delivery of regulation itself. It instituted broader and deeper White House review of agency actions and increased the importance of political loyalty when staffing agencies' upper echelons. At the same time, its Office of Legal Counsel operated as an intellectual hub for what was becoming known as the unitary executive theory. At the Supreme Court, the *Chevron* decision offered the president's political accountability, and thus his political preferences, as a justification for deferring to agencies' interpretations of vague statutes. Other doctrinal developments similarly recognized the political nature of agencies' regulatory decisions, and thus rendered them more susceptible to claims of presidential control.

None of these developments necessarily had staying power. Innovations from the Reagan White House ultimately could have been discarded as artifacts of a deregulatory administration's struggle against an oppositional bureaucracy, and, in the case of the unitary executive theory, a passing intellectual fad. As for *Chevron* and the other cases discussed at the end of chapter 2, their ambiguous rationales might have tilted away from presidential control over the bureaucracy.[1] But instead, these developments lasted. As a result, they played a longer-term and larger role in the decline of administrative expertise.

From Regulatory Review to Presidential Administration

Reagan-era White House regulatory review, largely carried over into the George H.W. Bush administration,[2] was controversial. Critiques ranged

from constitutional arguments that Executive Order 12,291 unconstitutionally extended presidential power, institutional arguments that
OIRA review reduced the scope for expertise-based administrative
decision-making, and policy arguments that OIRA's mandated cost-
benefit analysis pushed too hard in a deregulatory direction. Because
at least some of those critiques mapped onto philosophical and policy
differences between Republicans and Democrats, when Democrats
recaptured the White House in 1992 it was widely expected that President Clinton would end the practice.

To the surprise of many, he did not.[3] Instead, he issued his own executive order, Number 12,866, instituting his administration's own version of
White House regulatory review. To be sure, the Clinton order differed from
its predecessor. It contained transparency features to mitigate the secrecy
problems that arose under the prior order, when private interests funneled
arguments and information to OIRA which would in turn forward them
to agencies outside the public rulemaking process. It also softened around
the edges the Reagan order's cost-benefit mandate. On the other hand, the
Clinton order's provision giving the president final authority to resolve
disputes between OIRA and agencies implied a significant increase in the
White House's asserted authority. So did the order's inclusion of independent agencies in its provisions for regulatory agenda review.[4]

Despite these differences, the most important point is that the Clinton administration reaffirmed the Reagan-era practice of White House
regulatory review. That reaffirmation solidified that practice as bipartisan. While presidents since Clinton added their own tweaks, the practice of such review has now remained in place for a generation.

Beyond institutionalizing regulatory review, President Clinton took
additional steps to strengthen the identification between himself and the
bureaucracy's regulatory initiatives. Justice Elena Kagan, before ascending to the Court but after serving in the Clinton administration, wrote
a now-canonical recounting and analysis of those steps—steps that together she called "presidential administration."[5] She described President
Clinton's innovations as issuing directives that agencies take particular
actions and appropriating agency actions—that is, associating himself
with and taking credit for them.

The directives Kagan discussed could be quite specific, not only mandating that agencies commence a rulemaking process on a particular

topic, but specifying the outlines of the rule he preferred. Consider an example she discussed.[6] In 1999, President Clinton issued a memorandum "direct[ing]" the Secretary of Labor to promulgate rules allowing states to use their unemployment insurance systems to provide leave for new parents. Six months later, Clinton announced the agency's promulgation of rules that followed the principles his memorandum had expressed.

What is remarkable about presidential action like that is that it purports to direct agencies on how they should use the discretionary power Congress gave them. Chapter 2 explained that those agencies are creatures of Congress and derive their regulatory powers from congressional authorizations. By directing those agencies to commence particular regulatory actions, and indeed, specifying their content, the Clinton administration could be understood as asserting for itself the power to decide how agencies should use their congressionally delegated power.

Of course, the White House could not direct an agency to take actions for which it lacked authority. Nor could it forbid an agency from taking actions Congress required the agency to take. The administration seemed to recognize these limitations on its power, at least in its regulatory review order, which acknowledged "the primacy of Federal agencies in the regulatory decision-making process"[7] and conceded that "[n]othing in this order shall be construed as displacing the agencies' authority or responsibilities, as authorized by law."[8] Those acknowledgments and concessions reflected the administration's understanding of the limits of its power to intrude on congressional mandates to agencies.

Nevertheless, much of the authority Congress gives agencies is discretionary—that is, Congress often *authorizes* the agency to act, but does not *require* that it do so or specify the details of the action. To the extent Congress grants agencies such discretionary power, White House directives to agencies to use that discretion to take particular actions inevitably pushed agency decision-making toward the administration's political priorities. Unsurprisingly, for the administration, that was the point.[9]

Consider now the regulatory appropriations Kagan discussed: the president's public association with and credit-taking for agency action. Those steps included events such as Rose Garden press conferences in which the president, flanked by an agency head, announced a regulatory initiative. Such appropriations could be dismissed as mere public relations—the president simply taking credit for regulatory actions he anticipated would be favorably received. Nevertheless, as Kagan suggested, presidential associations with preliminary actions (such as a highly publicized rollout of a proposed rule) constituted de facto directives to the agency to complete that rule—presumably without making major substantive changes. She also pointed out that the demand for actions that Clinton could publicly promote led administration officials to prod agencies to move forward on actions the president might wish to trumpet.[10]

The upshot is that the eight years of the Clinton administration marked an increased identification of the incumbent administration with the bureaucracy's work product. The administration may have had many reasons to strengthen that connection. The ascension of Republican congressional majorities after the 1994 elections made legislative initiatives much less attractive, especially on topics on which the president wished to take more progressive positions (compared with, say, the 1996 welfare reform bill, which passed with broad Republican support but which split Democrats). Moreover, administrative initiatives are far more common than legislative ones, making them attractive for a president who was perhaps unusually committed to remaining in the public eye. Regardless of the reasons, Clinton's innovations took the form of both presidential direction of the bureaucracy's work and closer presidential identification with it. Thus, they further politicized it.

Presidential Administration in the George W. Bush and Obama Administrations

Presidential power continued to grow in the sixteen years between the end of the Clinton administration and the start of the Trump administration. The George W. Bush administration pressed claims of strong presidential control that reflected his legal advisors' unitary executive sympathies. Many of those claims focused on post-9/11 foreign and domestic security issues, while others focused on Bush's increased use of presidential signing statements to signal his refusal to consider himself bound by components of bills he signed into law but nevertheless thought were unconstitutional. The administration also continued the

Clinton practice of exerting control over the bureaucracy. Indeed, it was entangled in several situations where it was accused of suppressing agency-developed information contradicting its regulatory positions,[11] conducting regulatory business in secret,[12] and attempting to remove high-level officials considered unsympathetic to the administration's priorities.[13]

More to our current purposes, toward the end of his second term, President Bush issued an executive order (13,422) that required the approval of a political appointee before an agency could begin a rulemaking, and required that that appointee herself be approved by OMB. While major rulemakings would naturally have to be approved by politically appointed agency leadership, scholars nevertheless remarked that this order inserted the White House into the administrative rulemaking process at an earlier stage, and in a broader and more formalized way than ever before.[14] Indeed, one way to understand this provision of the Bush executive order is that it stopped just short of direct and formal White House commanding of particular administrative action.[15]

President Obama continued the practice of presidential control over the bureaucracy. Perhaps most notable was his administration's tight public embrace of high-profile regulatory measures in environmental and immigration law—for example, when it characterized EPA's finalization of auto fuel efficiency standards as the work of "the Obama Administration."[16] Such public actions distinctly echoed the "presidential administration" Kagan described as characterizing the Clinton administration, as did his use of the Internet (and social media in particular) to communicate directly with the American people.[17] Conversely, the president—or at least members of his cabinet—also exerted political pressure to delay regulatory actions. A notable example occurred in late 2011, when Health and Human Services Secretary Kathleen Sebelius directed the FDA to deny a citizen petition to certify a controversial contraceptive, "Plan B," for over-the-counter use, despite the FDA's conclusion that Plan B met the criteria for over-the-counter availability. Indeed, the Plan B episode also featured a presidential *denial* of responsibility for that decision—a denial that was presumably grounded in a desire to both avoid creating a campaign issue in an election year while also assuring his pro-reproductive rights supporters that he was not personally responsible for the petition's denial.[18] Finally, Obama also made liberal use of regulatory "czars"—White House officials tasked with overseeing regulation of a particular subject area, such as the recovery of the auto industry following the 2008 financial collapse.[19]

The Trump Years: Where to Begin?

This section's title is snarky. But it reflects a sincere truth: there was much—very much—about the Trump administration's approach to the bureaucracy that was qualitatively different from what came before, from any previous administration of either party.[20]

Begin with ham-fisted attempts to control agency output. Very early in his term, President Trump issued an executive order that, among other things, prohibited an agency from promulgating a new regulation unless it identified two regulations for rescission.[21] Observers panned this order as a thoughtless way to accomplish the ostensibly reasonable goal of minimizing regulatory burdens. Consider how it would play out in practice. An agency—say, the Securities and Exchange Commission—decides that it really needs to promulgate a new regulation. Perhaps a new financial product needs reining in or a new market manipulation needs stopping. In order to promulgate that regulation, the SEC has to find two regulations—somewhere—to rescind. But rescinding a regulation must satisfy the same reasoned decision-making requirement as promulgating one. (Recall from chapter 2 the *State Farm* airbags case, which reversed an agency's rescission of a regulation because it was unreasoned.) What will the agency say when a court requests a reasoned explanation for why it decided to rescind the existing regulations? To make room for another regulation, on a totally different topic? You would not want to be the agency lawyer having to defend that reasoning.

But it gets worse. The executive order speaks of regulations. Could an agency seeking to comply with it rescind the requisite number of regulations, but then re-announce them as merely policy guidance documents, which are not legally binding and thus do not have to go through the process for promulgating "regulations"? Relatedly, could the agency rescind the regulation, but simply make it informally clear to the regulated community that it considers the rule of conduct that regulation established to constitute an appropriate implementation or interpretation of the relevant statute? Could it also make clear that it will enforce that rule of conduct in a lawsuit that would allege a violation, not of the regulation (which no longer exists) but of the underlying statute on which the regulation had been based? In these cases, all the executive order will have accomplished is to drive regulation underground, to nobody's benefit. Alternatively, could an enterprising agency dutifully rescind four regulations, and combine them into two larger ones? In that case, the net tally would be two fewer regulations on the books, and, voila!—the agency is now free to promulgate the new regulation it wants.

To be sure, some of these tricks may not work, at least not all the time. Indeed, later clarification from OMB tried to clean up some of the mess the two-out-for-one-in mandate created. But this is no way to run a railroad—or regulatory policy.

But that order wasn't done. *The same executive order* required that, for 2017, no agency, without special permission, impose an overall increase in regulatory costs. Think about that requirement. It's not a requirement that an agency not impose a net increase in regulatory costs, *when compared to regulatory benefits*. Rather, it appeared to require consideration of costs alone, *without any reference to regulatory benefits*. Thus, it would prevent an agency from promulgating a regulation that, say, imposed costs of $1 million even if it provided benefits of $100 million, unless it found some other regulation costing $1 million that it was willing to rescind—even if that other regulation *also* provided massive benefits in relation to its costs.

Cost-benefit analysis is often described and defended as "smart regulation." What the Trump executive order imposed was dumb regulation.

Move on now, and consider other features of the Trump administration's regulatory policy. First, it had an absolutely atrocious win-loss percentage when its regulations were challenged in court. The average administration's win rate in such cases is 70 percent. Trump's? According to scorekeepers at New York University, a shade higher than 20 percent.[22] Not because it was only "Obama judges" deciding those cases. The Trump administration lost because it, and the agency leadership it selected, were unusually sloppy in their regulatory initiatives. They were, in fact, the very opposite of regulatory experts.

Consider now the administration's treatment of the real experts. We likely all remember Colonel Alexander Vindman, who was unceremoniously removed from his White House position, and ultimately had to leave the military, when, *following legally prescribed channels*, he reported what persons in those channels concluded were reasonable and serious concerns about the president's conduct in his dealing with Ukraine. But even if we put that notorious example aside, given its connection to Trump's alleged personal wrongdoing, the history still reveals a pattern of the administration belittling the bureaucracy (calling it "the Deep State"), silencing experts when they sought to speak in public about important issues, and scrubbing agency websites of well-accepted terminology it didn't like. Or just remember the president's year-long and often very public fight with public health officials during the COVID-19 pandemic: sidelining key figures in the public health bureaucracy, refusing to meet with them, and even retweeting calls for their ouster. A president may not like the message the experts bring him, but very publicly shooting the messengers is no way to reassure Americans that the experts are on the job.

Or consider the president's relationship to truth. A basic requirement of a president who, among other things, heads an expert apparatus tasked with protecting and improving the country is that he not utter howlers about the topics of those experts' work. Calling climate change and the COVID-19 virus hoaxes doesn't reflect trust in and encouragement of government expertise. Nor, for that matter, does taking a sharpie and visibly changing the weather service's cone of uncertainty for a hurricane, apparently just to reinforce the plausibility of his own earlier tweet about the storm's path.

Nor were Trump's attacks on truth confined to large questions of climate change, the pandemic, and similar Page 1 issues. One study concluded that it took President Trump just two and one-half years to tell the number of lies about scientific information that President George W. Bush, until Trump considered the most science-hostile president of the modern era, told over a full eight years.[23] As a final indication of the scale of the problem, in the fall of 2020, the *New England Journal of Medicine* endorsed Joe Biden's candidacy for the presidency. Stubbornly non-partisan, the *Journal* had never before endorsed a presidential candidate. But Trump was different.

President Trump's record merits this extended treatment because there's no guarantee he, or someone like him, won't again occupy the White House. While it may not always be a good idea to make policy in response to worst-case possibilities, his example nevertheless justifies considering the broader picture. Presidents since Clinton continued and in important ways expanded his innovations in presidential administration. One scholar, for example, has written that "President Obama's proliferation of high-profile czars is his particular instantiation of a policy, common to all modern Presidents, of seeking to magnify his control over agency action in domestic policy."[24] Another scholar of the science-law interface, writing in 2013, concluded that "Overall, the expertise-based understanding of administrative law has, at least since the 1980s, struggled against the political control model."[25]

Much more recently, two other scholars have implicitly agreed with that observation when they called upon then President-elect Biden to "abandon[] presidential administration."[26] Their call emerged in the aftermath of the Trump administration's particular pathologies, but their concerns were broader. Chapter 5 will evaluate the merits of presidential administration. For this chapter's more descriptive purpose, it suffices to observe that, if in early 2021 scholars were calling for abandonment of presidential administration, we can safely conclude that it is still around.

Reinventing Government—and Claiming to Shrink It

As with White House attempts to influence the rulemaking process, the push to remake the bureaucracy also survived the end of the Reagan/ Bush I era. In addition to reaffirming the basics of Reagan-style White House regulatory review and inaugurating what Justice Kagan called "presidential administration," President Clinton also attempted to demonstrate his small government, market-oriented bona fides by seeking to reduce and reimagine the civil service.

The Clinton administration's attitude toward the civil service raised different issues than its other regulatory actions. As a "New Democrat," Bill Clinton was not a classic New Dealer; indeed, he famously declared that "the era of big government is over." In some ways, he was as good as his word, deregulating large swaths of the financial sector and signing welfare reform legislation that many liberals criticized. But as a Democrat committed to many traditional Democratic political goals, he needed government. Indeed, while the "era of big government is over" phrase is well-known, consider what Clinton said in a 1996 campaign speech: After boasting about reductions in the civil service head count that had occurred during his first term, and stating "There is not a big government issue out there anymore," he then stated, later in the speech, "But we have to keep working to give you a Government that you feel you can trust and have confidence in."[27]

To create that trust and confidence in government, he sought to reinvent it. But his pledge to "reinvent government"—a core part of his New Democrat image—was thought to require a pledge to downsize the bureaucracy, which in turn required him to outsource regulatory tasks.[28] Outsourcing was necessary to keep government operating with a smaller civil service head count. But it was also necessary to implement the promise of his administration's "Reinventing Government" initiative: to convert the civil service from "rowers" who actually implemented regulation to "steerers" who simply supervised contractors who performed the "rowing" task more cheaply and efficiently.[29]

Regardless of whether he succeeded in reinventing government, Clinton appeared to have kept his word about reducing the size of the bureaucracy—between 1993 and 1999, the civil service workforce fell by 400,000, from 2.2 million to 1.8 million. To be sure, scholars question those figures' significance, citing everything from the post–Cold War "peace dividend" to the increasing use of contractors as reasons to suspect that government's true domestic size had not shrunk. Still, perceptions and rhetoric mattered. A Democratic president's embrace of at least the rhetorical goal of reducing the civil service established that idea as a bipartisan one. When combined with his deregulatory initiatives, that rhetoric and its follow-on encouragement of outsourcing helped cement the neoliberal, market-driven philosophy of the Reagan/Bush I years. His precedent made it hard for future Democratic presidents to openly champion the cause of strengthening or increasing the size of the bureaucracy, at least if the Democratic president in question was a centrist—as both Democratic presidents since Clinton have been. The cause of limiting the bureaucracy's size—and thus, necessarily, looking more favorably on outsourcing, since government's responsibilities have only grown since 2000—has become bipartisan.[30]

"I'm from the Government . . .": Bureaucracy Bashing and Its Consequences for Public Trust

The aggressive presidential control of the bureaucracy described both in chapter 2 and so far in this chapter clearly tilts the regulatory balance in favor of politics and away from bureaucratic expertise. As chapter 9 will explain, so has the outsourcing of regulatory work that accelerated in the 1980s and has since continued apace, again discussed in the prior chapter and immediately above. But leave those realities aside for the moment (or, in the case of outsourcing, until chapter 9). This book addresses not just the reality but also the public perception of such expertise. How have these regulatory moves affected that perception, and thus the public's trust in bureaucracy?

Survey data suggest that trust in government responds, at least to a significant degree, to changes in economic conditions.[31] In addition to helping explain the decline in public trust during the stagflation-plagued 1970s, this conclusion also helps explain why trust in government rebounded during the first two years of the Reagan administration, when the American economy began recovering from the Second Oil Shock.[32] While that rebound in trust might therefore seem unsurprising, it remains striking in light of the administration's rhetoric—in particular, its skepticism about government regulation and its insistence that individuals could do a better job promoting their own interests.[33] As Reagan often said, "the nine scariest words in the English language are 'I'm from the government and I'm here to help.'" The partial success of the Reagan administration—ultimately, it succeeded only partially—requires that we decouple public confidence in a politician or political program from public confidence in the government more generally.

While public confidence in the bureaucracy is, perhaps surprisingly, understudied,[34] scholars have done at least some research. One recent study concluded that declines in expertise caused a more serious drop in public trust in a bureaucracy than did declines in regulatory capacity (that is, the resources needed to regulate) or the appointment of officials with ideologies that conflict with the agency's core mission.[35] The study measured expertise—or, more precisely, its absence—in terms of employees who lacked training or background in the subject of the agency's concern.[36] Extrapolating from that static measure of expertise allows us to speculate about a connection between capacity, expertise, and overall public trust: At some point, a decline in capacity will surely affect performance, which will in turn damage the public's perception of the agency's expertise, and in turn, its trust in the agency. Indeed, the relationship between trust and expertise runs in the other direction as well: As one scholar observed, "successful governance" depends on public trust in "the implementation of policy programs."[37]

Politicians can influence all of these factors, directly or indirectly. For example, a study of the effect of "bureaucracy bashing" on bureaucratic institutions concluded that political attacks on the bureaucracy "foster a work environment that threatens effective policy implementation"— that is, bureaucratic performance.[38] The 1980s witnessed particularly severe bureaucracy bashing. Candidate and later President Ronald Reagan criticized "big government" as wasteful, inefficient, and incompetent.[39] Influential anti-tax groups promoted policies designed to "drown big government in the bathtub"; indeed, activists were quite frank about their desire to cut taxes so as to reduce the revenue available to fund regulatory programs—that is, to reduce bureaucratic capacity.[40] One prominent scholar of the bureaucracy described the bathtub slogan as one that "inspired the anti-bureaucracy movement."[41]

It is also easy to understand the close connection between such rhetoric and moves to both control the bureaucracy's output (via White House regulatory review) and divest it of regulatory authority (via outsourcing). President Reagan's statement that "Every once in a while, somebody has to get the bureaucracy by its neck and shake it loose and say, stop what you're doing"[42] fits neatly with the regulatory review that, by requiring agencies to cost-benefit justify their actions, attempts to get them to "stop what [they're] doing." Similarly, outsourcing regulation to assertedly lean, efficient, responsive, profit-driven organizations fits nearly perfectly with a critique of the bureaucracy as bloated, inefficient, and hostile to the administration's goals.

Later administrations, especially Democratic ones, were more measured in their critiques. Still, Clintonesque disavowal of "big government" and embrace of downsizing and marketizing regulation raise the same suspicions of traditional bureaucracies regulating in traditional ways. No administration since Clinton's has attempted to allay those suspicions. While muted since Reagan's fanciful claim of hundreds of

OSHA ladder-climbing regulations, the rhetoric of distrust, when combined with policies that impair bureaucratic effectiveness, likely generate such distrust—if not directly, then by setting the bureaucracy up for failures that prove their untrustworthiness.

Legal Evolution

The Rehnquist Court, which sat from 1986 until Chief Justice William Rehnquist's death in 2005, introduced many changes into constitutional jurisprudence. But one area in which it did not innovate was administrative law.[43] In most areas relevant to the expertise of the administrative apparatus, the Court left largely intact the administrative state it found in the later Reagan years. First, Congress remained free to delegate broad swaths of regulatory power to agencies, subject, at most, to limiting interpretations of the statutes that accomplished those delegations.[44] Second, the Court left undisturbed Congress's broad power to immunize agency heads from presidential at-will removal and thus create independent agencies.[45] The result was congressional latitude both to delegate broad authority to agencies and to structure those agencies in ways that reduced presidential control.

At the sub-constitutional level, the Rehnquist Court continued to require courts to defer to administrative agencies' interpretations of vague authorizing statutes. While the justices sometimes disagreed on how to apply the deference doctrine announced in the 1984 *Chevron* case discussed in chapter 2, it showed no interest in revisiting that decision. Indeed, if anything, the Court strengthened *Chevron*'s idea of deferring to administrative interpretations when in a 1997 case, *Auer v. Robbins*, it reaffirmed the deference agencies enjoy when they interpret not their authorizing statutes, but their own regulations.[46]

It would overstate the case to argue that the Rehnquist Court's administrative law jurisprudence unqualifiedly endorsed either expertise-based or politics-based understandings of regulation. Agencies, especially those whose leadership enjoyed immunity from at-will removal, could use broad delegations to retreat into their expertise-based cocoons and promulgate regulations based on their staff's best understanding of the relevant regulatory issue.[47] But broad delegations to executive (i.e., non-independent) agencies could also be understood as providing a similarly expansive set of regulatory options to presidents who wished to control the regulatory process. That same presidential policymaking discretion results from the Court's reaffirmation of broad judicial deference to both agencies' statutory interpretations and interpretations of their own regulations. Here again, though, that deference could also cut in the direction of expertise, if presidents refrained from aggressively intervening in the regulatory process.[48]

But 2005 heralded a change. That year, Chief Justice Rehnquist died and was replaced by John Roberts. While that replacement caused little change on some constitutional issues, it soon became clear that Chief Justice Roberts—and, gradually, other newcomers to the Court—differed from Rehnquist and his Court on issues relating to presidential control over the bureaucracy. Most notably, the Roberts Court soon began to express skepticism about congressional attempts to immunize agency officials from direct presidential control. In cases from 2010 and 2020, the Court, speaking through Roberts himself, struck down agency structures featuring immunized agency heads.[49] While those cases did not overrule Rehnquist-era precedent, they cabined and limited it, setting it up for eventual overruling if a majority wished.[50] Perhaps most important, in reaching these results the Chief Justice spoke explicitly about the importance—indeed, the constitutional imperative—of significant presidential authority over administrative agencies.[51]

On other issues, the Roberts Court has sent more uncertain signals about presidential control of the administrative apparatus. In 2019, the justices came closer than they had for two generations to striking down federal legislation as violating the non-delegation doctrine—the doctrine that requires Congress to include an "intelligible principle" in legislation that delegates regulatory power to agencies. A strengthened non-delegation doctrine could conceivably have momentous impacts on our regulatory system, especially if—as seems likely—Congress continues to find itself unable to muster the will to reach consensus on more detailed standards for regulatory action. One might think that a strengthened non-delegation rule would impair agencies' ability to use their expertise, if Congress was prohibited from handing over the broad power it could before. On the other hand, more precise congressional standards would arguably reduce presidential politicization of agency action, by reducing the latitude presidents enjoy to push agency action toward the president's preferred policies.

Relatedly, the Roberts Court has, to the surprise of many observers, shown real interest in reducing the deference courts owe to agencies' legal interpretations. In 2019, the Court split badly on whether to reaffirm its earlier precedent according agencies broad deference when they interpret their own regulations.[52] Even more surprisingly, over the last several years rumblings have arisen among the justices about whether to overrule or limit the deference *Chevron* accords agencies' interpretations of their authorizing statutes.[53] Limiting or rejecting such deference would impair presidential control over agency action if the agency would otherwise have been able to claim deference for the statutory interpretation the president favored for political reasons.

As the prior several paragraphs have explained, the ferment at the Court on these administrative law questions cuts in different directions for purposes of political accountability-justified—and politically motivated—presidential control over agency action. Thus, as the nation stands on the threshold of a likely attempt by the Biden administration to rebuild the reality and the perception of agency expertise, the Court lurks in the wings, primed to hand down decisions that may impact that effort in unpredictable ways.

Expertise and the Public

So far, this chapter has discussed the continuation of trends, begun in the 1980s, that focused on signals about the bureaucracy sent from political and legal elites to citizens. It closes with another trend that started in the 1980s, this one focused more directly on Americans' attitudes. Despite that different focus, the vector is the same—in the direction of more political control of regulatory decisions, at the expense of expertise.

In recent years, some observers have concluded that Americans, and westerners more generally, have become more resistant to claims of expert knowledge. The argument here is that they reject, not the general concept of expertise, but rather the idea that expertise resides exclusively within small groups of highly trained and credentialed specialists.[54] Observers who perceive this trend find support for it in basic human phenomena such as confirmation bias (that is, people's tendency to seek out information that confirms their pre-existing views) and people's over-estimation of their knowledge. But they also identify causes in aspects of modern American culture, such as education systems that refuse to ac-knowledge the possibility of student ignorance and an egalitarian ethos that extends beyond political rights to knowledge claims. According to some observers, those latter phenomena encourage resistance to claims that specially trained and highly knowledgeable experts merit special deference to their views about matters within their expertise, by denying that such knowledge in fact resides within specialized groups.[55]

The resulting conception of expertise as something that everyone can have shifts the question from "does expertise merit trust?" to one that asks, "*whose* expertise merits trust?" This latter question—especially, its intimation that expertise is available to all—is a fraught one in a society steeped in anti-elitist thinking that has only become more prevalent in recent decades. After all, if the converse is true and specialized, creden-tialed "experts" really do know more about social and scientific prob-lems and thus merit deference to their proposed solutions, then what has become of democratic self-government?[56]

One can resolve this conundrum if an informed public uses what it knows to acknowledge the complexity of many problems and defer to the experts it identifies, even while insisting on a democratic right to make the basic value judgments regarding such issues. A hundred years ago, the columnist Walter Lippman, pondering the complex regulatory problems industrialization and technological innovation posed for dem-ocratic government, offered a strikingly similar prescription. He urged that we

> strip public opinion of any implied duty to deal with the substance of a problem, [or] to make technical decisions. . . . And instead we say that the ideal of public opinion is to align men during the crisis of a problem in such a way as to favor the action of those individuals who may be able to compose the crisis.[57]

But Lippman's admonition to "align" the public "to favor . . . those indi-viduals who may be able to compose the crisis" encounters a problem. As sociologist Gil Eyal points out, educating laypersons sufficiently to persuade them to trust expertise simultaneously empowers them to question experts' authority and legitimacy.[58] Eyal's point was anecdotally reinforced by a March 2021 focus group of Trump voters, conducted by Republican pollster Frank Luntz, who were unsure about getting the COVID-19 vaccine. Members of that group insisted that they admired CDC scientists and wanted information about the vaccine. At the same time, though, they critiqued the CDC's leadership for issuing shifting guidance. Perhaps more fundamentally, they wanted that information so they could make their own decisions—not so they could decide who to trust.[59]

One can over-read Luntz's brief summary of one focus group. Still, it reflects hints of Eyal's critique: persons who consider themselves capable of evaluating scientific information about the vaccine, and who wanted to learn more about it, but also felt qualified to question the CDC's conduct. Of course, blind deference to credentialed experts is not the answer, if for no other reason than its political unacceptability. Rather, as Lippman realized a century ago, the challenge becomes educating or otherwise persuading persons to make informed deference decisions. Unfortunately, this prescription runs headlong into the politicization of expertise that arises from the information bubbles modern technology allows.

News from (and inside) the Bubble

As we all know, information technology has changed drastically in the last quarter-century. In 1997, the first Supreme Court case to consider the Internet's First Amendment implications spoke of "newsgroups" and "mail exploders"—concepts that seem to us as quaint as telegrams.[60] Today, the Internet, in particular social media, has become many Americans' main source of information. That development has triggered a heated debate about the impact of online media on the project of informed self-government. That debate has focused on the alleged prevalence in that media of both flat-out disinformation and one-sided information. But the immediate precursors of Facebook, Twitter, and their more fringe cousins have been just as problematic in misinforming Americans about the bureaucracy and its work and causing even more foundational mischief.

Just as with the other phenomena this book has discussed, the modern story of mass media's role in politicizing discussions of expertise

began in earnest in the late 1970s. Around then, a variety of technological and policy innovations began to change both the sources and character of the news and information Americans received. In the late 1970s,
Americans received their news in ways that had become settled over
the previous quarter-century: local newspapers, national magazines,
nightly (and sometimes morning) local and national television news
broadcasts, and short radio reports. But around then, the migration of
music broadcasting from the AM band to the richer sound emanating
from FM broadcasts created a programming hole for the owners of AM
radio stations. Talk radio, a recognizable medium since at least the early
1960s,[61] began to fill the gap.[62]

To be sure, until well into the 1980s that format focused less on exclusively political discussions with obvious ideological leanings.[63] Part
of the reason was the Fairness Doctrine, the Federal Communications
Commission rule that required presentations of political opinion to provide time or space for the presentation of opposing viewpoints. However,
the FCC's repeal of the Fairness Doctrine in 1987 removed that barrier
to the frank presentation of a single political viewpoint throughout a
broadcast. Perhaps not coincidentally, the next year, Rush Limbaugh,
the progenitor of today's ideologically slanted political talk show, began
his nationally syndicated broadcast. Eight years later, the 1996 Telecommunications Act significantly liberalized radio station cross-ownership
rules and eliminated limits on the total number of stations a corporation
could own. Together, these regulatory changes enabled the political talk
radio format, and created the business conditions under which nationally scoped corporations could vertically integrate, by supplying the content for the (now multiple) stations they themselves owned.[64] Political
talk radio could get big.

Beyond persuading Americans to adopt one political viewpoint over
another (a phenomenon studies have discerned),[65] has ideologically
one-sided political talk radio exacerbated the public's distrust of expertise? Certainly, in persuading listeners to oppose particular regulatory
programs, or regulation in general, talk radio—which undeniably skews
conservative[66]—has likely helped bring into disrepute the general enterprise of regulation. But to the extent that opposition focuses not on the
merits of a particular program, or even the very idea of regulating, but
instead on skepticism about the underlying facts justifying such regula-

tion or the credibility and honesty of regulators and scientists, talk radio's critique has deeper implications.

Indeed, much of talk radio's focus has been on undermining the factual foundations for regulation. Limbaugh himself named "the four corners of deceit": "government, academia, science, and the media."[67] Given that major functions of those institutions involve informing and regulating, allegations of not just malfeasance but systematic deceit necessarily imply an attack on the foundations of fact-based regulating and can only harm the trust listeners have in those institutions' fact presentations. As one observer concluded:

> The rise of talk radio challenged the role of experts by reinforcing the popular belief that the established media were dishonest and unreliable. Radio talkers . . . attacked everything, plunging their listeners into an alternate universe where facts of any kind were unreliable unless verified by the host.[68]

Talk radio was not alone. Its rise in the early 1990s occurred as opinion cable television was becoming a fixture. Political television shows had always existed, but before the 1980s had mostly taken the form of journalists questioning newsmakers in a subdued setting, such as *Meet the Press*, or slightly more aggressive and ideological, but still polite, questioning on shows such as *Firing Line*. But by the early 1980s, *The McLaughlin Group* had pioneered the format of commentators (albeit of differing political persuasions) yelling at each other rather than engaging in calm, measured conversation.

Such shows were entertaining—but they sowed the seeds not just for Rush Limbaugh and his imitators on radio, but for an entire television network focused on a particular viewpoint—Fox News. The story of Fox News—its format and content, its critics, and its liberal imitator in the form of MSNBC—is well-known. (Whether Fox and MSNBC are equivalent is a political fight we can, thankfully, avoid. But we can say that Fox's ideological position in the partisan wars of the 1990s and beyond made it presumptively anti-regulation.) Fox's presence on television rather than radio, its deep marketplace penetration, and, ironically, its protestations to be "fair and balanced" (unlike Limbaugh himself, who made no secret of his conservative orientation) all combined to complement the impact of talk radio as a source of information. Information and, when it chose, misinformation.

The Internet and social media have completed this revolution. In its infancy, the Internet spawned much utopian speculation about the impact of nearly unlimited knowledge diffusion and access. Today, of course, those hopes have been seeded with a heavy dose of pessimism. Ironically, that pessimism has arisen largely because the Internet kept its original promise to bypass traditional media gatekeepers and allow anyone to speak and to select the speakers to whom they will listen. In that sense, the Internet (and social media in particular) has perfected the availability of an epistemic bubble in which listeners or readers can avoid encountering unpleasant, contradictory, or worldview-questioning information, in favor of nonstop information that reinforces and justifies the listener's existing views.

In addition to allowing such epistemic closure, scholars argue that the ability to gather online in like-minded groups reinforces and hardens those views, thus further strengthening one's convictions. The polarization this epistemic closure creates encourages citizens to believe that their side on an issue must be right, all the time—almost literally, no questions asked. Further, it combines with the human tendency to hold unwarrantedly favorable views about one's own knowledge to incentivize persons to mount the ramparts and defend one's position, rather than to recognize one's own fallibility and intentionally seek out confounding information.[69]

These dynamics, if real,[70] bode poorly for calls to accept the superior expertise of government agencies on regulatory issues, especially if the agency's general orientation or its specific proposals conflict with the individual's own interests or values.[71] They bode similarly poorly for Walter Lippmann's call for a public role focused on "aligning" its opinion with those most able to solve a given problem. An attitude open to carefully selecting the experts to which it is willing to defer is not an attitude that is sure of its own correctness, convinced that other views are corrupt, and accustomed only to hearing a chorus of agreement and validation.[72]

More generally, the media environment, much of which aims at sowing doubt and anger about the established order (including about conventional ideas of experts and expertise), capitalizes on the confused state of expertise to encourage political, and even populist, reassertion of governmental control in the name of democratic accountability. Political scientist Yascha Mounk describes the result as "the antidemocratic dilemma": Bureaucratic elites (among other entities) regulate in ways that are socially necessary but raise anxieties about the people losing democratic control over their government.[73] A media environment that feeds those anxieties, by casting doubt about regulators' competence and basic good faith and allowing retreats into epistemic bubbles, is one that will encourage people to resist expert regulation and instead embrace populist politicians. Again, these are hardly the conditions conducive to the flourishing of bureaucratic expertise—or, indeed, of democracy itself.

These developments provide the final piece of the puzzle that has been under assembly since candidate Ronald Reagan decried the fictional hundred-plus OSHA ladder-climbing regulations. The emerging picture is one in which regulators—and, by extension, regulation—cannot be trusted. Instead, faith must be placed in one's preferred political leader—the one who reflects a citizen's own views back onto her. Whether that leader is President Reagan imposing his own deregulatory will, President Clinton personalizing regulation through presidential administration, or President Trump asserting that only he can rescue the American people from a corrupt deep state, the leader promises to provide what the people want. In other words, they politicize regulation and the regulatory process. While the strength of that politicization will vary with the particular leader and his populist aggressiveness, the experience of the Trump administration reveals the extent to which that dynamic can impact the bureaucracy's ability to regulate. What these final two sections have added is the phenomenon of facts not getting in the way.

Overconfidence in our own expertise, epistemic closure, and polarization raise serious problems for our democracy. The aftermath of the 2020 presidential election, in which Americans remained divided not only on which candidate *should* have won the election, but which candidate actually *did* win, illustrates the risk: The Biden administration began its term in office with a sizable percentage of the population believing it to be fundamentally illegitimate.

These phenomena pose equally serious challenges for the programs our democracy carries out—including regulatory programs. Such programs rest on intricate analyses of complex phenomena. That fact does not justify regulation that is publicly unexplained and, in some way, unapproved by the democratic process. But, as Walter Lippman realized a hundred years ago, the complexity of modern regulatory issues does require public trust in the regulators. It is that trust that has been undermined by a media landscape that finds it more profitable to enrage than inform, the Internet's capacity to allow persons to select their own news sources (and news), and our inherent resistance to experts. For regulators who are tasked with crafting and implementing solutions to difficult problems that are expensive to resolve, and which often impose costs that fall unequally on different parts of American society, that lack of trust is an existential challenge.

Conclusion

This chapter has covered a variety of developments, occurring over a long period—essentially, the last three decades. That period encompassed presidential administrations of very different types, a Supreme Court that has completely turned over, and an information landscape that would have been largely unrecognizable at its start. But a quick, and not too simplified, summary of these developments would reveal the following. First, many of the regulatory trends from the Reagan years have become more or less settled wisdom: reliance on market forces, increased White House control over regulatory decisions, and critiques and neglect of the career bureaucracy. Second, judicial doctrine, while initially resistant to increased presidential control of regulation, has begun to warm to the idea. Third, the media and broader information environments have sharpened the political divide and accentuated Americans' predispositions to distrust elites and the expertise they represent.

Until the Court shows its hand more clearly, the Biden administration can look out on a landscape in which its predecessors' innovations in increasing presidential influence over regulation remain legally viable options. Indeed, they remain not just legally viable but perhaps practically necessary, given the close political divide in Congress and the nation that makes significant legislative action excruciatingly hard to achieve. But also facing the administration are public attitudes liberally sprinkled with distrust of regulation, regulators, and the facts on which both rely.

This is the landscape the administration faces as it confronts the nation's regulatory challenges. This is where we are. The rest of this book looks for a path to a better place.

PART II

A Framework for Expertise

Chapters 4–7 examine how administrative agency expertise should appropriately relate to the federal government's major institutions. Chapter 4 considers Congress. In particular, it considers whether Congress should be required to be more specific when it delegates authority to agencies, to prevent a dynamic in which agencies find themselves making politically fraught decisions that invite presidential interference. It concludes that neither constitutional nor statutory interpretation analysis can succeed in forcing Congress's hand.

In turn, chapter 5 considers presidential involvement in agency rule-making. It critiques the most aggressive forms of that involvement—not just formalized White House regulatory review, but also more informal mechanisms presidents since Reagan have used to control agencies and their regulatory work product. Chapter 5 seeks to preserve a proper realm for presidential influence while reducing inappropriately intrusive presidential interference in the workings of agencies.

Chapter 6 turns its gaze to agencies themselves. It examines how politically appointed agency officials—including but not exclusively the actual agency heads—should work with career agency staff in the regulation-crafting process. It attempts to carve out appropriate roles for both agencies' political leadership and career experts. In particular, it seeks to ensure that those career experts enjoy the latitude to perform the informational and deliberative functions for which their expertise well trains them.

Chapter 7 considers federal courts. It urges them to tweak their current approach to judicial review of agency action, with the aim of using judicial review to reinforce the structural and procedural reforms chapter 6 urged. Thus, it urges courts to focus their scrutiny toward reinforcing agency expertise.

4

A Call to Congress

Part I set the scene for our current regulatory predicament by recounting a set of distinct but interrelated phenomena that have occurred since at least 1980 and that, together, have damaged both the reality and the public perception of administrative expertise. Those developments have combined to create a situation in which the executive branch wields significant control over the bureaucracy and its outputs, often—although not always—in pursuit of deregulatory goals. Conversely, during this period claims of administrative autonomy have enjoyed at best mixed success. Added to this accretion of executive power is the public distrust in the administrative apparatus—a distrust that, unsurprisingly, strengthens the president's claims for control over that apparatus.

If these factors suggest the inappropriate politicization of the science that underlies regulatory expertise, then a logical reaction to this problem is to suggest, straightforwardly enough, that science should be separated from politics in federal regulation. This would in turn suggest that the explicitly political branch responsible for setting regulatory policy— Congress—be required to make those political choices. If Congress does that, the theory goes, agencies would no longer be required to make them—or at least not to the same degree. In turn, agencies might be able to recover their status as pure expertise-driven implementers of clear policy choices Congress expresses in legislation.

Of course, Congress could always decide on its own to enact more precise statutes. But because it clearly has chosen not to (or shown itself unable to), the question becomes whether the judiciary could force the issue, either at the level of constitutional law or statutory interpretation. The constitutional option raises the specter of a resurrected nondelegation doctrine. The statutory interpretation option would take the form of a judicial refusal to uphold administrative regulations that are unusually important or socially significant unless they are clearly authorized by statute. This latter concept is sometimes understood as a version of the "major questions" doctrine.

Both of these ideas are intuitive. Both of them end up failing.

The Non-Delegation Doctrine

As its name suggests, the non-delegation doctrine holds that Congress may not delegate its legislative power to another entity. This principle derives both from the Constitution's text and its underlying assumptions. As to text, the idea is that, because Article I of the Constitution gives Congress "All legislative Powers herein granted" (i.e., granted in the rest of the document), Congress may not take that power and give it away—i.e., delegate it—to someone else. That textual argument—which not all scholars accept[1]—provides the foundation for a deeper justification. That justification flows from the document's underlying assumption that ultimate sovereignty rests with the people of the United States. Thus, when "We the People" vested in Congress "All legislative Powers" we granted to the federal government, we accomplished the first act of delegation. That decision—to delegate these powers to Congress—thus prohibits the delegate—Congress—from re-delegating that power somewhere else. Or so the theory goes.[2]

This is not to say that the doctrine is uncontroversial. Legal historians have clashed sharply on the question of whether the framers understood themselves to have enacted a non-delegation principle.[3] Other scholars have concluded that any constitutional non-delegation principle consists simply of the prohibition on Congress delegating to others the power to vote on legislation—literally, delegating away the power to legislate—rather than as a limitation on what decisions Congress can authorize another institution, such as an administrative agency, to make.[4] Scholars have also sharply clashed over the policy benefits of a strong non-delegation doctrine and, conversely, the current regime under which Congress retains broad latitude to delegate important decisions to administrative agencies. Many scholars argue that such delegations are not only necessary as a practical matter, given Congress's inability to comprehend, let alone reach consensus on addressing, the enormously complex issues that confront the nation, but also affirmatively desirable. Beyond agencies' acknowledged expertise, those scholars compare Congress's democratic responsiveness unfavorably with agencies', given the former's careful attention to special interests and the latter's required focus on regulatory rationality and procedural openness under the rule-making process mandated by the Administrative Procedure Act.[5] By contrast, scholars such as Theodore Lowi and David Schoenbrod have vociferously attacked the current regime, arguing that it allows Congress to evade responsibility for making hard choices, which end up getting made by agencies as part of a bargaining process among powerful entities that ignores the public interest.[6]

Despite disagreements about both its legal foundation and its policy wisdom, the mainstream understanding holds that the non-delegation principle does indeed limit the scope of Congress's authority to authorize administrative agencies to make decisions that come too close to legislative judgments. This is where the problems start. That principle—that some grants of power to agencies to act are simply too close to grants of legislative power—creates serious line-drawing problems. Indeed, "serious" hardly does those problems justice; perhaps it is better to describe them as insoluble. Administrative agencies promulgate rules that have massive impacts on American life. (Consider fuel efficiency and safety regulations that have transformed the cars Americans drive.) They also promulgate trivial rules that order minor aspects of Americans' social and economic lives. Finding a principled line between them is a tall order. Even if it were possible to draw such a line, the fact remains that Congress, if it chooses, can legislate even trivial rules of conduct. That realization confronts us with yet another problem: How can the same policy choice be a legitimate exercise of Congress's legislative power when Congress makes that choice itself, but non-legislative (that is, not a delegation of "legislative" power) when an agency makes it?[7]

In fairness, the Supreme Court's current non-delegation doctrine does not require courts to distinguish between valid and invalid delegations based on the magnitude of the resulting rules. Instead, the Court has focused on the nature of Congress's directions to the agency—in particular, whether those directions are sufficiently precise to guide the agency's use of its discretion. Since 1928, it has implemented this approach by requiring that any statute delegating such authority contain "an intelligible principle."[8] The idea behind the intelligible principle requirement is straightforward: Including such a principle in the statute indicates that Congress has indeed made a policy choice—i.e., it has leg-islated. In turn, the existence of that choice limits the agency's discretion to select any policy it wishes, and instead renders the agency's action something closer to an implementation of the choice Congress made. It also allows courts to determine whether the agency has acted according to Congress's will.[9]

But embracing the intelligible principle standard, as the Court has now done for nearly a century, merely pushes the line-drawing questions to another level. What, exactly, counts as an intelligible principle? How "intelligible" does a given principle have to be? If a statute embraces potentially conflicting goals, say, cleaning up the air and maintaining a vibrant industrial economy, does the principle therefore become unin-telligible? What if that statute issues guidance on how those conflicting goals are to be balanced—for example, by requiring that the agency im-pose air quality standards that are "requisite to protect the public health" with "an adequate margin of safety"?[10] Does such vague language, clearly vesting significant discretion in the agency, constitute an intelligible principle? Can we say that Congress has truly made a policy choice in such circumstances? Can we say that such language truly allows courts to determine whether the agency has acted pursuant to Congress's will?

Given these difficulties, one can easily understand why the Court has not strictly enforced the non-delegation doctrine since the 1930s, and perhaps not even then. To be sure, in 1935, the Court did issue two de-cisions striking down provisions of an early New Deal statute, the Na-tional Industrial Recovery Act (NIRA), on the ground that they failed the intelligible principle requirement.[11] But the NIRA was a uniquely broad statute. One of the provisions struck down in the 1935 cases autho-rized the president to promulgate "codes of fair competition" governing every aspect of an industry's operations, guided only by an exceptionally broad and internally contradictory set of goals. The other provision that was struck down gave the president more limited power, but prescribed essentially no guidance on how he should use it. Since 1935, however, the Court has failed to strike down any federal statute on non-delegation grounds.[12] Instead, it has upheld, for example, laws authorizing the FCC to regulate the airwaves in "the public interest" and the SEC to regulate securities structures to ensure that they do not "unfairly or inequitably" distribute shareholder voting power.[13] Considering the vagueness of the intelligible principle standard, it's not surprising that the Court has failed to apply it in a meaningful way.

Nevertheless, since the 1930s individual justices on the Court have indicated a willingness to try. To date, these attempts have taken the form of separate opinions, usually speaking for only one or two justices, in cases dealing with unusually broad or fraught delegations. In recent years, however, their numbers have increased. Consider the SORNA case. In 2019, the Court heard a non-delegation challenge to a statute regulating the registration of sex offenders. That law, the Sexual Offender Registration and Notification Act (SORNA), prescribed detailed registration and reporting requirements for sex offenders released from prison after the law's 2006 enactment date. However, arranging such requirements for offenders released before that date—so-called pre-Act offenders—presented difficult logistical problems, since some of them had been out of prison for years or decades. SORNA's seeming answer was simply to authorize the Attorney General to prescribe whatever requirements he thought best.

To be sure, a four-justice plurality, squinting at SORNA's language, did find the requisite intelligible principle lurking in the statute. But three justices would have struck the law down—the biggest tally for a non-delegation strike-down since the 1930s. However, their proposed test—asking whether the challenged law merely required administrative fact-finding or "filling in the details" of a regulatory scheme, or whether the law delegated power already partially shared by the executive—was itself rife with vagueness. Ironically, their proposed strengthening of the doctrine revealed the problem with drawing any non-delegation lines at all.[14]

Beyond that vagueness lies an even deeper problem. If the ultimate goal of enforcing a non-delegation principle is to remove politically fraught questions from the agency's plate, the fact is that the dissent's test won't accomplish that. "Details"—assuming we know how to distinguish them from more important delegated decisions—can be fraught. So can fact-finding. Indeed, one of the more important regulatory decisions made by the Obama administration—and one of its most controversial—was the so-called endangerment finding that greenhouse gases endanger the environment or public health. That finding authorized the EPA to regulate greenhouse gases—thus, it was surely a significant, high-stakes political decision. Would the dissenters in the

SORNA case nevertheless have understood it as a mere fact-finding that Congress could delegate to the EPA?[15]

In theory, it might be desirable to enforce a meaningful non-delegation principle. Such a principle would ensure that society's basic value choices are made by elected legislatures. But even this straightforward justification for a non-delegation limit on legislation encounters an objection. Scholars have argued that the administrative rulemaking process may in fact be a superior venue for obtaining citizen input into federal policymaking, given both the well-known maladies afflicting Congress and the statutorily required participation rights citizens enjoy when an agency considers promulgating a regulation.[16] Moreover, insisting that Congress make the basic choices about the regulatory policy it wants an agency to implement assumes that Congress can muster the energy and political will to reach a consensus on such (more detailed) legislation. In our partisan times, that is a heroic assumption.[17] When Congress's supposedly superior democratic pedigree is open to debate, when a strengthened non-delegation doctrine might call into question the federal government's ability to enact meaningful regulation addressing pressing social problems, and when judicial enforcement of a strengthened doctrine would likely devolve into conclusory and circular statements about "details" and "fact-finding," the argument that agencies can avoid political choices if courts require Congress to make them starts to look problematic indeed.

Statutory Interpretation: The Major Problems with the Major Questions Doctrine

A primary tool today's Court uses to defeat non-delegation challenges is to interpret the challenged statute narrowly enough that it survives intelligible principle review. Most recently, the plurality in the 2019 SORNA case did just that. In recent years, the Court has used a variant of that same idea, to similar effect, while purporting to avoid the constitutional non-delegation question altogether.

Recall from chapter 2 that, as a general matter, under the *Chevron* doctrine a court must defer to any reasonable agency interpretation of a statutory ambiguity. Within a decade of that 1984 decision, however, the Supreme Court was beginning to suggest that when the statutory interpretation question in the case raised a particularly important issue of federal policy, it would decide the issue itself, rather than deferring to an agency. Sometimes it reached that conclusion on the theory that the statute did in fact clearly answer the question, thus making it unnecessary to apply *Chevron*'s deference formula. Other times, it simply concluded that Congress did not intend for agencies to enjoy deference when making such a high-stakes interpretation. This approach became known among scholars as the "major questions" doctrine, since the Court seemed to apply it when the interpretive issue raised a "major" policy question. Scholars have traced this judicial approach at least as far back as 1994, exactly a decade after the *Chevron* decision.[18]

An example illustrates the major questions idea. In 2015, the Court faced the question whether the Affordable Care Act (ACA) provided tax credits for persons who bought insurance on the federal healthcare exchanges the law established, or whether such credits were available only to persons who purchased insurance on a state-run exchange. In *King v. Burwell*, the Court held that the credits were available to purchasers on both types of exchanges. For our purposes, the important point is that the Court reached this decision independently, rather than according the agency—in this case, the IRS—the normal deference *Chevron* would call for if the statute was ambiguous.

Why didn't it defer? Here is what Chief Justice Roberts said:

> When analyzing an agency's interpretation of a statute, we often apply the two-step framework announced in *Chevron*. . . . This approach is premised on the theory that a statute's ambiguity constitutes an implicit delegation from Congress to the agency to fill in the statutory gaps. In extraordinary cases, however, there may be reason to hesitate before concluding that Congress has intended such an implicit delegation. This is one of those cases. The tax credits are among the [ACA]'s key reforms, involving billions of dollars in spending each year and affecting the price of health insurance for millions of people. Whether those credits are available on Federal Exchanges is thus a question of deep economic and political significance that is central to this statutory scheme; had Congress wished to assign that question to an agency, it surely would have done so expressly. . . . This is not a case for the IRS. It is instead our task to determine the correct reading of [the ACA].[19]

In *King*, the importance of the question on the table—its "deep economic and political significance"—meant that, unless Congress was crystal clear about giving the agency the decisional authority, the Court would conclude that it itself must decide the interpretive issue. Under the major questions doctrine, therefore, "major" statutory interpretation "questions" are usually for courts to decide. As it turned out, the Court agreed with the government's position—under the ACA, tax credits were indeed available on the federal exchanges. But the Court decided that question for itself, rather than simply deferring to the IRS's interpretation. Notably, the Court did not assert that power for itself because it thought the statute was clear; at least twice, the Court concluded that the relevant provision was ambiguous.[20] Normally, such ambiguity means that the agency enjoys *Chevron* deference—but not when the question on the table is a "major" one.

The major questions doctrine thus presents another alternative for a court that wishes to preclude agencies from making decisions that could be described as foundational or politically fraught. On its face, it offers an attractive option: By insisting that agencies not be allowed leeway to interpret statutory ambiguities that implicate important policy issues, this approach seems an elegant way to avoid having agencies making high-stakes political decisions, without calling out the constitutional heavy artillery of the non-delegation doctrine.

Unfortunately, it doesn't work. Analogize the situation to the follow-the-ball shell games Times Square barkers used back in the day to separate tourists from their money. Just like in those games, the statutory interpretation ball has to be somewhere. If the Court is going to refuse to defer to agency statutory interpretations on major questions, then it will end up deciding the meaning of the statute itself, as it did in *King*. That result promises to absolve the agency of the political heat it would otherwise feel for taking a politically fraught step based on its own interpretation of a vague statute. But the agency still must take the first crack at the interpretive question; the major questions doctrine does not allow the agency simply to sit back and say nothing.

But the major questions doctrine does more than fail to remove agencies from all politically fraught issues. As the previous paragraph noted, the analogy to the follow-the-ball game teaches that interpretive authority has to rest somewhere when Congress writes a statute that lacks an obvious meaning. Under *Chevron*, that responsibility lies with agencies themselves, as long as the agency interpretation is reasonable. Under the major questions doctrine, that responsibility falls to courts, as in *King*. In other words, because *someone* has to figure out what a statute means on an important issue, if the major questions doctrine removes that authority from agencies, it ends up under the court's shell. That's where the ball lands at the end of the major questions shell game.

There is good reason to be skeptical about that placement of interpretive responsibility. If one considers the two fundamental reasons Congress delegates important decisions to agencies, rather than courts— agencies' superior expertise and their control by a politically accountable president—there emerges little reason to favor courts as deciders of those questions. On both counts—expertise in the given regulatory field and political accountability—judges are inferior to agencies. (Moreover, agencies provide opportunities for public input into the statutory interpretation decision that courts simply cannot match.) To be sure, judges *are* well-versed in statutory interpretation—literally, that's where their expertise lay. But *Chevron* deference—the deference that disappears in major questions cases—is triggered only when the statute fails to provide a clear answer to the particular interpretive question on the table. Thus, courts' expertise in statutory interpretation is not triggered in major questions cases that would otherwise call for deference to the agency.

But if the act of finding meaning in a vague statute is not exactly "statutory interpretation," then what is it? According to *Chevron* itself, it is policymaking. As Justice Stevens explained in *Chevron*, when a court concludes that the statute is ambiguous, what an agency (or court) is doing when it "interprets" the statute is policymaking—taking whatever meaning can be found in the statute, filtering it through the interpreter's conception of good policy, and reaching a result. That's exactly what happened in *King*, where the Court observed that a contrary conclusion about tax credit availability on the federal insurance exchanges would trigger a cascade that would destroy the insurance markets the law established. That may be excellent policy analysis. But it's not straight-up statutory interpretation, and thus not something in which judges have a comparative advantage. If anyone has a comparative advantage in policymaking, one would think it would be the expert and politically accountable agency.[21] Thus, the major questions doctrine, a tool we might have picked up in order to promote agency expertise, ends up, if anything, impairing it.

A defender of the doctrine might retort that the entire point of the major questions doctrine is to assume that, in fact, Congress did not intend to delegate such important decisions to the agency. In other words, the doctrine assumes that the statute must answer the (major) question on the table, because Congress would not have delegated such a big decision to an agency, at least not without saying so explicitly. But starting the analysis with that assumption constitutes an act of brute force. Simply insisting that the statute must contain a clear meaning somewhere does not make it so.

To be sure, a court could still "find" a meaning in a vague statute without deferring to an agency. Sometimes courts must do just that—for example, when Congress writes a vague statute but does not delegate to an agency the power to implement it. Think of federal antitrust laws, which are written very broadly but which end up having to be "interpreted" by the courts, with those interpretations looking a lot like judicial policymaking. But when an agency *is* available, it makes no good sense for a court to deny it the authority to make policy and instead to assert that policymaking power for itself. Such an assertion would mean one of two things: Either courts are a more natural place than agencies to make "major" policy decisions, or the importance of the issue means that there just has to be a clear meaning waiting for judicial discovery, if only courts look hard enough. The first justification is simply wrong—in fact, there are many reasons that agencies are better than courts at policymaking. The second justification—that the importance of the issue must mean that there exists a clear answer somewhere—simply wills that clear meaning into existence. That latter justification for not deferring to the agency would amount to moving the shells around the barker's table but assuring the tourist that the ball—the statutory vagueness in need of policy-based "interpretation"—has magically disappeared. It hasn't.

New and Strengthened—But Not Improved

A variant of the major questions doctrine poses an even more problematic hurdle for effective expertise-based administrative regulation. In recent years, judges have begun suggesting that the lack of a clear statutory meaning on an important question of agency authority means, not that the court decides the interpretive question, but instead that Congress should be understood as having denied the agency the authority at issue. In other words, this variant of the major questions doctrine essentially puts the decisional ball back under Congress's shell: If a statute does not explicitly authorize the agency to take an important regulatory action, then the statute should be read as denying it that authority.

This is not just a denial of interpretive authority to agencies. Rather, it is a denial of substantive regulatory power. Rather than simply taking away from agencies the authority to interpret their authorizing statutes, this stronger version of the major questions doctrine presumes that, failing an explicit statutory grant of authorization, an agency lacks the power to regulate in that way. It's not just that the agency doesn't get deference for its reading of the statute and has to take its chances with the court's interpretation. In that case, an agency might still ultimately win, as it did in *King*. Rather, under this stronger version of the doctrine, the agency loses on the merits.

One might wonder what the problem is. For example, one might think that it makes sense to deny an agency important or fraught regulatory authority unless Congress is clear about bestowing it. Indeed, such "clear statement" rules abound in constitutional law. For example, when the Court wishes to protect the federal-state balance it often does so by requiring Congress to be extremely clear if it wishes to regulate state governments.

But that's the problem. This stronger version of the major questions doctrine implements a presumption against aggressive agency regulation, just like its constitutional law cousins implement an analogous presumption against federal regulation of the states. This stronger, more substantive version of the doctrine thus reflects a bias against aggressive regulation that Congress must provide a clear statement to overcome. Aggressive regulation may be a good thing or a bad thing. But the anti-regulation bias this version of the major questions doctrine encodes hearkens back to old, pre–New Deal judicial philosophy that greeted aggressive government regulation with similar skepticism. To be sure, those old cases focused on the constitutionality of legislative action. By contrast, the stronger version of the major questions doctrine does not deny Congress's authority to grant agencies broad regulatory powers, but "merely" insists that it do so clearly. Nevertheless, the skepticism reflected in that stronger version of the doctrine echoes the early twentieth-century Court's skepticism about regulation. As such, it itself should be greeted skeptically.

One might seek to justify this stronger version of the doctrine as an application of the non-delegation doctrine discussed earlier in this chapter.[22] On this theory, the presumption against finding Congress to have given agencies broad regulatory authority rests on concerns about concluding that Congress has delegated away the power to decide the "major questions" that constitute the core of its Article I legislative power. While the current non-delegation doctrine itself focuses more on whether Congress has provided *standards* guiding agency regulation (via the "intelligible principle" requirement), this emphasis on the *scope* of the power Congress has delegated certainly has played a role in the Court's actual application of the intelligible principle requirement.[23] Nevertheless, focusing too heavily on the scope of the asserted delegation, as opposed to the existence of guidance on how the agency should use its statutorily granted authority, risks turning the non-delegation doctrine—a tool for ensuring that Congress makes the foundational policy decisions that the agency then interprets—into a tool for making it harder for Congress to make *particular* policy decisions—i.e., those favoring agency regulatory authority.

Moving beyond such conceptual points, consider the practicalities. By placing a thumb on the judicial scales against finding broad statutory grants of power to agencies, the stronger version of the major questions doctrine makes it harder for legislative advocates of such grants. It imposes on those advocates the burden, not just of securing congressional majorities for those grants, but majorities for explicitly worded versions of such grants. That latter hurdle is different, and higher, than the hurdle advocates must usually surmount when they seek passage of legislation. Congresspersons often vote to delegate broad authority to agencies under vaguely worded statutes exactly because of that vague wording. The vagueness allows congresspersons to take credit for "solving" a problem without being held responsible for particular wording that might be controversial. It also allows them to criticize the agency later for "misinterpreting" the statutory grant.[24] Finally, as Justice Stevens recognized in *Chevron* itself, Congress may choose to word its grants vaguely because its members could not agree on more specific language. What the stronger version of the major questions doctrine means is that, whatever the reason for them, vaguely worded grants of important regulatory authority will be rejected as insufficient. Thus, advocates for such authority must muster a stronger consensus than normally required to win enactment of legislation, in order to overcome congresspersons' preferences for vaguely worded grants.

There's no good reason for such a requirement, unless, again, the system is properly understood as encoding a presumption against regulation. Other basic statements of regulatory law contradict such a presumption. For example, recall the *State Farm* airbags case from chapter 2. In *State Farm*, the Supreme Court rejected the argument that an agency's rescission of a regulation—and thus, its return of the marketplace to a deregulated state—merited lesser judicial scrutiny than an agency's imposition of a regulation.[25] Similarly, it is settled law that a decision to rescind a regulation must go through the same rulemaking procedure as the decision to promulgate one. Thus, deregulatory decisions get no shortcut, and the Court places no favorable thumb on the scale because of an action's deregulatory effect. But the stronger version of the major questions doctrine does just that. To conclude the Times Square shell game analogy, the strong version of the major question doctrine doesn't just hide the ball—it changes the game entirely.

A Solution from Congress?

Of course, neither the non-delegation doctrine itself nor either version of the major questions doctrine would be necessary if Congress did in fact legislate with more specificity. The judicial doctrines this chapter has discussed all respond to congressional failure—in the non-delegation context, failure to specify adequate guidance for agency action, and in the major questions context, failure to speak with clarity about whether the agency has the authority to act. If Congress did speak with more detail and clarity, there would be no need for such doctrines. As this chapter noted at the start, such statutory precision would remove at least some of the pressure agencies face to make decisions that everyone recognizes as political. If one wanted to promote both the reality and the public perception that regulation is based on expertise rather than politics, one might hope that Congress could provide agencies with clearer guidance on the policies they should implement.

Unfortunately, that is not likely to happen. Legislating is hard work under the best of circumstances. The Constitution erects a series of vetogates that opponents of legislation can deploy to derail a bill. On top of those constitutional hurdles lurk the internal legislative rules—most notably but not only the filibuster—that demand even greater consensus than required by the Constitution's formal requirements. Add to these hurdles the close but intense partisan divide that characterizes the nation and Congress—in other words, a situation in which Congress is closely but sharply divided, thus making bipartisan agreement among centrists both critical for most legislation and simultaneously a much harder proposition than in earlier decades. Finally, consider the fact that many regulatory problems today are intensely complex and contested. (What risks are posed by the current amount of human-generated climate change? What effect would net neutrality have on the nation's telecommunications network? What changes would improve Americans' access to health care?)

Given all these factors, we should not be surprised that Congress's output of major regulatory legislation has declined markedly over the last several decades. Consider, for example, that the last major amendments to the Clean Air Act were enacted thirty years ago, as was the last major civil rights bill addressing a new type of discrimination. Given these facts, perhaps we should not be surprised that non-congressional actors have taken the lead. It was an agency, not Congress, that took the first halting federal steps to combat climate change, via its interpretation of the Clean Air Act (enacted in 1970 and amended in 1977 and 1991), and it was the Supreme Court that guaranteed employment non-discrimination for LGBT employees, via its interpretation of the Civil Rights Act of 1964 (which also saw its last major amendments in 1991).

This dynamic will not change simply because the Court insists that any major legislation Congress enacts be more specific. Indeed, by requiring such specificity, whether via the non-delegation doctrine or the stronger version of the major questions doctrine, the Court would only make legislating harder. Anyone expecting a dynamic in which the

Court figuratively knocks heads together and forces Congress to reach more specific legislative compromises would likely be disappointed.[26] Indeed, the doctrines this chapter has discussed might well incentivize opponents of regulatory legislation to refuse to accept such specificity. Without these doctrines, the resulting statutory vagueness might in turn bring them unpleasant surprises, if the agency wields those vague statutory grants aggressively and wins judicial deference for those interpretations. They might thus be incentivized to fight for clear but more restrictive language. But with these doctrines, anti-regulation forces may try to compel Congress to settle for broadly worded laws, hopeful that such legislation either would be struck down as violating the non-delegation doctrine or (more likely) would be interpreted as not featuring the precise statements needed to authorize aggressive agency action.

In sum, both the non-delegation doctrine and the stronger version of the major questions doctrine seem conceptually problematic, institutionally unwieldly (from the perspectives of both the courts that would have to enforce them and the Congress that would have to enact more specific legislation), and conducive to more regulatory stasis. The weaker version of the major questions doctrine might be justifiable, even though it features the major drawback of shifting interpretive authority away from the expert and politically accountable agency charged with policymaking and toward the federal judiciary, which is neither an expert on the topics of such regulation nor politically accountable. (And, again, agency deliberations on those issues are open to broad public participation in a way that judicial deliberations are not.) But even if courts adopt that weaker version of the doctrine, agencies initially will still be confronted with the politically fraught question of how intensively to regulate, even if that decision is reviewed by the federal courts without any deference. Ultimately, judicial doctrines that seek to force congressional precision will likely not save agencies from having to make politically controversial decisions. Neither will insisting that Congress act on its own accord.[27]

Looking Forward

This chapter addressed a reasonable question about agency expertise: If broad statutes force agencies to make politically fraught decisions, could expertise be served by forcing Congress to give agencies more policy guidance, thus allowing agencies to accentuate their expertise? It turns out the answer is no. Anyone hoping to promote agency expertise will have to look elsewhere. That is where this book now turns—elsewhere, in successive chapters, to the White House, then to agencies themselves, and then to the courts.

5

Curbing Political Control

Elections have consequences. Over the last generation, presidents have cited this seemingly obvious truth to insist on increased political control over administrative agencies. Chapters 2 and 3 described the mechanisms by which presidents have sought that tightened control: regulatory review requirements, Clinton-style "presidential administration," increased political vetting of larger numbers of political appointees parachuted into agencies, and deemphasis of the career civil service bureaucracy in favor of contractors. Those developments reflect presidents' desires to strengthen the already strong influence of their political and regulatory philosophy within the agency. This increased power allows presidents to influence agencies' regulatory output at a much deeper level than would be the case if the president were limited merely to appointing agency heads, let alone being limited to (figuratively) shouting at agencies' headquarters from the White House portico.[1] It allows them to politicize regulation, at the expense of regulatory expertise.

This chapter considers the possibilities for reducing inappropriate White House influence over the bureaucracy. The focus is on *inappropriate* influence. Nobody should believe that it is possible to erase all presidential influence over what administrative agencies do. More important, nobody should want that. Elections have consequences for a good reason: When conducted fairly and competently, their results are presumed to reflect the policy preferences of the American people.[2] Thus, to the extent administrative action reflects decisions about contested values, the administrative process should at the least account for the incumbent administration's positions on those issues. Of course, those positions cannot justify a decision that conflicts with a duly enacted statute, since that statute is presumed to reflect even more clearly the public's values (even if, as in a long-standing law, the values are those of an earlier generation). But when a broadly worded statute allows different value choices, the political values of the administration that most recently succeeded at the polls should play a significant role in determining agency action.

The hard question is determining what constitutes *inappropriate* influence, and how to excise it while retaining an appropriate role for presidential values and priorities. As a political scientist in the late nineteenth century, Woodrow Wilson explained that the goal of administration should be to distinguish between apolitical expertise and political values, assigning the former to the bureaucracy and the latter to the president.[3] More than a century's worth of experience has revealed the impossibility of a hard and fast division between the two, even assuming that that was something Wilson and his contemporaries desired or even thought possible.[4] Thus, again, the question becomes finding the appropriate balance between expertise and politics, and creating structures and procedures that can best implement that balance. This task is necessary because, as this chapter seeks to demonstrate, the balance has become skewed in favor of politics.

Crafting the Balance

A starting point in crafting that balance should be a rejection of extreme positions on either side. At one extreme, denying any role for presidential influence is a non-starter. As a constitutional matter, Article II's vesting of "the executive power" in the president, and its admonition that the president "take Care that the Laws be faithfully executed,"[5] requires that the president play at least some role in implementing laws. To grant the president that role but then deny that he can export any of his own values into the myriad discretionary judgments such implementation requires is effectively to deny him that power—or perhaps simply to ask the impossible of him.[6]

Beyond constitutional concerns, it would also be undesirable as a policy matter to place the responsibility of making such value judgments solely in the hands of unelected administrators. At least as long as we accept Congress's power to delegate exceptionally broad legislative power to agencies, removing the president from any politically inflected influence on how agencies implement their statutory authority would create a system in which unelected civil servants make fundamental value judgments, unsupervised by a politically accountable actor. Unless one is willing to rely entirely on statutorily required administrative procedures to generate democratic accountability, such a system's lack of control either by Congress (via statute, oversight, and budgetary control) or the president (via formal and informal control measures) would suffer from a significant accountability deficit.[7]

The opposite extreme—complete presidential control—is also unacceptable. Leave aside the risk that such control could lead agencies to violate their statutory mandates. The most notable presidential initiatives designed to control the bureaucracy—the White House regulatory review orders discussed in chapters 2 and 3—disclaimed any pretension to authority to command an agency to violate its authorizing statute. But assume away such presidential self-control. The fact remains that Congress usually chooses to delegate power not to the president himself, but instead to an administrative agency. As one scholar has observed, complete presidential control over how that agency administers the statute in question would transform that congressional delegation decision into a mere suggestion.[8] Indeed, that transformation would raise yet another legality concern.

Moreover, as a policy matter one should desire an independent agency voice on regulatory matters. It is a basic assumption of American administrative law—and a basic justification for it—that agencies are repositories of various types of expertise. Recall the introduction's discussion of expertise. To summarize that discussion, beyond technical expertise, such as NHTSA auto engineers' knowledge about auto collision dynamics, or SEC economists' understanding of capital markets, agencies also possess what this book has called regulatory expertise— that is, expertise in the job of regulating. That expertise is what one scholar called the "unique wisdom" of regulatory agencies, honed by experience in doing actual regulatory work.[9] The character and location of such expertise make the bureaucracy an indispensable part of the regulatory process. This realization in turn requires a conclusion that a regulatory role must remain for agencies in their capacity as possessors of regulatory expertise—not simply agencies as mechanical implementers of presidential will.[10]

How then, to craft the balance between presidential control and agency autonomy? Thinking about the analysis so far helps point the way. At a basic level, presidential control is thought to be legitimate because it transmits to agencies the policy preferences presumed to be those of the American people. On the other hand, administrative autonomy is considered appropriate primarily because it reflects expertise and, perhaps secondarily, because administrative procedures are considered sufficiently fair to legitimate the resulting agency action.[11]

By itself, the politics/expertise distinction this balance reflects simply restates the perhaps-simplistic description of Woodrow Wilson's and his Progressive Era colleagues' attempt to distinguish political decision-making from apolitical public administration. Nevertheless, keeping an eye on these two ideal types—on the one hand, the explicitly (and appropriately) political process of selecting one value over another, and, on the other, the apolitical use of expertise to analyze a regulatory issue—provides us with overall guidance when striking the balance.

The remainder of this chapter uses that fundamental distinction to consider the appropriate role for politics in public administration, and, conversely, the role for expertise. It will consider that balance in the course of thinking about three ways in which presidents seek to exert control over bureaucracies' work product: White House regulatory review, "presidential administration" of the sort Justice Kagan recounted and chapter 3 discussed, and presidential (or otherwise political) selection of agency heads and agency personnel under the agency head level.[12] The next chapter continues this narrative of agencies' structures and their relationships with political actors by moving the focus inside the agency, to consider how political appointees within agencies interact with career civil servants.

OIRA Regulatory Review

White House review of administrative regulatory action is the most formal and explicit control mechanism this chapter considers. That review rests on formal presidential documents: the executive orders mandating such review (discussed in chapters 2 and 3), and the variety of other executive orders, circulars, and sundry documents that reflect presidents' attempts to stamp the bureaucracy with the incumbent administration's views of wise (or politically expedient) administration.

This book focuses on the regulatory review executive orders. Recall from chapter 2 that the Reagan order, Executive Order 12,291, required that important regulatory steps—not just the promulgation of final regulations but even notices of proposed rulemakings—be subject to review by the White House Office of Information and Regulatory Affairs (OIRA). That order required agencies to submit to OIRA cost-benefit analyses of important regulatory actions, which OIRA would then review along with the proposed rule. The executive order prevented agencies from promulgating final regulations until OIRA consulted with the agency, if OIRA informed the agency that it wanted such a consultation. OIRA's delay authority of course enabled it to exert politically motivated influence over the agency action in question.

Given this book's focus on expertise, its consideration of OIRA regulatory review will emphasize how that review affects the expertise content of agency actions and, if relevant, public perceptions of agency expertise.[13] However, it is still important to consider the legal questions surrounding OIRA review, as those questions provide a backdrop to the expertise inquiry. The fundamental legal question OIRA review poses concerns the legality of White House direction of agency action that statutes delegate to the agencies themselves. Recall from earlier chapters that the foundation for any agency regulatory activity lies in the authority Congress gives the agency. For example, the EPA's authority to regulate air pollution derives from the Clean Air Act. OIRA review, to the extent it results in the White House directing an agency to use its regulatory authority in particular ways, risks violating Congress's decision to delegate that authority to the agency, not to OIRA or the president.

Confronted with this argument, defenders of OIRA review offer essentially two responses. One response maintains that congressional delegations of authority to executive branch agencies are best interpreted as authorizing some degree of White House control over how agencies use that authority.[14] Even though this is an argument about statutory interpretation, it rests on an assumption about the president's constitutional authority to superintend the bureaucracy. Essentially, this response argues that, when Congress delegates power to administrative agencies, it does so fully aware of the president's constitutionally grounded authority to control how those agencies use such authority. It observes that, given the option of delegating regulatory authority to an independent agency, a congressional decision to delegate such power instead to an agency whose head serves at the president's pleasure implies consent or implicit authorization to the president to influence how the recipient agency uses that power.[15]

Beyond this constitutionally inflected statutory interpretation argument, defenders of OIRA review also rely more directly on the Constitution. As noted earlier in the book, such defenders of presidential authority argue that Article II's conferral on the president of "the executive power" and its admonition that he "take Care that the Laws be faithfully executed"[16] create presidential power over how administrative agencies implement, or "execute," federal law. As the book also explained earlier, this argument is pressed with particular force by adherents of the so-called unitary executive theory, which reads Article II as granting the president complete control over the implementation of federal law.[17] Opposing this view are those who insist that Congress's broad power to make federal law and create the agencies that are tasked with implementing it authorizes Congress to bestow implementation discretion on federal officials other than the president, with that discretion remaining free of direct interference, even from the president himself.[18]

The clash these legal arguments address—boiled down, a clash between the president's and Congress's opposing claims to control administrative agencies and direct their output—is a matter of pointed disagreement among scholars and judges. Evaluating it would require enormous space and effort and would take the book far afield from its more practical concerns. For our purposes, the most important consequence of those opposing claims is that White House defenses of OIRA review have acknowledged a role for agencies in implementing the statutory mandates Congress imposes on them. That acknowledgment surfaced in the Department of Justice's 1981 memo defending the legality of OIRA review.[19] It also appeared in Executive Order 12,291 itself, in its numerous cautions that particular provisions of that order apply only to the extent permitted by law.[20]

Despite this genuflection toward agency authority, practice during the Reagan administration featured clashes between OIRA and agencies, in which OIRA attempted to prevent or delay agencies from promulgating regulations.[21] In one particularly egregious case, OSHA, acting a mere 24 hours before a court-ordered deadline, sent OIRA a workplace chemical exposure standard that included a particular exposure limit. When OIRA objected to that limit, OSHA simply crossed it out and finalized the regulation without it. Unsurprisingly, a reviewing court rejected the standard's lack of such a limit as unsupported by the record—a record that had been compiled under the assumption that the limit in question was part of the regulation.[22]

In response to such incidents, the Clinton administration's analogous regulatory review order included a more explicit provision recognizing agencies' statutory authority.[23] On the other hand, the Clinton order also provided that disputes between OIRA and agencies would be resolved by the vice president or the president himself, thus suggesting that the Clinton White House retained ultimate authority to decide the relevant regulatory question.[24] Regardless of these details, or the proper resolution of the larger dispute about presidential legal authority to impose such review, the existence of legal and political controversies surrounding OIRA review has shaped that review toward White House guidance and direction of agencies, rather than out-and-out appropriation of agencies' regulatory prerogatives. For example, a court decision that OIRA had illegally blocked an agency from promulgating a congressionally required rule caused a political storm that forced OIRA in 1989 to promise not to use its review power to delay a regulation.[25]

Given the resulting shape of OIRA regulatory review, how has it affected agencies' ability to use their expertise? Assume for the moment that, absent White House review, those outputs would reflect both technical and regulatory expertise. How does White House review change that characteristic, if at all?

In several possible ways, it turns out. First, consider the cost-benefit analysis such review mandates. The discussion in chapter 2 of cost-benefit analysis during the Reagan years explained that, despite sounding like a rational—indeed, an expertise-promoting—exercise, its implementation and even the decision to perform it at all reflected political value choices, largely cloaked under a veneer of technocratic analysis. Indeed, one gets a sense of CBA's foundation in value judgments when one thinks about how it has been performed. Recall from chapter 3 that the Clinton order took a softer approach to such analysis than the Reagan order, acknowledging the difficulty of quantifying many regulatory benefits and extending the scope of the benefits to be considered to non-quantifiable values such as equity. The Obama order went even farther, including dignity as a factor to consider.[26] These tweaks may be good policy—but that is what they are: policy.

Unfortunately, the dark side of such policy choices comes along with the bright side. Decisions about arcane inputs such as the assumed discount rate have the potential to create massive skews in CBA results. Recall chapter 2's example of an OSHA workplace exposure standard whose draft analysis found workplace injuries to cost ten times more than the final rule did, with the difference explainable simply by the selection of different discount rates. That selection is as much a political as it is a scientific decision.

None of this even broaches the possibility of incompetent (or willfully bad) performance of CBA. For example, in 2017 the Trump administration suspended an Obama-era regulation requiring reduced natural gas flaring during some oil and gas extraction, a rule the Obama administration concluded would create $204 million in benefits. The Trump agency's suspension decision recognized the cost savings to the industry of suspending the rule, but completely failed to consider the regulation's benefits, even to critique or evaluate the prior rule's calculations. As one can imagine, the reviewing court was not impressed.[27]

Move on now to consider how CBA distorts not just regulatory results, but regulatory processes. Critics of White House review have argued that the cost-benefit mandate (even a "soft" mandate of the sort reflected in the Clinton order) imposes a final requirement for agency action—a final hurdle to surmount—that diverts attention from the issues that the agency feels appropriate to consider as part of its internal regulatory process. That internal process is an intricate one, requiring the agency to consider a wide variety of factors, which might range from the proposed regulation's technological feasibility, to its impact on other values (including other values that might matter to the president), the agency's ability to marshal the type and quantity of data that would be necessary to support it in a judicial challenge, and the likely reaction of key external constituencies.

Of course, a tally of the proposed regulation's costs and benefits may well be one of those considerations the agency has already considered. Indeed, presumably it should be: Even laws that mandate regulation up to the point of "technical feasibility" have been understood to require a consideration of costs.[28] But elevating that one consideration to the level of a final, standalone factor, as the regulatory review orders do, risks distorting the agency's decision-making process. At best, it requires a final consideration of a single factor, plucked out from the mix of factors that had gone into the agency's earlier analysis. So understood, the executive orders' cost-benefit mandate risks turning the enterprise of cost-benefit analysis into a game of after-the-fact justification for a decision reached through a different process that considered a broader set of considerations.[29] Beyond the obvious flaws with this dynamic as a matter of good decision-making procedures, the ex post nature of the agency's reasoning could seep into its final justification for the rule and thus damage the regulation's odds of surviving judicial review.[30] As an extreme example, recall how OSHA responded to OIRA's concerns about one element of the agency's proposed chemical workplace exposure standard by simply deleting that element from its final rule, a choice that resulted in having the entire rule struck down.

Such after-the-fact distortion of the agency's rule is the best case. At worst, the cost-benefit mandate has the potential to infect the entire rulemaking process by emphasizing one overriding consideration. In so doing, it potentially disrupts the intricate process of weighing competing factors that otherwise goes into making regulatory decisions. Again, recall the introduction's discussion of regulatory expertise, which it explained essentially as the agency staff's acquired skill at balancing the multitude of factors that enter into a regulatory decision. Given the need to balance a variety of factors, a single-minded mandate that regulations survive a cost-benefit analysis threatens to disturb that intricate process. And this observation does not even consider the capabilities of the OIRA staff who implement that narrow mandate—capabilities that at least one scholar has identified as lacking in understanding of this regulatory expertise.[31]

Thus, even aside from concerns about its competent performance, the very requirement of a final cost-benefit check on regulatory action threatens that action's expertise content. In addition to disturbing the intricate balancing and deliberative intra-agency process described above, OIRA's performance of regulatory review essentially creates two rulemaking processes: an internal process that considers evidence, balances factors, consults stakeholders, and weighs options, and a second process conducted at OIRA itself. That second process is performed by outsiders, emphasizes either one consideration (costs and benefits) or costs and benefits and other idiosyncratic priorities the president happens to value, and features none of the informal consultation and option-weighing that marked the internal process.

That second rulemaking process is also sudden and potentially avulsive. Rather than constituting part of the rulemaking process from its inception, OIRA review, as Jon Michaels puts it, "swoops in" at a particular moment in time—potentially, "at the last possible minute."[32] To be sure, agencies presumably anticipate at least the possibility of OIRA taking a special interest in a particular rule. But even that anticipation is a crap shoot, given what two scholars concluded was OIRA's "idiosyncratic" interest in carefully reviewing some rules but not others.[33] Moreover, OIRA input focuses heavily on only one or at most a limited number of the rule's aspects; indeed, a Reagan-era study of the OIRA process found widespread agency complaints that OIRA review "is often focused on 'nit-picking.'"[34] It thus threatens to distort the agency's more broad-ranging balancing process that emerges from its regulatory expertise.

OIRA review is also opaque. Experience under the Reagan administration's order revealed a dynamic in which influential groups enjoying privileged access to the White House funneled information and arguments to the agency via OIRA. That process occurred both out of view of the public rulemaking process and divorced from the agency's organic internal process.[35] It's quite likely that such well-connected private entities prefer a back-channel OIRA-enabled funnel to the agency over the public rulemaking process, since privately generated arguments and data that OIRA chooses to funnel to the agency presumably come with the administration's imprimatur. The very weight added by that additional thumb on the scale distorts the force that information would otherwise merit in the agency's expert evaluation of those arguments and that information.[36]

These phenomena combine to paint a troubling picture of OIRA review. Episodic—indeed, "idiosyncratic"[37]—review that is narrowly focused, opaque, and outside the agency's organic internal decision-making process, almost assuredly disrupts the normal rulemaking process. It is hard to see how it can promote the agency's ability to use its expertise. It is easy to see how it can impair it.

Despite these problems, White House review has its defenders. At a policy level, they observe that it allows a deregulation-minded administration to push back against an agency that would otherwise be inclined, for reasons of institutional mission and culture, to err on the side of over-regulating.[38] At a more structural level, they argue that White House review allows the president to ensure that his administration presents a unified regulatory program to the nation.[39] Relatedly, scholars and officials argue that such review gives the administration a chance to influence the agency to the same degree as congressional committees and private stakeholders, the two groups that, along with the agency itself, constitute Washington's notorious "iron triangle."[40] Boring down to the level of intra-agency operations, such defenses also suggest that White House review allows the president to monitor the conduct, not just of the agency, but of the political appointees who run it and who might be tempted to stray from the president's course. If those officials remain loyal to the president, such review is justified as providing them backup in their asserted struggles against a hostile or at least unaccommodating bureaucracy.[41]

Many of these concerns are reasonable. Given that regulation requires not just technocratic judgments or regulatory expertise, but also political value choices, it is appropriate for political values to influence the choices agencies make. These defenses thus require us to consider two questions: whether White House review is necessary to promote the administration's political values, and whether that review, regardless of its usefulness in promoting those values, exacts unacceptable costs.

On the first question, some scholars argue that the president's control over his political appointees—his ability to select them, to remove them, and to influence them informally—suffices to transmit the administration's political values into the agency's decision-making process.[42] This argument holds that such informal controls are more than adequate to ensure that the president's priorities influence an agency's output. Trends in the selection of political appointees bear this argument out. Recall from chapter 2 that the last forty years have witnessed a revolution in how presidents view their cabinet officials. For example, when introducing his cabinet to the nation in December 1968, Richard Nixon made a point of stressing the independence of the persons he had chosen.[43] By contrast, today, cabinet members are chosen primarily for their fealty to the president and his political program. Still, one must concede that some political scientists have identified inherent tensions between the president and his cabinet heads, the latter of which inevitably have to look to many persons and institutions for support.[44] Such tensions arguably reduce the president's influence over his cabinet heads and support the argument for OIRA review as a substitute method of control.

A variant of this argument holds that OIRA review reinforces agencies' political appointees in their struggles against hostile staffs.[45] But the picture of beleaguered and out-gunned agency heads in need of presidential backup appears at least overstated. If Professor Golden's study of Reagan-era agencies has shown anything, it is that career officials' motivations do not single-mindedly point toward frustrating political appointees' agendas, even when those agendas conflict with the careerists' own preferences.[46] Given the authority political appointees wield, and the at-least presumptive duty careerists feel toward their political appointee supervisors, the argument that those appointees need White House regulatory review as a backup seems, at the very least, unproven. Indeed, if anything, experience during the Reagan administration demonstrated that the power to make a large number of sub-cabinet political appointments provides the president with significant power to counteract any such careerist undermining.[47]

At any rate, it is fair to ask whether OIRA review successfully transmits systematic presidential preferences about regulation to agencies. Two scholars question that claim, given the unpredictable selectivity of OIRA review.[48] Other scholars question whether OIRA inherently reflects the president's priorities.[49]

Consider now the second point, about the policy costs of OIRA review. The earlier discussion about the effects of White House review on the rulemaking process raises serious questions about those costs. The concerns that discussion raised—about the distorting effect White House review imposes on both the agency's internal decision-making process and its regulatory output (not to mention its blunt preference for deregulation)—have led some scholars to urge ending or at least overhauling the practice.[50] It's hard to disagree with these critiques, especially when one recognizes the myriad tools presidents retain to influence agency action and the unavoidable tension regulatory review creates with Congress's authority to give agencies their marching orders.

The hard fact for fans of presidential power is that Congress enjoys the ultimate authority to direct the course of agency regulation, via its legislative power. When Congress wields that authority by providing very broad discretion to agencies, White House review of proposed regulations, and especially review for compliance with White House preferences on a single criterion, threatens to wrest that discretion away from the agency. No compelling arguments justify that conduct.

Another Role for OIRA

None of the foregoing is intended to suggest that the president lacks any constitutional justification to interest himself in how agencies use their statutorily granted discretion. To the contrary, his Article II power to enforce the laws clearly gives him a stake in agency action. But, as Rena Steinzor and others have argued, the president's ability to select—and remove—the upper echelons of the agency's bureaucracy, not to mention the informal influence he retains over those persons, likely provides the president all the control that Article II demands.[51] To be blunt, OIRA review may not be unconstitutional. But neither is it constitutionally required.

In fact, other types of presidential control may be more appropriate to the president's Article II duties. For example, scholars have suggested that White House review might appropriately focus on the agency's interpretation and application of its authorizing statute.[52] Such review by definition would respect Congress's ultimate authority to set the terms under which an agency acts. Yet it also fits comfortably within the president's Article II authority to "take Care that the Laws be faithfully executed," and even allows the White House to exert some measure of politically inflected influence on the agency's regulatory choices. In many cases, such review would focus the White House's attention on the variety of factors Congress often requires agencies to consider when regulating. OIRA review that focused on how the agency has considered those factors would likely also reinforce the agency's own attention to them, since it would be aware of the impending White House review.

In addition, more programmatic decisions by the agency—for example, to set its future regulatory agenda—may legitimately be subject to White House review. President Reagan again led the way on this point, when in 1985 he issued another executive order, this one requiring each agency to forward to OIRA its regulatory agenda for the coming year.[53] Such White House review of regulatory planning involves OIRA at an earlier and more programmatic stage of the agency's work. At that stage, White House direction has a less disruptive effect on agencies' action and is also more justifiable as presidential coordination of their work.

By focusing on that earlier stage when the agency is not yet deliberating about particular regulations, such agenda review and coordination may be more appropriate for the White House, because it avoids direct review and thus interference with the agency's use of its congressionally granted power to actually promulgate regulations. At the same time, earlier-stage White House review helps the president present a coherent regulatory policy to the nation, by coordinating different agencies' regulatory plans and ensuring their conformance with the president's overall priorities—for example, regulatory relief during the Reagan administration, homeland security after 9/11, or pandemic recovery in 2022. It thus provides the democratic accountability often cited by defenders of OIRA review of individual regulations.[54]

Indeed, scholars otherwise unsympathetic to OIRA's role in reviewing regulatory action have acknowledged the potential usefulness of inter-agency coordination beyond OIRA review of any particular agency's regulatory agenda.[55] So has the Administrative Conference of the United States (ACUS), a government agency comprised of regulatory lawyers, administrative law scholars, and government officials, which studies the administrative process. In 2012, ACUS offered a set of recommendations aimed at improving agency coordination when more than one agency shares responsibility for a regulatory program.[56] (For example, under federal law, EPA and NHTSA share responsibility for promulgating auto fuel efficiency standards.) While ACUS's recommendations focused on the details of inter-agency coordination on regulatory issues that explicitly encompass multiple agencies, their inclusion of White House offices, including OIRA,[57] as suggested participants in that process reflects the role those offices can play more generally in the process of coordinating agency action, both with that of other agencies and with the president's own priorities.[58] White House offices, including but not limited to OIRA, are natural candidates for that coordination role, given both their bureaucracy-wide perspective and their superior place in the governmental hierarchy. The benefits of such coordination are there for the reaping.

Presidential—and White House—Administration

Presidential administration constitutes another, more informal, vehicle for influence over agency action. Chapter 3 described this phenomenon, as recounted by then-Professor Kagan, reflecting on her time in the Clinton White House. Recall from that chapter that presidential administration includes public relations events such as White House ceremonies touting proposed or completed rulemakings—for example, Rose Garden press conferences where the president, flanked by the agency head, announces a regulatory initiative—but also more official actions such as directives to agencies to commence particular regulatory actions.[59]

When thinking about presidential administration, it is important to keep in mind a distinct but closely related phenomenon: influence exerted by White House officials other than the president (and through means other than OIRA's regulatory review). These officials can occupy positions either on the president's own staff or in other White House offices, such as the Council on Economic Quality and the various "czar" staffs that have been established over the last two decades. These non-presidential (and non-OIRA) actors can play broad and significant roles in influencing agencies.[60] For example, President Biden's climate czar will likely be interested in a large variety of regulatory programs and agencies—everything from obvious ones like the Clean Air Act and the EPA to less obvious ones like the SEC, via that agency's program requiring climate risk–related securities disclosures. This section discusses both types of non-OIRA influence—from the president himself and from White House offices other than OIRA—as "White House administration."

This book is concerned primarily with the policy effects of such influence—in particular, the extent to which the exertion of such influence promotes or impairs agencies' ability to wield their expertise. Nevertheless, legality questions necessarily influence the ultimate verdict on these tools' usefulness, just as similar legality questions influenced the ultimate verdict on OIRA review. Thus, consider first the legality of presidential directives, like those Justice Kagan described, requiring agencies to commence or complete a regulatory action. The debate over the legality of such directives recalls the analogous debate about the legality of President Reagan's regulatory review executive order, discussed in the previous section. That earlier debate pitted adherents of strong presidential power to control the bureaucracy with those who cite Congress's role in creating agencies and delegating authority to them.

That same debate resurfaces here. Indeed, presidential directives that agencies commence particular rulemakings reflect even greater presidential intrusion on agency discretion than the OIRA regulatory review orders. Justice Kagan's defense of Clinton's "presidential administration" concedes the point: "President Clinton's assertion of directive authority over administration, more than President Reagan's assertion of a general supervisory authority [via OIRA regulatory review], raises serious constitutional questions."[61] It is easy to see why: Reagan-style regulatory review merely mandates OIRA review of agency action for compliance with cost-benefit and other criteria. Thus, it involves the White House only after the agency has decided to begin a rulemaking process, and does not purport to direct the content of the resulting regulations. By contrast, Clinton-style rulemaking directives command the agency to commence a particular rulemaking and often specify those regulations' content. As such, they involve deeper presidential influence over how agencies utilize their congressionally granted authority.

Recall an example from chapter 3's discussion of the Clinton years. In 1999, President Clinton issued a memorandum "direct[ing]" the Secretary of Labor to promulgate rules allowing states to use their unemployment insurance systems to provide leave for new parents. Six months later, Clinton announced the agency's promulgation of rules that followed the principles his memorandum had set forth. It should not be surprising that those original, presidentially declared principles survived into the final regulations. Indeed, it would have been surprising if they had not, given the memorandum's mandatory form and, more informally, the president's unmistakable interest in the promulgation of regulations reflecting those principles. One can easily understand the concern about presidential control over, not just the Department of Labor's agenda, but the actual substance of its regulations.

Ultimately, Kagan concluded that it made sense to read most regulatory statutes (those that delegated power to executive agencies, rather than independent ones) as implicitly authorizing presidential control over how those agencies wielded the power Congress bestowed. Courts often use aggressive—or, if you wish, innovative—statutory interpretations to resolve tricky constitutional problems: Recall from chapter 4 that for the last two generations the Court has rejected non-delegation arguments by giving narrowing interpretations to alleged over-broad delegations. (Some might describe those narrowing interpretations as aggressive, or even willful.)

So too here: Justice Kagan deftly avoided the constitutional issue confronting Clinton-style regulatory directives by finding that Congress authorized them by statute.[62] Interestingly, though, she read those statutes as granting the president the authority to issue such mandates (like the parental leave rulemaking directive) because she thought that presidential administration was effective as a policy. In other words, the original constitutional question was answered by a statutory interpretation analysis, which was itself answered by a policy analysis. So that is where we will go, too: to examine whether presidential—and, more generally, White House—administration is good policy, and, in particular, whether it likely leads to more expertise-grounded decision-making.

But first, consider more informal White House influence. Such influence presents different legal issues. Luckily, they need not detain us long, because it is impossible to condemn as categorically illegal the informal influence and credit-taking Justice Kagan described. Freezing out the president from even informally influencing agencies' work would deprive him of any ability to informally influence how they execute the laws, in a way that would not apply to Congress. Such limits would render the president helpless to shape his own administration's policy, short of the extremes of using the nuclear option of removing the agency head or the very mild option of participating, like everyone else, in the public rulemaking process. Such restrictions would be irrational. That is why nobody advocates for them.[63]

But what about the policy wisdom of any of this—presidential or White House influence, or presidential mandates such as the Clinton directive to the Labor Secretary?[64] Does it generate more publicly accountable regulation? One might intuitively suspect that such influence benefits the regulatory process by impressing upon agencies the president's broader understanding of his administration's regulatory policy preferences—as noted earlier, a preference, say, for regulatory relief in the Reagan years or for prioritizing homeland security in the years after 9/11.[65] Such influence may be even more profound if it transmits the administration's preferences, *which are then presumed to reflect the preferences of the electorate that chose that president.*[66] As one critic of this idea explained it:

> To its defenders, presidential administration gives the electorate a powerful voice in federal regulation. Presidents serve as proxies for the people, translating general public preferences into specific directives to administrative agencies. The more influence presidents exercise in agency rulemaking, the theory goes, the more likely federal regulations will reflect majoritarian preferences and thereby advance the will of the people in agency rulemaking.[67]

Indeed, step back from such conceptual thinking and realize that most Americans naturally associate agency action with the incumbent administration. If that action is publicized enough, it can impact the president himself—just consider how President Bush's popularity took a serious hit after the Federal Emergency Management Agency's (FEMA's) botched response to Hurricane Katrina in 2005. This connection makes the accountability argument for presidential influence even more straightforward. If the American people hold the president accountable for what agencies do on his watch, shouldn't he have influence over what they do?

Critics challenge these justifications. They doubt whether presidential influence creates a consistent administration-wide regulatory program, given what they allege is the president's only episodic and scattershot interest in the workings of the bureaucracy. Indeed, Justice Kagan, even while applauding President Clinton's regulatory involvement, described it as "haphazard[]"; another scholar described presidential influence over rulemaking as "political oversight of the most sporadic and fortuitous sort." Of course, there may be a good explanation for those unflattering descriptions: Demands for more systematic presidential influence over regulations may be asking too much of a person whose responsibilities are as broad and time-consuming as the president's. Put bluntly, between everything else to which he must attend, the president may simply be too busy to do more than give "sporadic" and "haphazard" attention to regulatory action.[68]

But that's the problem. If the president really is too busy to provide systematic input into regulatory action, then one should question any empirical linkage between him and the regulations the bureaucracy churns out. Other scholars mount even more direct attacks on the accountability claim, questioning whether presidential intervention on a given regulatory question necessarily reflects public opinion on that issue.[69] This latter critique is a powerful one: It is often thought that presidents win or lose elections mainly based on economic conditions, with other policy issues—even important ones—often playing distinctly secondary roles. For example, despite his overwhelming election victories, President Reagan faced public opinion that continued supporting the regulatory and social welfare initiatives he had campaigned against.[70] These critiques should give us pause before uncritically accepting any intuition that White House influence over rulemaking generates the claimed accountability benefits.

Does the analysis change if the influence flows, not from the president himself but rather from his staff? If Kagan's "presidential administration" is hard to justify as a politically accountable president's methodical supervision of agency action to reflect Americans' preferences, nonpresidential White House influence presumably rests on similarly unstable foundations. To be sure, the White House staff—a multiperson entity—may have the time to focus on regulatory activity that the president does not. That luxury may make staffers' influence more methodical than "haphazard[]"[71] presidential influence, from the perspective of imposing on the bureaucracy a coherent overall regulatory program. Nor is any democratic accountability lost by the fact that the influence emanates not from the president but from his staff, since the public quite likely does not distinguish between the two.

These factors may incrementally improve the case for White House administration. But they hardly seal it. Two scholars have questioned whether White House staff are any more attuned to the president's wishes than the agency's; after all, the agency is headed by a presidential selection and features large numbers of other political appointees.[72] Relatedly, one can wonder whether a given White House office—say, the office of the climate czar or the Council of Economic Advisors—really does have the same broad perspective we might attribute to the president himself, or whether instead its perspective, while still potentially broad, remains limited to its substantive subject (here, respectively, climate change or the economy).

Finally, one can ask basic questions about the conformity of such influence with Americans' preferences. As the previously cited two scholars note, agencies must engage the public through a rulemaking process that allows for direct submission of public views on regulatory issues.[73] The resulting transmission of at least some Americans' views (through their own participation or that of like-minded interest groups), and agencies' legal obligation to respond to those views, may render agencies' everyday operations more democratically accountable than the sporadic influence of a president who may not even speak for a majority of Americans on any given issue.

Independent Agencies

This discussion has already mentioned independent agencies, but it's time to bring them explicitly into the conversation, if only briefly. Any examination of administrative expertise must account for independent agencies—that is, agencies whose heads serve fixed terms and are not removable at will by the president. As chapter 2 explained, such agencies' heyday was the period stretching from the late nineteenth century through the first four decades of the twentieth. That period was marked by a faith in science, including the social sciences. Such a faith naturally led to reliance on experts to solve social and economic problems, such as railroad regulation and control of the money supply. In turn, trust in experts pushed congressional architects to create many regulatory agencies using the independence model.

Beyond the immunization those agency heads enjoy from presidential removal-at-will, the independence model also usually features leadership by a multi-member board (rather than a single agency head) and broad, legislatively granted authority. These features all support a vision in which experts, unencumbered by politics, are given latitude to solve regulatory problems.[74] Among the better-known independent agencies are the Federal Reserve Board (the "Fed"), the Federal Communications Commission (FCC), and the National Labor Relations Board (NLRB).

The national faith in expertise has corroded since then. (Indeed, that corrosion furnishes much of this book's impetus.) Nevertheless, the independent agencies created earlier in our history have survived. As chapters 2 and 3 explained, courts have (thus far) rejected attacks on their constitutionality. Just as important, presidents have largely respected their independent status. President Reagan's regulatory review order did not apply to them, and, while President Clinton did require them to submit their annual regulatory agendas, he nevertheless refrained from subjecting them to his "presidential administration" tactics.[75] To be sure, Reagan and Clinton may have had political reasons for extending that respect.[76] But the important thing is that they did, as have their successors.

Given the existence of agencies who have (thus far) escaped the more explicit attempts at presidential control, the obvious question is whether, like Oliver Twist, we should ask for "more, please"—that is, more independent agencies. It's a complex question. Scholars sometimes argue that, rather than being truly independent, "independent" agencies simply fall more under Congress's sway.[77] Such congressional control may be even worse than the inappropriately strong presidential control this chapter has been critiquing. Critics of congressional influence over agencies often note that such influence usually emanates from particular committees or even highly interested or powerful individual congresspersons, all of whom may have parochial axes to grind when exerting their control. The result is oversight that may be even more distorted than presidential influence.

Other scholars scramble the question even more deeply by suggesting that a given agency's true independence is a function not so much of formal legal rules (such as statutory tenure protections for the agency head) but rather of informal norms that often turn on long-standing political arrangements. For example, one such scholar suggests that the NLRB, despite its leaders enjoying immunity from presidential at-will firing, is quite political, given how political labor relations questions—and thus appointments to the Board—have become.[78]

If this analysis is correct, then the entire question of "independent agencies" must be reconceptualized as a series of agency-specific, politically contingent, and empirically complex questions. Ironically, that complexity simplifies our task, because it means that we can push on with our consideration of presidential influence as a general matter, without worrying (at least not too much) about the formal status of an agency as independent. What matters instead is the reality of presidential influence, and whether that influence is a good thing.

White House Administration and Agency Expertise

Beyond the legality and accountability questions discussed immediately above, we must also consider whether presidential regulatory mandates or informal White House influence promotes agency expertise. Recall this chapter's earlier discussion of the effects on agency expertise of OIRA regulatory review. That discussion worried that OIRA review was avulsive, single-issue focused, and procedurally opaque, and thus contributed little to—indeed, likely detracted from—agencies' ability to utilize their expertise.

Both presidential directives of the Clinton-era sort and more informal presidential and White House staff influence raise some of these same concerns. To the extent an agency's decision to commence a rulemaking constitutes part of its unified, coherent program of regulation emerging from a deliberative, multifactored reasoning process, a presidential mandate to begin a particular rulemaking is at least as disruptive to the agency's expertise-driven regulatory process as OIRA review.[79] Informal presidential or White House influence is likely similarly disruptive, if the White House's "suggestion" is taken essentially as a command. The effect is likely even worse if the mandate or suggestion directs that the rule feature particular content.

Either way—as a formal command or a mere presidential or White House staff "suggestion"—such influence likely reflects a strong emphasis on political considerations, which, if balanced with other factors at all, are balanced outside of the agency's regular process. Rather than a methodical insertion of legitimate political concerns into the process, such influence communicates a blunt message—"jump"—to which the agency's likely response is a compliant "how high?"[80] (Indeed, when the White House also specifies the content of the desired rule, as President Clinton did with his parental leave directive to the Labor Secretary, it essentially specifies the height of the jump, as well.) Given those char-acteristics, it is hard to see how such influence consistently promotes expertise-based agency action, if expertise is understood, as this book's introduction explained it should be, to encompass not just technical ex-pertise but methodological sophistication in the art of regulating.

To be sure, as noted earlier, entities and interest groups of all sorts continually seek to influence agencies toward their preferred outcomes. Few observers suggest that the White House be uniquely prevented from joining the parade passing in front of the agency's front door.[81] But the White House float in that parade may be particularly prominent, given agencies' heavy dependence on the White House (for example, for their budgets),[82] the president's power to appoint much of their leader-ship, and, for non-independent agencies, the ultimate control feature of presidential power to remove their leaders.[83] Nevertheless, regardless of any dysfunctions it might cause, informal White House influence over agencies is probably impossible to cabin formally, exactly because of its informality and ubiquity. But the likely continuation of such informal influence suggests that formal mechanisms of influence, from OIRA review to the more mandatory forms of presidential administration, should be limited.[84]

Still, it merits pausing to question this conclusion one last time. As we have noted, agencies face pressures and influence from many sides beyond the White House: the regulated community, Congress, reviewing courts, the press, and even their own staffs. Some of those influences—especially the first two—can be quite insistent. One might wonder, then, whether imposing any limits at all on presidential influ-ence weakens presidential control too much. Two scholars express this concern as follows: Given all these other influences on agencies, "It will be no surprise if, left to swim in these treacherous waters, the agency head loses sight, sooner or later, of the shore from which he set off to implement the president's general policy preferences."[85] Justice Kagan's defense of the Clinton administration's control tactics takes a slightly different tack. She emphasizes the partisan gridlock that already existed in the 1990s, and argues that presidential administration allows for ef-fective administration—what Alexander Hamilton called "energy" in government—when Congress is incapable of governing.[86] (Of course, the gridlock has only gotten worse since then, thus strengthening her argument.) These two defenses of presidential control complement each other: The first worries about the lack of presidential control, while Kagan's focuses on how that control can have beneficial effects.

These reminders caution us that the goal here must not be reducing presidential control as an end in itself. Rather, as this chapter began by setting forth, the goal is crafting the right balance between that control and expertise-promoting agency autonomy. We can recognize that presidents have a legitimate interest in influencing regulatory action. We can further recognize that that interest is a relative one, seeking to ensure adequate presidential influence, not in the abstract, but as compared with other influencers. We can also recognize that, since George Washington, the balance of forces confronting agencies has constantly shifted and will continue to do so.[87] Finally, we can recognize that such influence may have beneficial effects, both for democratic accountability and effective administration. The question then becomes: At this particular political moment, is the current balance distorted and, if so, how?

This chapter argues that the current level and type of presidential influence over agency action is poorly suited to restoring an appropriate level of expertise to regulation. The current regime of presidential mandates and OIRA review distorts the process by which agencies seek to satisfy external constituencies and reach an internal consensus on the proper regulatory course—that is, the process by which agencies utilize their regulatory expertise. This augmented presidential control weakens the effect of the agency expertise that emerges when career staffers digest technocratic data, translate it into policy and, using their regulatory skill, add into the mix the agency's sense of what is feasible in light of the agency's relationships with all of its external constituencies. Indeed, even Justice Kagan's defense of Clinton's "presidential administration" concedes that, when the relevant regulatory matters turn heavily on expertise, presidential control should play a lesser role. She is surely right.[88]

The President, His Appointees, and the Civil Service Staff

This chapter concludes with a brief discussion of the president's relationship with agencies' politically appointed leadership. That relationship involves both quantity—that is, the sheer number of political appointees the president can appoint—and what one might loosely call quality—not simply how effective political appointees are, but rather, how that political leadership interacts with career civil service staff. This section considers the quantity question, while the next chapter focuses on how political appointees (of whatever quantity) interact with their agencies' staff.

For our purposes, quantity refers, not to the number of agency heads, but to the number of high-ranking agency officials who are political appointees. That number increased remarkably over the last four decades of the twentieth century. While President Kennedy had 286 politically appointed slots to fill within the bureaucracy, forty years later President George W. Bush had 3,361; by one count, by 2016 the number had increased to 3,648.[89] These increases resulted from several developments, including a 1978 Civil Service reform law that created the "Senior Executive Service" (SES), a new category of top-level bureaucrat, 10 percent of which could be filled by political appointees, as well as presidents' liberal use of the power to create confidential advising positions, called "Schedule C" appointments. For example, President Carter increased the number of such appointed positions from 911 to 1,566; later presidents continued that practice of growing those numbers.[90]

This phenomenon is destructive from several perspectives, but consider this book's perspective—expertise. Begin with the basics. Filling such a large number of vacancies requires White House time and attention. Moreover, many of these positions—especially Schedule C positions—are the subject of high turnover, as these junior political appointees move on to other offices or the private sector.[91] This combination results in a large number of unfilled slots at any given moment, in positions that were created to provide political guidance to agencies.

The result is unsurprising, if still ironic: Increased reliance on political appointees designed to impart a clearer policy course for agencies instead creates agency inaction and confusion, as one might expect in any organization that experiences long-term or recurring vacancies in policymaking positions. The situation has only grown worse with time, as political polarization has stymied presidents seeking to fill even their cabinet-level slots, let alone lower-ranking positions.[92] Nevertheless, it is not a new problem, with one scholar identifying it as early as 1990—perhaps unsurprisingly, since he was writing in the immediate aftermath of the Reagan administration's increased use of such appointees.[93] But the problem hasn't gone away: As a May 2, 2021 op-ed in the *Washington Post* observed, by that date the Biden administration had managed to get forty-four Senate confirmations for high-ranking administration positions—out of 1,200 slots that need such confirmation.[94]

In addition to the problem caused by longer and more frequent vacancies, evidence also suggests that political appointees are less successful leaders. A study published in 2007 found that agency bureaus led by political appointees consistently scored lower than their analogues led by career civil servants on the George W. Bush administration's Program Assessment Rating Tool. This result held despite the author's findings that political appointees generally had slightly higher education and broader work experience. Strengthening the intuition that experience within that particular agency office is what matters for performance, the author also found that, at least up to a point, longer experience working in that particular bureau was positively correlated with competent performance, but experience working in a different bureau was not. That result supports a hypothesis in which the career civil servants who know their particular bureaucracy—who have the regulatory expertise that comes from long immersion in how that bureaucracy operates and long experience with its external environment—tend to do better as managers.[95]

Beyond faring more poorly, another scholar of the bureaucracy, Paul Verkuil, notes that political appointees may also be inclined to make greater use of contractors.[96] Contractors, and outsourcing of regulatory work more generally, are discussed later, in chapter 9. That discussion will argue that contractors are a problematic feature of today's federal government apparatus. For now, it suffices to suggest what chapter 9 will demonstrate—that contractors, while they have their place, raise serious concerns about regulatory expertise, just like the rise in the political appointees who (over)-utilize them.

A 2003 study of the federal bureaucracy led by former Fed Chairman Paul Volker urged at least a one-third reduction in the number of political appointees, calling that "an appropriate first target."[97] That figure may be startling, but it becomes comprehensible in light of the more than tenfold increase in their numbers between 1960 and 2000, in a bureaucracy whose overall size has remained approximately the same. The magnitude of the Volker Report's suggestion, made by an entity led by someone not known for casual exaggeration, suggests the scope of the problem.

One can understand a president's desire for the power to appoint large numbers of political appointees. Beyond the patronage benefit of having a great many offices to fill,[98] the president's ability to insert his own preferred personnel in high agency positions reinforces White House control over the direction of agency policy. For that reason, it should not be surprising that observers have identified the practice of parachuting large numbers of political appointees into agencies, along with the White House control of agency action discussed earlier in this chapter, as pillars of what has long been called "the administrative presidency."[99]

Nevertheless, as explained above, the explosion in politically appointed positions remains deeply problematic. Indeed, it is problematic in part precisely to the extent that political appointees play their intended role—as extensions, deep into the agency, of the president's own political preferences and desire for control. Just listen to a first-hand witness. In looking back at his tenure as President Reagan's first Secretary of Education, Terrel Bell strongly criticized White House-selected sub-cabinet officials, viewing them as political ideologues who did not understand government and had no use for rigorous analysis that might generate policy recommendations they disfavored.[100]

A Different Vantage Point

To repeat a point this chapter and this book more generally have made consistently, this critique should not be understood as denying the legitimacy of the president's desire to influence bureaucratic outcomes. Politics—and in particular the president's politics—is a legitimate factor in regulation. That imperative justifies, among other things, the presence of the president's men (and women) inside agencies.

The next chapter considers the critical question of how those political appointees should—and should not—work with the career staffs at those agencies. When considering the relationship between the president and the bureaucracy, and, more generally, the optimum balance between politics and expertise, this chapter considered the view from 1600 Pennsylvania Avenue. It's now time to consider the view from agency headquarters.

6

Relationships within the Agency

Following on chapter 5's discussion of the White House's relationship with agencies, this chapter turns to dynamics within the agency itself. Those internal dynamics are critical to improving expertise-based agency action. As one scholar explained, referring to some of the presidential control tools chapter 5 discussed: "Executive orders, and other forms of direct presidential action, are not self-executing. The question is . . . , when agencies are told, 'do this,' do they 'do that'?"[1] This chapter considers that question, but also the broader questions of how regulatory work is structured and how it *should* be structured.

What a Bureaucrat Wants

How (and how well) do political appointees work with career agency staff—and how (and how well) do staff work with political appointees? Begin with descriptions of ideal types, to get a sense of the spectrum of possible answers. Start with career agency staff. At one extreme, political scientists have sometimes posited a rational actor model of career staff, in which career bureaucrats seek to maximize their own welfare. Such welfare might include pay or prestige, one's ideological preferences, or even leisure.[2]

This assumption does not necessarily predict how such staff will interact with political appointees. For example, obtaining promotions or even simply keeping one's job may entail cooperating with political appointees' initiatives. On the other hand, promoting one's own ideological preferences might entail explicitly opposing or subtly undermining those initiatives, if they reflect preferences different from those of the career bureaucrat. The key point here is that, under this assumption, the way to understand civil servants' conduct is to figure out what they want, and the way to ensure effective implementation of a president's program is to structure bureaucrats' self-interested incentives in the direction of implementation rather than blockage or undermining.

At the other extreme lies the vision of the bureaucrat as public servant. On this theory, the career civil servant is motivated by a conception of her professional role as one that requires serving her duly installed superiors, from the president down to her fellow civil servant and political appointee supervisors. Thus, this theory posits that civil servants will sincerely attempt to serve the incumbent administration's program.[3] This understanding sounds similar to that of the bureaucrat as an apolitical expert, but it is different. For example, a view of bureaucracy as the application of apolitical expertise to a given regulatory problem might lead a bureaucrat to oppose the incumbent administration's policies if she believes them to conflict with her technical analysis of the issue.

By contrast, the idea of the bureaucrat as public servant rests on the career staffer's understanding that her job is to implement the will of incumbent administration, to the extent consistent with law. In *The Fifth Risk*, Michael Lewis's description of the Trump administration's encounter with the bureaucracy, Lewis wrote about a Department of Energy staffer who was quizzed by a Trump transition team member about which other DOE staffers had worked on climate change. Recounting the staffer's compliance with the information request, Lewis wrote:

> It says a great deal about the mind-set of career civil servants that the DOE employee in charge of overseeing the transition set out to answer even the most offensive questions. Her attitude, like the attitude of the permanent staff, was, *We are meant to serve our elected masters, however odious they might be.*[4]

That, in a nutshell, reflects the bureaucrat-as-public-servant vision.

When Ronald Reagan became president, speculation arose about the likely relationship between his administration and the federal bureaucracy, given the intuition that bureaucrats tended to favor regulation more than his administration would. There was good reason for that intuition. It's a standard understanding of career civil servants that they selected a career in government—and, indeed, in a particular agency— because they favored regulation in that particular area, or, as that idea is sometimes expressed, because they "believed in that agency's mission."[5]

For example, one scholar's interviews with civil servants at the Department of Agriculture's Food and Nutrition Service (FNS) (the office that administers the federal Food Stamp, school lunch, and Women's, Infants, and Children programs) revealed both a strong bias toward providing these food services and career paths that included stints in other service organizations with public health or nutrition missions.[6] One does not often choose a career in an institution that is dedicated to goals one deeply dislikes, at least if the institution does not provide countervailing material benefits that outweigh any resulting psychic displeasure. Additionally, it is often suggested that even civil servants without such pre-existing biases in favor of a given type of regulation eventually develop them, given that their workplace mission is to engage in exactly that type of regulation or service provision.[7]

Faithful Implementation, Open Revolt, or Guerilla Warfare?

As a candidate and then as president, Ronald Reagan espoused deregulation and cuts to social programs. Given their likely preferences, one might intuit that civil servants in regulatory and social service bureaucracies, such as the FNS discussed in the previous paragraph, would likely oppose the incoming administration's plans, at least as a matter of personal political orientation. Would such opposition carry over into their implementation of those plans? Would bureaucrats openly oppose or subtly undermine such deregulatory initiatives?

One scholar sought to find out. After the conclusion of the Reagan administration, Professor Marissa Golden interviewed a group of career civil servants in four agencies: the National Highway Transportation Safety Administration (NHTSA), the agency that regulates auto safety; the FNS, described earlier; the Civil Rights Division of the Department of Justice (CRD); and the Environmental Protection Agency (EPA). All four of these bureaucracies confronted a Reagan administration that was determined to shift their regulatory focuses, and that appointed agency heads and politically selected subordinates to accomplish that.[8]

Recognizing the limits of potentially self-serving or self-justifying survey responses, the results of Professor Golden's study cut a middle path between the rational actor and public servant models. On the one hand, she found a remarkable degree of bureaucratic compliance with their superiors' politically inflected initiatives. Her results suggested that that compliance flowed in part from rational actor–style concerns about self-preservation—not just the fear of being included in periodic "reductions in force," but also concern about not being promoted or otherwise having one's career sidetracked.[9] But she also found much to support the public servant idea—namely, statements from civil servants in those agencies that, whatever they might have thought personally about the new administration's policies, they saw their professional roles as requiring them to do their best to implement those policies as effectively as possible.[10]

To be sure, Professor Golden, using economist Albert Hirschman's famous taxonomy of "exit, voice, and loyalty,"[11] found instances of bureaucrats' "exit" and "voice"—respectively, departures from the agency based on policy disagreement and expressions of opposition to those new policies (mainly via internal discussions but occasionally through media leaks and other external outlets).[12] Adding a category to Hirschman's taxonomy, Golden also found examples of what she called "neglect"—that is, the passive performance of duties, or what one might colloquially describe as "going through the motions."[13] Nevertheless, she found that civil servants in these bureaucracies generally did what they could to implement the agency leadership's plans—plans that, of course, meshed with the administration's philosophy more generally.[14]

Interestingly, the bureaucracy's compliance with presumptively distasteful regulatory initiatives occurred in agencies led by very different types of managers. The EPA under its first Reagan-era administrator, Anne Gorsuch, suppressed dissent and intimidated dissenters. Under her leadership, the agency maintained a "hit list" of bureaucrats marked for dismissal, transfer, or demotion based on their perceived political views, reorganized and dispersed the division devoted to bringing enforcement actions against polluters, removed regulation-drafting tasks from career personnel and placed them with political appointees, and excluded career personnel from meetings where key information was discussed.[15] Professor Golden also found versions of these latter two tactics at NHTSA: Agency leadership removed to the highest (political) level the task of formulating regulations, rather than allowing proposed regulations to percolate up from the agency's technical and regulatory experts, and civil servants found themselves excluded from important meetings and their key tasks reassigned away from them.[16]

By contrast, a more cooperative, open environment prevailed under the EPA's two subsequent Reagan-era administrators, William Ruckelshaus and Lee Thomas.[17] But despite that difference in management style, interviewees reported similar willingness to implement political appointees' initiatives under both types of management regimes. Perhaps in between these two extremes, attorneys at the Justice Department's Civil Rights Division reported that the political appointee head of the division allowed debate and discussion on relevant policy issues, even if it became clear that that leader would not change his views. As with EPA bureaucrats, CRD interviewees reported a high level of "loyalty"—that is, faithful implementation of their superiors' policies. Such cooperation also existed at NHTSA and the FNS.[18]

Lessons Learned

These case studies suggest that a combination of self-interest and public-spiritedness largely caused otherwise-hostile civil servants to faithfully implement the programs pushed by their Reagan-appointed supervisors. What lessons does that teach? If Reagan-era agencies could obtain significant civil service compliance with White House initiatives, does it matter which path the agency head took to achieve such compliance?

There is reason to think that it does. Most important, shutting down discussion—and, indeed, suppressing dissemination of information to civil servants and, in several cases, to the general public—leads to regulatory missteps. In the 1983 *State Farm* airbags case discussed in chapter 2,[19] the Supreme Court handed NHTSA a humiliating defeat, striking down the agency's rescission of a regulation that had occupied the agency for the better part of a decade. Professor Golden's interviewees at NHTSA insisted that the agency's decision could have survived judicial review had its leadership made more use of the agency's technical and regulatory expertise.[20]

One might suspect that it is a shade too convenient for NHTSA personnel to blame the agency's loss on their exclusion from the decision-making process, and to insist that, had they been included, their public-spiritedness would have motivated them to do the quality job the agency needed to win. But their story gains plausibility when we recognize that the agency lost exactly because the Court faulted the agency's explanation for the rule—an explanation that, like all agency explanations of complex regulatory decisions, ideally emerges after a broadly inclusive discursive process that analyzes, balances, and reasons.[21] Simply put, NHTSA's loss in *State Farm* flowed from its failure to do exactly what expert bureaucracies are built to do—and what NHTSA's leadership failed to allow. While the stories have not yet been fully told, when one recalls from chapter 3 the Trump administration's horrendous win-loss record when its regulations were challenged in court, it would not be surprising if these same dynamics, perhaps magnified, played out more recently as well.

To be sure, beyond the claims of bureaucratic public-spiritedness revealed in incidents like the NHTSA episode, Professor Golden's case studies also suggest that self-interest played a role in bureaucrats' reactions to their Reagan-era bosses. But even self-interest might conduce to positive agency outcomes, if bureaucrats' incentives are aligned with the agency's goals. If they are not aligned—if instead, self-interest yields a response of hunkering down and doing the bare minimum to avoid being unfavorably noticed (what Professor Golden called "neglect")— the unsurprising result will be suboptimal work.

Either result is possible. As Professor Golden concluded, "self-interest is neither unidimensional [nor] unidirectional."[22] It can operate to promote the leadership's goals or frustrate them. To speak colloquially, bureaucrats' self-interest is what agency leaders make of it.

Implementing Incentives

The question thus becomes, can agency procedures be structured to promote both bureaucrats' self-interest and their self-perception as loyal implementers of the leadership's policies? Concededly, there may be an intractable conflict between those two concepts if bureaucrats' self-interest is defined in terms of their political beliefs, those beliefs clash with the administration's, and that self-interest trumps their conception of their role as loyal implementers of administration policy. In such a case, we can expect opposition, either open or masked. On the other hand, if self-interest speaks to bureaucrats' career satisfaction, then, to adapt a phrase from the Reagan administration, "letting bureaucrats be bureaucrats" might redound to the leadership's benefit.[23] That wisdom appears to be the lesson of the NHTSA staffers' insistence that, regardless of their personal beliefs on the issue, they could have helped the agency succeed in rescinding the airbag rule had they only been allowed into the process.

This reasoning triggers a follow-up question: Is there a way to structure agency decisional processes to allow bureaucrats to play their professional roles while also allowing the leadership to promote its own political agenda? Much of the remainder of this chapter seeks to answer that question. While the details of that answer will vary by agency and regulatory program, some general ideas suggest themselves.

Analysis of the appropriate role for experts—and expertise—should begin with the uncontroversial proposition that agency experts are, indeed, the experts, and should enjoy significant latitude to wield that expertise.[24] But conversely, politically appointed agency leaders are, indeed, the leaders. While they should not enjoy the freedom to ignore their agencies' expertise, when those leaders exercise that leadership and reach final decisions, they should enjoy the authority to account for their—and their White House patron's—political views.

These two complementary propositions create the framework for what follows. First, this chapter recommends that structures be created that incentivize experts to develop their expertise. That means freedom to create information and, within broad bounds, freedom to disseminate it. Chapter 8 will discuss information integrity in more detail; this chapter will confine its discussion of information to its role in structuring the agency's decision-making process. Second, this chapter maintains that, at the end of the process, the agency leader should enjoy the power to make the final decision on the agency's action, and to make it, within limits, based on political considerations.

If we map these two proposals on an administrative decision timeline stretching from initial fact-gathering to ultimate decision-making, we are left with a vast middle swath of agency activity between those initial and ultimate steps. (Note, though, that the idea of a timeline seriously over-simplifies the agency's process, in which fact-gathering and policy deliberation constitute iterative processes that overlap over the course of an agency's work on a regulation. Nevertheless, for simplicity's sake, this discussion uses the metaphor of a timeline.) With the metaphor of a timeline in hand, the next part of our task requires us to structure that middle-phase activity so as to respect both bureaucratic expertise and agency leaders' political considerations.

Those middle phases of the agency's decisional process are complex ones. They reflect the interface between expertise and politics, as well as the interface between different types of expertise. Consider EPA rule-making. Thomas McGarity, a scholar who thirty years ago conducted an in-depth study of EPA rulemaking, concluded that, given the complexity of environmental issues, no one person within the agency enjoys all the relevant expertise. One can easily understand his point once we realize that, for example, air pollution issues require knowledge of everything from atmospheric chemistry (to understand how pollutants interact in the air) to mechanical engineering (to understand how smokestacks work), and urban planning (to understand how regulatory decisions might affect commuting patterns). But expertise becomes an even more complicated concept once we remember that expertise goes beyond technical knowledge to include expertise in the regulatory process itself. That regulatory expertise (discussed in the book's introduction) helps connect the varieties of technical knowledge McGarity discerned in the EPA with the agency's skill in balancing all the relevant regulatory considerations.

The existence of these varied types of expertise means that assembling the components of the resulting analysis into a coherent and reasoned outcome will constitute an important part of that middle swath of the agency's regulatory timeline. That integration process entails more than simply superimposing one-dimensional scientific findings onto an equally one-dimensional policy template. Rather, it involves, in McGarity's words, the attempt "to integrate the contributions of widely varying professional perspectives into a single coherent product."[25] Clearly, the middle phases of the agency's regulatory timeline constitute a highly complex, intricate series of steps. That fact will be crucial to our analysis.

Information Development

Begin, though, with the initial fact-gathering phase. Even this initial phase, seemingly given over to the expert fact-gatherers, reflects a mixture of expertise and politics, considering the political nature of a decision even to commence a fact-gathering process and the follow-on decision to frame that process in a particular way.[26] But leave aside that complexity and consider the fact-gathering itself. First, and most fundamentally, because agency experts possess the requisite expert knowledge, they should enjoy relatively free rein to develop information the agency needs to implement its statutory mandates, without that information being suppressed or distorted.

Often, they have not enjoyed that latitude. For example, Professor Golden's study of Reagan-era agencies recounts an incident in which an FNS study was extensively rewritten by a political appointee to cast in a less favorable light a program the administration was hoping to cut.[27] Political appointees in the George W. Bush administration were accused of editing technical documents that examined the pace of climate change, while both that administration and the predecessor Clinton administration were accused of interfering with agency experts' testimony before Congress.[28] By no means a laggard on this score, the Trump administration was widely criticized for suppressing information agency experts had developed, perhaps most infamously, information about the COVID-19 pandemic.[29]

To be sure, an agency's information and research function implicates a wide variety of activities. It encompasses far more than an individual scientist reviewing academic papers and drawing conclusions from her study. It also requires creating models, adopting assumptions, and integrating what she has learned into other experts' knowledge from study of their own disciplines. The type of analysis those latter steps require comes dangerously close to the boundary between science and politics. Consider, for example, the process of creating a scientific model into which data are fed. Modeling requires making politically fraught assumptions. As one illustration, during the Trump administration the head of the US Geological Survey ordered that climate change modeling not account for effects beyond 2040, a departure from past practice that promised to alter conclusions about the ultimate impact of reducing greenhouse gas emissions.[30] Such decisions impact scientific analysis, but do not rest solely on scientific judgment.

Political considerations loom even larger as the resulting data encounter policy concerns. For that reason, a useful demarcation in the agency's regulatory timeline is between the time agency experts initially develop their information and the time that information becomes integrated with information from other disciplines and with broader regulatory considerations, to form the "single coherent whole" Professor McGarity identified as the goal of the regulatory process. Indeed, McGarity and Wendy Wagner, another prominent scholar of law and science, have proposed exactly this boundary for a rigid firewalling between agency expertise and political appointee influence. They suggest a strict separation of the information-gathering and assessment process and the process of crafting a regulatory response.[31]

Their proposal reflects an assumption that the information-processing realm is essentially the exclusive province of agency experts. Consequently, their proposed firewalling is stringent. It encompasses a near-prohibition on political appointee influence not just over the technical process itself (including the process of validating findings, for example, by presenting them for peer review), but also over the procedures by which that technical work is conducted. Under their proposal, political appointees would be walled off not only from the actual conduct of technical work, but also from management of those technical personnel—in McGarity's and Wagner's words, "their budget, their assignments, and their hiring and firing."[32] But even though it is rigid, their proposed firewall is also limited, as it seeks to wall off from political influence only information-gathering and analysis. Thus, they would expose other functions to political influence even though those functions may also rely on regulatory expertise.[33]

McGarity and Wagner recognize the practical difficulties inherent in enforcing such a demarcation, especially in the face of determined political appointees seeking to influence regulatory science.[34] But if the goal is modest—to create a structure that works adequately, if not perfectly—then a well-crafted policy, including guardrails mitigating violations, may help minimize impairments on agency informational integrity. Such guardrails could include explicit procedures creating such firewalls and legal protections for agency personnel who draw attention to violations through either formal whistleblowing or leaks to the media or Congress.[35] As the next chapter explains, they can also involve judicial review of the resulting agency action. On the other side of the ledger, in what Professor Wagner later described as a "quid pro quo" for such autonomy, the experts' information development could be subject to external peer review, to prevent either technical mistakes or, even worse, attempts by researchers to smuggle policy preferences into the analysis that otherwise enjoyed immunity from political meddling.[36]

One observer has built on McGarity's and Wagner's proposal and suggested the construction of particular intra-agency processes that expressly delineate the decisional steps that require policy choices and those that require the creation of information.[37] This delineation aims to establish the realms governed, respectively, by policymakers and experts; its explicitness helps protect against breaches of that division by either side.

Such structures sound useful, but they raise hard questions. Conceptually, the line between science and policy is deeply murky. Consider a scientific question—say, a suspected carcinogen's likely effect on humans. If ethical considerations make human experimentation impossible, we need to extrapolate from other information—for example, from animal testing. The assumptions grounding that extrapolation would strongly influence the ultimate conclusion about the effect of the substance on humans. But those assumptions may be susceptible to political influence, even if science provides their plausible boundaries.[38] Just remember the Geological Survey's mandate that its climate research assume no effects beyond 2040.

Practical challenges also abound. One challenge is the likely need for input and communication across the science-politics firewall. Indeed, the proponent of the decision-making process described above conceded that, "Without a doubt, policymakers will need the advice of staff scientists and staff scientists will need the advice of policymakers during certain phases of the fractured process."[39] This need prompted that commentator to propose that paths be created that allow consultation across the science/politics boundary.[40]

Unfortunately—but unsurprisingly—those pathways allow each side of the science/politics boundary to infect the other. Policymakers have particularly powerful incentives to transgress that boundary. Disguising a policy decision as one based in science—"scientizing" policy—limits the public's ability to take issue with the agency, by shifting the discussion toward terrain that most of the public (and indeed, Congress, courts, and even the White House) simply cannot scrutinize effectively. We have likely all experienced giving up trying to examine a technical explanation for something because we simply could not understand it. Imagine how tempting that prospect would be for an agency leader pushing a policy she suspects will engender opposition.[41] The examples Professor Golden provided of agency leaders interfering with their staff's technical analyses strongly suggest that many agency leaders would succumb to that temptation.

Ultimately, then, hard-and-fast firewalls and procedural rules may be both difficult to craft in meaningfully precise ways and prone to violations. However, conscientious agencies should encourage informal norms and practices respecting the principles offered by the scholars discussed above. Some norms and practices should be particularly strong. For example, as chapter 8 will explain in more detail, at the very least political appointees should respect the integrity of scientific information once they direct that it be created. That means refraining from editing or otherwise altering it once it is created. It also means refraining from suppressing or altering its presentation to Congress. Congress, even more than the public, has a constitutional oversight responsibility that demands such disclosures. When the material constitutes the agency's basic scientific work on the subjects Congress tasks the agency with regulating, presidents should be able to claim only a very limited non-disclosure privilege. In addition, as chapter 7's discussion of judicial review will explain, effective dissemination would also be assisted by a legal rule or agency practice of including important pre-decisional scientific information in the disclosures agencies must make to courts when a regulation is challenged.

This prescription for robust dissemination of information to Congress and the courts might strike some readers as weak tea. One obvious objection immediately arises: If this proposal calls for disclosing information the agency develops, wouldn't the agency's leadership have an incentive simply to direct agency experts away from studying areas where those leaders might fear the development of unfavorable information? But built-in checks can prevent such game-playing. First, Congress can probe the agency's decision-making and fact-gathering processes if it suspects that agency heads have directed their experts' gaze away from study topics that might embarrass the agency. Second, courts can scrutinize agencies' choices just like Congress can. As the next chapter discusses, courts reviewing agency action require that agencies take a "hard look" at the regulatory problem and consider reasonably available regulatory options. Those requirements effectively require agencies to develop information a court might reasonably consider relevant, if for no other reason than to justify their rejection of those alternative options. As that chapter will explain, those judicial review requirements could provide a powerful incentive to agency heads to allow the creation of information that then, under this chapter's analysis, presumptively would be available to reviewing courts and thus the public.

For these reasons, the suggestion that agency leadership respect the integrity of the information they direct be developed should not deteriorate into an incentive simply to direct experts to avert their eyes from information the agency head might wish to remain undiscovered.[42] Indeed, as noted above, congressional and (especially) judicial review of agency action can assist, not simply in publicizing the information agencies develop, but in incentivizing agencies to actually develop that information in the first place.

More generally, nothing prevents agencies from inculcating norms and practices reinforcing the boundaries this section has discussed, even if hard-and-fast rules remain elusive. For example, agencies should institute guidelines governing the pathways by which an agency's policy leaders can communicate with their scientific staff (and vice-versa). They can also empower auditors, such as the particular agency's inspector general, to investigate allegations of inappropriate transgressions of the science-politics border.[43] Indeed, since this issue arises in all agencies, this would be an area where OIRA's cross-agency coordinating capabilities could be put to good use. But beyond such informal guardrails, indirect means of policing these boundaries, such as judicial review calibrated to account for agency conduct on this issue, may be the most viable option.

Managing the Politics-Expertise Interface

The previous section, as intricate as its analysis might have been, nevertheless confined itself to the relatively straightforward question of experts' authority to generate and disseminate scientific information. Even more challenging questions arise once one realizes that such information, critical as it is, serves only as an input into the process of actual regulatory decision-making.

That decisional process raises many questions. How should scientific information, and those who possess it, interact with the selection and implementation of more overtly political values? How can that interaction be managed when one adds in the fact that the political appointees who run the agency will likely have been chosen exactly because of their political alignment with the current administration, and will feel that their job is to implement the incumbent administration's political priorities? Does the political basis for the leaders' positions in the agency give politics an inevitable advantage in the crafting of administrative policy? If so, *should* politics enjoy that advantage? These questions speak to the politics-expertise interface in regulation. Managing that interface is critical if regulation is to feature a coherent and legitimate combination of political accountability and expertise.

The challenge of managing that interface extends to the very end of the decision-making process. Even then, when the agency head metaphorically closes her office door behind her and decides whether or not to promulgate the regulation in question, her presumed political allegiance to the president does not allow her to ignore the agency expertise that has gone into the proposal. If she does ignore it, she does so at her own peril, as she would surely discover when the regulation is challenged in court and the judge demands a reasoned, expertise-grounded justification for her decision.

The fact that expertise and politics both play roles after the initial fact-gathering phase means that, at least up to the point that the agency head closes that door, representatives of both interests must participate fully in the process. Professor McGarity's description of EPA rulemaking depicts a complex, multi-perspective process involving both political appointees and offices possessing various types of expertise. The expertise that sits across the table from the politics in those EPA conference rooms—and conference rooms across Washington—is wide-ranging. It extends from technical knowledge to the sort of regulatory know-how the introduction called "regulatory expertise"—for example, understandings of the challenges agency enforcement officers will face when trying to ensure compliance with the resulting regulation. Robust participation by representatives of both politics and expertise (and, indeed, all relevant subspecialties of expertise) is critical to ensure that those perspectives do not get lost in the intricate, multi-step process of proceeding from information-gathering to presentation of the proposed action to the agency's top leadership.

This participation imperative means that there is no point in the process where agency experts should be excluded, until the agency head retires to her office to deliberate and make the final decision. Until that final point, one can visualize the process as one in which both politics and expertise constantly hover over the decision-making group. Politics demands its place in the process because it will necessarily play an important, and perhaps even a controlling, role in the agency head's final decision. But expertise also demands its due. Indeed, as noted earlier, expertise continues to influence the decision even when it reaches the agency head's desk, given the specter of a reviewing court inquiring into the regulation's foundation in expertise. Thus, even though the ultimate agency decider—the agency head—may be motivated primarily or even solely by politics, those motivations remain checked by the prospect of judicial review. Indeed, as the previous section proposed (and the next chapter will flesh out), that judicial review should be informed by the agency's expert information development, carried out safely behind a web of protective agency norms and practices.

This call for participation by both politics and expertise might seem obvious. By this time in the book, who could disagree that politics and expertise both deserve their due? But recall the stories Professor Golden's interviewees recounted: exclusion from critical meetings, placement of the rulemaking drafting function solely in the hands of political appointees, top-down mandates of regulatory initiatives and approaches rather than bottom-up percolation from agency staff closest to the issues, and the creation of cultures where experts tried to leave the agency or simply kept their heads down and passively acquiesced in decisions rather than actively participating in them. Unfortunately, we can update Professor Golden's data to paint similar, more recent pictures. In a 2018 survey of EPA scientists, only a minority disagreed with the statement that they had been excluded from discussions or decisions related to their work in which they normally would have expected to be included. (To translate that awkward survey verbiage, only a minority pushed back on a suggestion that they had been inappropriately excluded from meetings relevant to their expertise.)[44]

Some of these dysfunctions suggest simple bad management—surely, developing "hit lists" of disfavored staffers based on their suspected political views is no way to create a motivated workforce. But others, such as removing regulation-drafting responsibilities from experts and giving them to political appointees acting alone, and editing scientific reports to change their meaning, suggest more profound organizational pathologies. These stories, to which one can likely add others, caution us that seemingly obvious good organizational practices do not effortlessly emerge simply by virtue of their underlying good sense.

Nevertheless, at the end of the process the agency head does indeed close her door and make her decision. That fact might suggest that early stages of the process are for naught. Thus, a reader might dismiss all the suggestions this chapter has made on the ground that, in the end, the political leadership will do what it wants, based on politics. However, the existence of an external check—courts—insisting that such decisions be both reasoned and reasonable, helps ensure that when that door closes, expertise is not left completely outside, even if the agency head is primarily, or even solely, motivated by politics when she reaches her final decision.

The next chapter considers what that judicial review should look like, now that we have constructed the outlines of an agency process that accords proper respect to agency expertise. But before considering the external check of judicial review, we must consider one final protection from inappropriate internal agency procedures: protections for agency personnel who experience such malfeasance and want to do something about it.

Protecting Agency Personnel

Three types of protections could conceivably assist agency experts who experience either inappropriate politicization of agency information-gathering or exclusion from subsequent decision-making phases. First, such conduct could be made the subject of a whistleblower complaint. Second, agencies can provide informal channels for voicing concerns about such conduct. Third, agencies' inspectors general can investigate such concerns.

Start with whistleblowers. Whistleblowers are employees—here, of a federal agency—who, having witnessed illegality or other inappropriate conduct, disclose what they know, or "blow the whistle" on it. Federal and state laws protect whistleblowers in both the private and the public sector. The motivation for such laws is obvious: they incentivize employees to go public (or at least semi-public) with what they know, by protecting them from retaliation or other adverse action at the hands of the person on whom they are blowing the whistle—the person who is likely to be their supervisor.

Despite its seeming attractiveness, whistleblower law is a bad fit for the type of agency misconduct at issue here. First, federal whistleblower protections apply only if the agency imposes or threatens to impose on the whistleblower an adverse employment action, such as termination or an undesired transfer. To be sure, agency leaders are not above such tactics—recall EPA leadership's creation of "hit lists" of staffers targeted for just such actions because of their suspected political views.[45] Nevertheless, whistleblower protections apply only if an agency's leadership takes this extreme step. The mere use by an agency of an inappropriate decisional process, without more, does not trigger any protections since, literally, there is no need for the job protection that constitutes the core of the whistleblower protection idea.

Second, the subjects of whistleblowing are limited. Under federal whistleblower law, the subject of a whistleblower complaint must generally be something other than a policy decision reflecting the lawful exercise of an agency's discretionary authority.[46] In other words, policy disagreements are not the stuff of a whistleblower's protected disclosures. Instead, whistleblower law protects only disclosures that reveal legal violations, serious mismanagement, "an abuse of authority, or a substantial and specific danger to public health or safety."[47]

This structure makes intuitive sense. An agency's exercise of its discretion to select one policy or another must be respected—to be sure, challengeable by a staffer inside the agency before it is finalized and by a plaintiff in a lawsuit afterward, but not the sort of illegal, abusive, or dangerous conduct that whistleblower law targets. Indeed, this reasoning extends even further: Despite the seemingly clear words of the statute—that is, its protection of disclosures evidencing "any violation of any law"—courts have held that whistleblower protection does not apply to an agency decision that reflects a simple misreading of the law. Under the statute, making a mistake about the law is not the same thing as "violating" it.[48]

These principles presumably would exclude from whistleblower protection a claim that the agency has failed to comply with the type of expertise-respecting and inclusive decisional procedure this chapter has recommended. The only potential way for such a claim to be cognizable would be if the procedure in question was formalized into a statute or regulation that the agency then intentionally violated, or if the agency action otherwise rose to the level of seriousness reflected in the other statutory terms quoted above. Such high thresholds render whistleblower laws an ineffective means of deterring the problematic agency conduct with which we're concerned, or protecting bureaucrats who expose it.

Other, more promising protections beckon. Beyond the formality and limitations of whistleblower law, agencies should create internal procedures for exposing inappropriate political interference with actions that should be grounded in expertise. Several agencies have created so-called dissent channels that allow staffers to communicate dissenting views about agency policies, without fear of reprisal, when normal deliberative channels are unavailable. Such channels might be useful innovations for agencies seeking to implement desirable decisional procedures without creating a rigid set of rules that might, because of their very rigidity, become unworkable.[49]

To be sure, dissent channels are only as valuable as agencies' commitments to both take the "dissents" seriously and protect their users from the retaliation that whistleblower law protects against in other situations. A 2020 report on agency dissent channels raised questions about those commitments.[50] More generally, one might question whether such channels add much when the topic of dissent is not substantive policy but rather an agency's faithfulness to procedures designed to ensure inclusive decision-making. After all, if the agency is hostile to such an inclusive process (thus triggering the dissent), one can fairly ask why it would nevertheless be open to complaints about such exclusions.

A final mechanism to protect such informal whistleblowing is the institution of Inspectors General (IGs) offices. IGs are agency offices, usually established by statute, that hold mandates to investigate the agency itself for inefficiency or malfeasance.[51] Beyond routine efficiency audits and inspections, IGs are also empowered to investigate alleged abuse or mismanagement. Because investigations can be triggered by complaints from a variety of parties, including agency employees, they constitute a mechanism to ensure agency adherence, not just to formal procedures the agency might have promulgated governing the policymaker/expert relationship, but also to appropriate managerial and decision-making practices more generally.[52]

A 2006 IG investigation illustrates their potential usefulness. That year, a Department of the Interior IG investigation concluded that a political appointee in the Fish and Wildlife Service (FWS) had, among other things, bullied and harassed FWS scientific staff and inappropriately edited their scientific findings, despite her lack of education in the relevant discipline.[53] The fact that that investigation targeted exactly the sort of misconduct this discussion has focused on, and, indeed, was triggered by an anonymous complaint, reveals IGs' usefulness in ensuring political appointees' fidelity to principles that are otherwise difficult to reduce to precise, binding legal rules. The end of the story also reflects the potential for IG investigations to protect expertise-based decision-making: Beyond the report causing the official to resign, the agency subsequently reviewed more of her work and revised several decisions she had influenced, and a court, citing that official's conduct, ruled against an agency decision for failure to reflect the best science.[54]

Conclusion

Regulatory work is complex. Not just the technical part, and not even just the part this book has described as based in regulatory expertise, but also the organizational part. Such work involves its participants in a process that attempts to locate the appropriate middle ground between the extremes of purely apolitical expertise and purely political decision-making. We should want neither of those extremes. Hence, the challenge of finding the right balance.

No one response to this challenge can apply to all regulatory programs across all agencies for all time. Instead, that balance will fluctuate uneasily. Any guidelines governing it should be informed by the appropriate roles assigned to the experts and the politicians—respectively, information-gathering and analysis, and filtering political viewpoints into that analysis. But it's difficult to operationalize that intuitive function-based allocation of power: As this chapter has shown, in the real world this conceptually neat dividing line dissolves into a vague and messy blur.

Still, certain principles should guide agencies as they seek to draw that line. Information-gathering and basic research should remain as immune from politics as possible and should be subject to open dissemination as much as other legitimate values, for example, national security, allow. At the other end of the process, the final decision to act appropriately rests with the agency's political leadership, as long as that leadership understands that that decision will likely face judicial scrutiny into its foundation in expertise. Between these starting and ending points for the agency's action, the watchword should be robust internal participation, protected to the extent possible by internal procedural norms and external guardrails.

The next three chapters build on these ideas. Chapter 7 considers the judicial review that seeks to ensure that even politically motivated regulatory decisions rest on an adequate foundation of expertise. In turn, chapter 8 considers ways to strengthen that foundation by protecting the integrity of the information experts generate. Chapter 9 considers another way to strengthen that foundation—by maintaining and nurturing a career federal workforce that is capable of providing expertise and structured to do so.

7

Judicial Review

Chapter 6 closed with a promise that judicial review can perform a checking function on agencies, complementing the internal agency restructuring that chapter proposed. Recall that that restructuring aspires both to facilitate the creation and dissemination of accurate information indispensable to true expertise-based decision-making and also to ensure full participation by agency experts in the internal deliberation and debate over regulatory decisions. Judicial review should aspire to incentivize those same dynamics. If it succeeds, it will encourage agencies to accord appropriate weight to the regulatory expertise this book seeks to promote.

The Goals of Judicial Review

Judicial review—that is, courts' evaluation of the legality of government action—is controversial. When it involves review of statutes for their constitutionality, such as review of laws restricting abortion, it raises anxieties about the appropriateness of unelected federal judges overturning decisions made by democratically elected branches, sometimes, as with abortion, in order to vindicate vaguely worded constitutional restrictions.[1] Judicial review of agency action implicates somewhat different concerns. First, constitutional review is not the main focus (although plenty of plaintiffs bring claims that an agency has acted unconstitutionally).[2] Second, because agencies are not staffed by elected officials, the democratic accountability concern raised by judicial review of statutes arises only indirectly—although, as noted in the next paragraph, it surely does arise. Third, judicial review of agency action, as it has developed, rests mainly on statutorily prescribed standards rather than vague formulas such as "due process of law," even though those statutory standards themselves are quite general.

But such review triggers concerns nonetheless. First, because agencies are the acknowledged experts in their particular regulatory field, judicial scrutiny of agency action raises questions about generalist judges' competence to second-guess agencies' analyses of often excruciatingly complex issues. Second, the democratic accountability argument, while not as obvious when courts review agency action, nevertheless lurks just below the surface. After all, while not themselves democratically elected, most agencies are controlled by an elected official—the president—who is. They are also subject to congressional supervision.

Judges are neither elected nor supervised by those who are. Nor are they experts. These facts raise questions about the legitimacy of their scrutiny of expert agencies acting under elected officials' supervision. We have encountered those questions before. Recall chapter 4's discussion of the major questions doctrine, under which courts refuse to defer to agency interpretations of law that implicate large economic or social issues. Recall also that chapter's critique of that doctrine, which emphasized courts' inferior democratic accountability and expertise credentials, when compared with agencies. That same critique applies here, too—unsurprisingly, since the major questions doctrine is itself a judicial review doctrine.

To understand the issues judicial review raises, it helps to consider the agency functions it seeks to police. First, agencies act by wielding substantive power Congress delegates to them via statute. In order to use that power, the agency must interpret that statute. For example, the Clean Air Act authorizes the EPA to promulgate air quality standards to reduce air pollution. That power necessarily requires an agency to interpret that delegation to decide, for instance, whether it authorizes regulation of ranching operations, since cow-produced methane pollutes the air. Second, agencies conduct public procedures as part of any regulatory process that results in the creation of binding law. Statutory law—either the authorizing statute itself, the Administrative Procedure Act (APA), or a combination of the two—provides the procedure agencies must follow when they promulgate the regulations that constitute this book's topic.[3]

Both of these types of provisions—substantive delegations of authority and procedural requirements—play important roles in the regulatory process. A statute's grant of power to an agency is what authorizes it to act to begin with—thus, the agency's understanding of that authority is critical. Procedural provisions, such as those in the APA, are similarly critical, because they ensure that agencies accord the public a meaningful and appropriate opportunity to participate in reaching regulatory decisions that impose legally binding requirements. Such provisions thus ensure compliance with the basic American principle that law can only be made with public participation. Public input also helps agencies make better substantive decisions, by ensuring that all relevant issues are ventilated and considered.

That last point—about the quality of the agency's ultimate decision—reveals the third function agencies play when they regulate. Beyond understanding their statutory mandate and following the required procedures lies the actual making of a regulatory decision—a step often called "policymaking." As obvious as it sounds, it merits a moment to unpack this concept. Policymaking amounts to the agency's use of its expertise to combine its statutory authority and its understanding of the state of the world to reach a regulatory result. For example, if (hypothetically) the Clean Air Act required the EPA to "impose reasonable regulations to mitigate severe threats to human health caused by air pollution," the agency would have to come to understand the meaning of those statutory terms (e.g., "reasonable" and "severe"). It would also have to understand the state of the world (e.g., to what extent does airborne soot trigger asthma attacks?). It would then have to filter those understandings through its expertise—and presumably, through any political preferences that might be appropriate to include in the decision-making process—to decide whether and how to regulate soot emissions.[4]

Judicial review of agency action aims at all three of these functions. The APA authorizes courts to strike down any agency action that violates statutory (or constitutional) legal requirements, fails to comply with the required procedures, or is otherwise "arbitrary" or "capricious."[5] Leave aside for the moment judicial review of agencies' statutory interpretation decisions. As we saw in earlier chapters, the deference agencies enjoy when they interpret vague statutory authorizations constitutes an important question, which this chapter will address later. For now, concentrate on the judicial review of the procedures agencies employ and their use of expertise when deciding how exactly to regulate—that is, agency policymaking. It turns out that these latter two types of review play intricate and interlocking roles in administrative law. Indeed, as this chapter will explain later, they also relate to the statutory interpretation question, thus creating a unified structure of judicial review. That structure will have much to say about how courts can incentivize agencies to use their expertise.

Different Styles of Judicial Review

Thinking about judicial review of agency action requires a very quick lesson in the history of that review. Before the late 1960s, judicial review of agency action was generally quite deferential. One might intuit that that deference grew out of the Supreme Court's surrender to the New Deal, the often-told tale of Franklin Roosevelt's triumph over a Court that was suspicious of government power. But the matter is not quite as simple as that: Even before that surrender, courts had often been extremely deferential toward administrative agency action.[6] Regardless of the origins of this early deference, the legitimacy agency action earned after 1946, when the APA imposed uniform procedural requirements on such action, ensured that courts would largely respect agencies' regulatory decisions.

That deference started to erode in the 1960s. Around that time, scholars and judges began worrying that agencies had been captured by the special interests they were tasked with regulating and were ignoring the public welfare they were tasked with safeguarding. In response, judges began exploring ways to open up the regulatory process. During the late 1960s and early '70s, they made judicial review more accessible, giving very narrow readings to the APA provisions precluding judicial review, loosening up limitations on "standing" doctrine (the rules governing who could sue), and making judicial review available earlier in the regulatory process.[7]

In addition to making judicial review more widely available, courts during the 1970s also made it more stringent.[8] But determining the proper shape of that more stringent review raised difficult questions. It could have taken the form of courts inquiring more carefully into the substantive rationality of the challenged regulation. Alternatively, that review could have examined more closely the process by which the

agency reached that decision, to ensure that it engaged in a robust decisional process that one could expect to yield the good results careful
procedures normally do. To put it in terms of the three agency functions
the prior section identified, judges in this era faced a choice between
focusing on agencies' substantive policy choices and the procedures they
used to make them.

Judges debated this choice for most of the 1970s. One line of cases that
focused on procedures required agencies to follow procedures beyond
those set forth in the APA. Those courts examined whether the nature
or importance of the particular regulatory issue required the agency to
provide public participatory procedures beyond those the APA mandated. The Supreme Court halted this practice in 1978. In a unanimous
opinion in *Vermont Yankee Nuclear Power Corp. v. Natural Resources
Defense Council*,[9] the Court held that the APA provided not just the
minimum, but also the maximum procedures a court could require an
agency to follow. Courts could certainly enforce additional procedures
Congress had enacted in the particular regulatory statute itself. But the
basic idea remained that Congress, not courts, decided what procedures
agencies had to follow.

Beyond making this point about congressional supremacy, *Vermont
Yankee* also observed that if judges could impose procedural requirements beyond those required by statute, agencies would face a constant
guessing game about the procedures a reviewing court would eventually
require. No agency wants to lose a case on the ground of inadequate
process, since that result requires the agency to start that process all over
again. Thus, agencies facing the sort of guessing game *Vermont Yankee*
described would likely err on the side of caution and adopt elaborate
procedures not required by the APA or the agency's authorizing statute.
The result would be that the threat of judicial review incentivized agencies to go beyond the procedural structure Congress saw fit to impose.
Or so the Court reasoned.

Vermont Yankee remains controversial.[10] But regardless of what one
thinks of it, its attempt to push judicial review of agency action away
from a focus on procedure has enjoyed, at best, mixed success. First,
courts have accomplished a de facto expansion of procedural requirements by giving broad readings to the APA's bare-bones rulemaking
provisions.[11] But more important for our purposes, the alternative ap-

proach to judicial review in the 1970s—the one that dueled with the approach the Court squelched in *Vermont Yankee*—opened an additional pathway to judicial scrutiny of agency procedures. Ironically, this second path to judicial review of those procedures emerged from judicial review of the *substance* of agency action.

A Hard Look at "Hard Look" Review

This irony arose from what became known as "hard look" review. Hard look review is a style of judicial review of regulatory policymaking. It is governed by Section 706 of the APA, which authorizes courts to strike down agency actions they find to be "arbitrary and capricious." Consistent with the history of judicial review presented earlier, "arbitrary and capricious" review was originally thought to be quite deferential. Recall, however, that by the early 1970s concerns had grown that such deferential review was insufficient to police agency conduct that many feared had evolved mainly to serve the special interests—usually, the regulated industry itself—that possessed both the resources and the incentives to continually engage with the agency. As a response, courts developed hard look review.

Originally, "hard look" review meant that a reviewing court would examine whether the agency had taken a hard look at its regulatory options. But by the end of the 1970s it had come to stand for the proposition that *courts themselves* should be the ones taking a hard look at those options. But neither that linguistic shift nor its underlying reality—the heightened stringency of the judicial review that shift implied—need detain us. The more interesting question for us is, what should hard look review focus on?

Throughout the 1970s, judges on the DC Circuit—the federal court that hears most administrative law cases and is considered quite influential on those issues[12]—debated that question. Indeed, two judges on that court engaged that question in an ongoing judicial dialogue that has become renowned in administrative law circles. On one side, Chief Judge David Bazelon argued that hard look review should focus on ensuring that the agency followed a decisional process that was most likely to yield the correct, or at least a reasonable, result. Note that this process review was not driven by process values per se. Instead, it rested on a belief that judges could best guarantee *acceptable results* by focusing on *acceptable procedures*. As Judge Bazelon wrote in a concurring opinion in an important case early in this debate:

> My brethren and I are reaching for the same end—a "reasoned decision"—through different means. They would have us examine the substance of the decision before us. . . . But in cases of great technological complexity, the best way for courts to guard against unreasonable or erroneous administrative decisions is not for the judges themselves to scrutinize the technical merits of each decision. Rather, it is to establish a decision-making process which assures a reasoned decision that can be held up to the scrutiny of the scientific community and the public.[13]

By contrast, Judge Harold Leventhal urged that courts performing hard look review concern themselves with the agency's actual substantive output. (He wrote the majority opinion in the same case above, and was thus one of Bazelon's "brethren" who sought to "examine the substance" of the agency's decision.) Leventhal championed a style of judicial review that insisted on examining the agency's action for substantive rationality, even if that required judges to steep themselves in the (often complex) technical details of the matter at hand. He and his like-minded colleagues developed a jurisprudence that required agencies to demonstrate that their regulatory choices rested on evidence, and that the agency had carefully and expertly considered the regulatory alternatives confronting it. In contrast to Judge Bazelon's approach, this review focused primarily on judicial scrutiny of the agency's output, not the process from which that output emerged.

As scholars have noted, the Bazelon (process)/Leventhal (substance) distinction can be overstated.[14] Most notably, judicial review of the agency's *reasoning*, which can be construed as a form of process review, often shades into review of the substantive *reasonableness* of the decision that resulted from that reasoning. The close connection between the two approaches also influences how judicial review can promote agency expertise. Judicial review focused on ensuring that agencies make appropriate use of their expertise includes components of both procedural and substantive review. Process, of course, is relevant to judicial promotion of expert decision-making: Indeed, in a sense, the entire point of process review is to ensure that the deliberative procedure the agency used effectively mobilized its in-house expertise. But substance also matters: Judicial review that seeks to ensure that agencies utilize their expertise will inevitably scrutinize agencies' regulatory output, if for no other reason than to ensure that the agency leadership's final, presumably politically influenced decision retains an adequate foundation in expert judgment.[15]

The Court's ruling in *State Farm*, the 1983 airbags case discussed in previous chapters, illustrates many of these points. Recall that the Court unanimously rejected NHTSA's decision to rescind completely its passive restraint regulation. The agency justified its decision on its newfound doubts about a particular passive restraint the regulation envisioned (automatic seat belts); however, it failed even to consider the possibility of reissuing a more targeted regulation requiring installation of another passive restraint (airbags) that the original regulation had also viewed as acceptable compliance. In a unanimous decision, the Court ruled that the agency's failure to even consider an airbags-only rule was arbitrary because it reflected a flawed reasoning process.

One can easily understand the Court's logic, and its conclusion that the problem lay in the failure of the agency's reasoning process—that is, its failure even to consider an obvious regulatory option. But what made it a reasoning failure? After all, the agency also failed to consider a rule requiring drivers to encase themselves in bubble wrap. Of course, the bubble wrap option is silly, and thus it was not arbitrary for the agency to ignore it. But that's the point: An agency's (procedural) reasoning failure is only a reasoning failure when the ignored option is substantively reasonable. The Court thus had to conclude (or assume) that airbags were a substantively reasonable option that therefore should have been (procedurally) considered. Process, in other words, depends on underlying substance.[16]

Focus now on the potential intensity of this sort of review for adequate reasoning. We can probably agree that NHTSA's failure even to consider an airbags-only rule was arbitrary, regardless of whether we call that a process failure or a substantive mistake. But another part of NHTSA's analysis was more defensible. (Even the narrow five-justice majority that condemned this latter reasoning conceded that the issue was "closer."[17])

That part focused on the safety benefits of automatic seat belts, and concluded that increased seat belt usage in vehicles specially equipped with automatic safety belts was not generalizable to the broader public. Even though it was possible to understand how the agency understood that data, the Court insisted on its own interpretation and found the agency's competing understanding to be arbitrary and capricious.[18]

This latter part of the opinion spoke only for five justices, while the agency's more egregious failure on the airbags question elicited rejection from all nine justices. Nevertheless, the fact that a majority of the Court—even a bare majority—second-guessed the agency's interpretation of its own data reflected seriously stringent judicial review of agencies' regulatory analyses. Since then, such stringent scrutiny has become, if not an inevitable fact of life facing agencies, then at least a lurking threat. Even if a particular judge or appellate panel ultimately declines to review an agency's reasoning as skeptically as the five-justice majority did in *State Farm*, the risk of encountering such a judge or panel may well incentivize a risk-averse agency to assume the worst when contemplating judicial review, and to act accordingly.

In this context, the worst case is a reviewing court that nitpicks every possible flaw in the agency's reasoning and every hole in the regulation's empirical support. The logical agency response to that prospect? Load up on reasoning, resolve any ambiguities, and address every empirical possibility. Of course, that level of care requires time and money—resources that are always in short supply and needed for other regulatory initiatives, that will now be delayed or canceled in order to ensure the regulation in question survives *State Farm*-style skeptical review.[19]

Hard look review is controversial. Critics allege that is has triggered "ossification" of administrative rulemaking—that is, the dynamic described immediately above, in which the prospect of nitpicky judicial review of every piece of agency evidence and every aspect of its reasoning causes a risk-averse agency to spend scarce time and money tying down every conceivable analytical detail and factual loose end.[20] More to our focus on expertise, courts' insistence on such bureaucratic care, in an era of increased agency responsibility but stagnant budgets, leads to embarrassing reversals of agency action that only feed the public narrative of bureaucratic incompetence.[21]

State Farm–style hard look review may also cause ironic procedural effects. The Court insisted it was not requiring the agency to adopt any particular public procedure beyond that set forth in the APA, and thus was not reneging on *Vermont Yankee*.[22] Still, the fact remains that satisfying *State Farm*'s reasoned decision-making requirement essentially requires agencies to do things that necessarily complicate their procedural paths. This should not be surprising, once we remember our earlier insight that inquiries into the substance of the agency's action easily shade into inquiries into its reasoning process. As our *State Farm* bubble wrap hypothetical demonstrated, courts cannot critique an agency's failure to consider certain factors without implicitly concluding that those factors were relevant to the substantive reasonableness of the agency's action and thus should have been considered. The connection runs in the other direction as well: Scrutinizing an agency's substantive resolution of a complex regulatory issue almost necessarily requires reviewing how (procedurally) carefully it thought about it.

State Farm's ironies continue. Critics have also argued that hard look review has caused agencies largely to abandon rulemaking in favor of other decision-making formats. One such format is case-by-case adjudication, which allows agencies to shroud policy decisions behind a veil of factual particularities about the particular defendant, thus blunting careful judicial review of those broader judgments.[23] An agency might also choose to promulgate so-called non-legislative rules, such as general statements of agency policy, which are somewhat more resistant to judicial review. Perversely, because neither of these alternatives requires the agency to solicit participation from the general public, the imperative to avoid hard look review may lead agencies to act in ways that may be flawed exactly because they lacked public input that would have improved the action's quality.

But hard look review also has its defenders. They contend that the critics have overstated both the extent to which lower courts have imposed inappropriately stringent scrutiny, and, to the extent they do impose it, the deleterious effects such review has had on agencies.[24] They also insist that judicial review for reasoned administrative decision-making—the foundation of hard look review—constitutes an essential element of the rule of law.[25] Finally, it's worth remembering that hard look review arose in response to the perception of agency capture. To the extent such capture was real—that is, to the extent agency action really did respond mainly to the wishes of regulated parties rather than the needs of the public—it raised serious concerns about the legitimacy of an administrative process founded on both democratic accountability to the general public and a vision of apolitical expertise applied in service of the public interest.

It is, of course, this last imperative—that judicial review reinforce agency expertise—that motivates this book, and thus this chapter's proposal for reforming judicial review. That proposal is next.

Expertise-Reinforcing Judicial Review

There are many ways to approach the question of judicial review in general, and judicial review of agency action in particular. This book's concern with promoting both the reality and perception of expertise-based decision-making suggests a particular approach to the judicial review problem.[26] This approach focuses on incentivizing the expertise-promoting reforms chapter 6 suggested. Recall that those reforms seek to create internal agency processes that guarantee experts' relative freedom to create and disseminate information and inclusion in the agency's deliberations, while recognizing the agency head's ultimate authority to reach the final decision, even one heavily influenced by politics. Boiled down, those reforms call for an administrative process that, while not free from political influence, confines such influence to its proper sphere while also providing room for the application of apolitical expertise to regulatory problems.

The judicial review this chapter proposes does not seek to directly police those procedural reforms. Thus, this proposal does not envision pure procedural review of the type some judges urged in the 1970s. Leave aside the fact that such review runs headlong into *Vermont Yankee*'s admonition to courts not to impose procedural requirements Congress has seen fit to omit: If direct procedural review was so helpful, this book would call on Congress to authorize it. Rather, the reason for shying away from such procedural review is straightforward: Very few, if any, of the reforms proposed in chapter 6 are capable of judicial enforcement as binding legal rules in their own right. Agencies and their regulatory challenges come in all shapes and sizes; even within one agency the appropriate informational and deliberative procedures and structures will vary with the features of the particular statutory program and regulatory issue on the table. Those procedures and structures may also evolve as the agency's learning about the problem advances and its external environment changes. For these reasons, any legal rule mandating the details of a procedure or structure would likely have to be too general to be judicially enforceable. If not—if the rule was detailed enough to enable judicial review—it likely would quickly obsolesce and become subject to circumvention, even by an agency leadership that was in good faith trying to do the right thing.

Despite courts' inability to aim their scrutiny squarely at agencies' structures and procedures, it remains possible to steer their attention toward them. Under this approach, courts would review the substance of the agency action with a presumption in its favor when the agency could demonstrate that it both gave its experts appropriate latitude regarding information generation and dissemination, and conducted an inclusive decision-making process. (That demonstration might require the agency to include more material in the record it submits to the court, an issue this chapter discusses later.) If the agency failed to make that demonstration, courts would review its action more skeptically.[27] Of course, the final step in the agency's process—the political one where, metaphorically, the agency head closes her office door and contemplates her final decision—remains one that is made by a political appointee. Presumably, that decision rests, at least in part, on political considerations. But even a politically motivated decision is subject to judicial review, to ensure that it was *justifiable* based on the agency's decisional record, even if, as a matter of fact, political considerations constituted the real reason for the decision.

That last phrase might give some readers pause. One might ask whether judicial review is worth the effort if at the end of the day a court can uphold, as an appropriate exercise of agency expertise, an agency decision that was in fact politically motivated. It's a fair question. But two responses should mitigate the concern. First, politics *is* a legitimate justification for agency action. Chapter 5's conclusions about White House influence over agency decision-making concede a legitimate role for politics—just not the overweening role it plays today.[28]

Second, and just as important, modulating judicial review based on the degree to which the agency's decisional process involved experts and allowed the creation and dissemination of expert information incentivizes agencies to reduce the role of politics—or, perhaps more accurately, to increase the role of expertise. Ratcheting up judicial scrutiny when the agency's decision reveals danger signals about its deemphasis of expertise thus serves to make it harder for an agency rule to survive a judicial challenge when it is justified on expertise grounds but is really based on politics.

This type of review—unlike the insistence on judge-created procedures rejected in *Vermont Yankee*—is consistent with the APA. As this chapter explained earlier, the generality of the APA's "arbitrary and capricious" standard has allowed judicial review to evolve from the deferential review that prevailed in the APA's early decades to the hard look review that began to predominate in the 1970s. Likewise, the vagueness and generality of that standard is also sufficiently broad to accommodate the modulated judicial review proposed here.[29]

Indeed, we know that the APA can accommodate this approach to judicial review because it largely already does. As currently practiced, hard look review aspires to similar expertise-reinforcing goals as those set forth above. As the Court stated in *State Farm*, hard look review requires that the agency "examine the relevant data and articulate a satisfactory explanation for its action including a rational connection between the facts found and the choice made." It also explained that "[n]ormally, an agency rule would be arbitrary and capricious if the agency has relied on factors which Congress has not intended it to consider, entirely failed to consider an important aspect of the problem, offered an explanation for its decision that runs counter to the evidence before the agency, or is so implausible that it could not be ascribed to a difference in view or the product of agency expertise."[30]

Consider some of the verbs in those quotations. The current version of hard look review requires an agency to "*examine* the relevant data," and cautions that an agency action will flunk judicial review if it "failed to *consider* an important aspect of the problem," or "*offered an explanation* for its decision" that either contradicted the evidence or was "so implausible that it could not be ascribed to . . . the product of agency expertise." Examining data, considering all important aspects of the problem, and offering an explanation that could plausibly be ascribed to the agency's expertise: These are hallmarks of an agency process that is informed by its expert analysis of accurate data. It is just that sort of process that chapter 6's reforms called for, and just the sort of process that judicial review should incentivize.

This is not to say that this proposal would leave current judicial review doctrine unchanged. The dysfunctions chapter 6 identified are largely process dysfunctions: failing to create information, suppressing information, and excluding experts from decision-making deliberations. Undoubtedly, such failures create the kind of reasoning failures *State Farm* warned about: failures to examine the data, consider all aspects of the problem, or offer an expertise-grounded interpretation of the evidence. But there's still a difference between the two: Rather than focusing exclusively on agency reason-*giving*—the agency's articulation and explanation of its reasons—this proposal modulates review of that reason-giving by explicitly examining the process by which the agency *generates* its reasons.

State Farm's facts illustrate this difference. Recall from chapter 6 that NHTSA staffers reflecting on the *State Farm* debacle insisted to Professor Golden that had they been brought more into the decision-making process they could have crafted an administrative record that justified the agency's rescission of the passive restraint rule.[31] Leave aside any possibility that those statements were intentionally self-serving; the interviewees' motivations are not the point. What they were claiming was that the agency's process—in particular, their exclusion from the decision-making—generated an insufficiently explained (and thus arbitrary) decision. In other words, those staffers were lamenting the lack of a process that would have generated reasons the Court would have accepted.

The judicial review this chapter proposes still focuses on the agency's reasons. However, it ratchets its scrutiny up or down based on the court's evaluation of the process that generated those reasons. It asks whether that process allowed experts to generate and disseminate information and participate in the agency's deliberations. Thus, it seeks ultimately to correct failures in that process, even if it does so by focusing the judicial eye on the *outcomes* of those dysfunctional processes—the reasons the agency presents to the court.

Procedural Review?

The just-completed analysis clearly suggests this proposal's affinity with process-style review. In turn, that suggestion raises questions about its permissibility, given the Supreme Court's admonition in *Vermont Yankee* that lower courts should not expand agencies' procedural obligations. In 1985, Merrick Garland—at that point a lawyer (indeed, the lawyer who won *State Farm* at the Supreme Court), then a DC Circuit judge, then a Supreme Court nominee, and, ultimately, Attorney General—offered a helpful taxonomy of the types of judicial review of agency action that courts were performing around the time of *Vermont Yankee*.[32] That taxonomy helps us locate this chapter's proposal on the spectrum of judicial review options.

First, Garland described as "purely procedural" the type of review *Vermont Yankee* forbade—judicial scrutiny of whether agencies should have provided more robust procedures than those the APA required. He then described as "quasi-procedural" the review the Court performed in *State Farm* itself. That review insisted that the agency consider its regulatory alternatives and explain its ultimate decision. As he observed, the Court rejected the government's argument that such review violated *Vermont Yankee*, with Justice White explaining that it was not requiring NHTSA to adopt any particular procedures but rather was simply insisting that it engage in reasoned decision-making. Finally, reflecting our own earlier insight about how such reasoned decision-making shades into substantive review, Garland discerned in the Court's decision notes of such substantive review.[33]

This taxonomy establishes that this chapter's proposal for judicial review is consistent with Supreme Court precedent and its underlying policy. The type of review this chapter calls for scrutinizes the agency's reasoning, just like the Court in *State Farm* scrutinized NHTSA's reasoning (or lack thereof). Thus, it does not directly train a reviewing court's eye on the particular internal procedures the agency followed. At the same time, *State Farm*–style review is in some ways still "procedural," because it focuses the court not just on the rationality of the ultimate outcome but on the reasoning path the agency took to get there. But it merits the "quasi" prefix Garland attached to the "procedure" label, since, as he explains, the Court's requirements "focus not on the kind of procedure that an agency must use to generate a record, but rather on the kind of decisionmaking record the agency must produce to survive judicial review; the method of generating the record is left to the agency itself."[34] So too with this chapter's proposal.

Concededly, the type of review this chapter proposes is closer to purely procedural review than the "quasi-procedural" review performed in *State Farm*. Taking Justice White at his word, the Court in *State Farm* did not particularly care what procedures NHTSA utilized, as long as it demonstrated that it had performed a reasoned analysis of the passive restraint issue. By (slight) contrast, our type of review cares a bit more about those procedures: It is those procedures that determine how stringently or leniently the court reviews the agency's reasoning. Indeed, to be fair, our type of review aims ultimately at ensuring the integrity of those procedures. Nevertheless, it aims at that goal indirectly, via scrutiny of the reasoning that emerged from those procedures. Perhaps one could call it "procedure-reinforcing quasi-procedural review." That's an awkward mouthful, but it captures the idea.

More important than its label is the fact that this type of review fits the problem. Recall the problem: agency procedures that fail to fully utilize agency expertise—the types of procedures chapter 6 critiqued. But recall also, from this chapter, the difficulty of a direct judicial fix, given the variability of the types of internal agency procedures that arise from the wide variety of agency structures, authorizing statutes, and regulatory problems agencies confront.[35] Thus, the proposed fix: judicial review that modulates its scrutiny of an agency's reasoning based on evidence that the agency has employed an appropriate procedure to generate that reasoning. To repeat: Courts should not review those procedures themselves; judicially workable standards distinguishing between acceptable and unacceptable procedures simply don't exist when the procedural questions at issue are as nuanced as these. But it is still possible for courts to take account of potentially problematic procedures when they unearth them. (Tips for those archeology projects are provided later in this chapter.) When they do uncover them, courts know to ratchet up the kind of scrutiny they *are* capable of doing—scrutiny of the agency's reasoning path, as in *State Farm*.

A Word about Statutory Interpretation

Early on, this chapter identified statutory interpretation as one of the functions an agency performs when it regulates, along with implementing decisional procedures and performing policy analysis. So far, it has not discussed judicial review of how an agency interprets its authorizing statute (for example, how the EPA interprets the Clean Air Act). (Recall, though, that earlier chapters discussed the *Chevron* deference doctrine and the "major questions" doctrine that limits *Chevron*.) There are reasons for that hesitation and delay. First, oceans of ink have been spilled on that question, much of it nuanced work of very high quality. Engaging that work with any detail would quickly overwhelm not just this chapter, but the entire book.

Luckily, a second reason for that delay is that what we have said up to now largely says all we need to say about the statutory interpretation question. Begin by clearing away a preliminary piece of underbrush. Scholars generally accept that the conceptually hard questions about judicial review of agencies' statutory interpretations arise when the statute is ambiguous. A statute that clearly answers the relevant interpretive question does not pose a problem for judicial review, since the obvious impulse is simply for courts to enforce that clear meaning, regardless of how an agency might have interpreted that law.

But what should happen when an agency interprets an ambiguous statute? By definition, the statute does not provide a clear answer to the interpretive question on the table. How should a court review an agency interpretation of such a law? As earlier chapters have already noted, under *Chevron* deference, a court must accept the agency's reading of any ambiguous statutory provision, as long as that reading is reasonable. In a very helpful statement from a 2011 case called *Judulang v. Holder*, the Court reasoned that this "*Chevron* deference" review is equivalent to the arbitrary and capricious standard we have already encountered in this chapter.[36] Thus, what this chapter has said about judicial review of policymaking also applies to judicial review of agency interpretations of ambiguous statutes.

There's good reason for these two review standards to be equivalent, because what the agency is doing in those two situations (making policy and interpreting an ambiguous statute) amount to the same thing. For example, when the Court in *Chevron* itself applied the deference it established, it inquired into the care the agency took in its reasoning—just like it did the year before in *State Farm*, when it applied arbitrary and capricious review to agency policymaking. To be sure, the agency's reasoning in those two cases might focus on somewhat different questions, depending on whether its task was making sense of an ambiguous statute (governed by *Chevron*) or producing a policy result implementing a clear statute (governed by *State Farm*). But as *Judulang* stated and *Chevron* itself demonstrated, those two reasoning tasks imposed on agencies require very similar analysis, and thus justify judicial review that asks very similar questions.[37]

There's one final piece of simplifying good news. Recall that judicial review of agency policymaking focuses on the agency's presumed expertise while still attempting to make room for politically influenced agency action. (Remember the expertise-grounded demands the Court imposed on the agency in *State Farm*: To rely on the appropriate factors, consider all important aspects of the issue, and offer a plausible explanation for its decision. Remember also from chapter 2 the politics-based leeway four justices were willing to give the agency as it tried to satisfy those demands.) *Chevron*'s review of agency statutory interpretations does the same. In explaining the *Chevron* standard, the opinion's author, Justice Stevens, cited both agencies' expertise and their political accountability as the reasons courts must defer to agencies' interpretations of ambiguous statutes, rather than simply forcing their own interpretations on agencies.[38]

Thus, both controlling precedent and logic draw a tight connection between courts' review of agency interpretations of ambiguous statutes and their review of agencies' policymaking. Both are reviewed under a reasonableness standard that inquires into the quality of the agency's reasoning. In addition, the two versions of that (same) standard rest on identical ideas of agency expertise and political accountability. Thus, when this chapter calls for procedure-reinforcing judicial review of agencies' policymaking, the same review can be understood as appropriate for agency statutory interpretations.[39]

Implementing This Review

Even if this chapter's proposed approach to judicial review makes sense, implementing it raises serious challenges. Judicial review of the agency's outward-facing procedures—that is, review of how the agency interacted with members of the public—is conceptually straightforward, since such outward-facing procedures are relatively easy to identify and measure. However, scrutinizing an agency's *internal* procedures, even indirectly, as a trigger for either more relaxed or more skeptical review of the agency's reasoning, presents a more complex problem. As chapter 6 explained, the great variety across agencies, statutory programs, and regulatory issues means that those internal procedures could take a limitless number of forms. Thus, determining exactly what process the agency actually followed and what that process means for the court's ultimate review of the agency's reasoning requires much more granular judicial scrutiny.

Still, benchmarks guiding judicial review are possible. Agencies have created general guidelines for other areas of administrative procedure where clear lines are hard to find and even harder for courts to enforce or impose.[40] It may be that courts performing this review must limit themselves to placing a thumb on the scale in the agency's favor if the agency has established such guidelines, at least in the absence of a plaintiff's credible claim that the agency has ignored them. In the absence of such guidelines, courts may entertain an argument that the substance of or reasoning behind the challenged action suggests an internal procedural problem of the sort this type of judicial review is concerned with.

Consider an example. Hypothesize an agency action that appears at first glance not fully supported by the scientific data or any plausible reasoning about that data—an action like the airbag rule rescission in *State Farm*. On judicial review, a court performing this chapter's proposed review might suspect one of two things: either something had gone wrong with the agency's internal process of utilizing its expertise, or the agency head simply had made a political choice at the end of the process. The first suspicion—that the agency had employed defective procedures—would justify a harder look at the agency's reasoning, as part of this chapter's proposal for expertise-promoting review.

The latter suspicion—that the agency head simply made a political decision—raises an interesting situation. Relying on politics might be perfectly legitimate; remember the metaphor of the agency head closing her office door at the end of the process and making a decision informed by political considerations. But to establish that political considerations really were the reason for the decision, the agency should be required to embrace those political considerations publicly. To continue the *State Farm* example, NHTSA should have been required to state explicitly that the philosophy of the Reagan administration disfavored regulation unless the pro-regulation case was overwhelming.

If the agency fails to be so forthright—if it fails, in other words, to acknowledge the role politics played—then politics is "hiding behind science" in one of two ways: Either political factors triggered manipulation of the expertise-based process that should precede any final consideration of politics, or those political factors caused the agency head to pretend to make an expertise-grounded decision that was really a political one. The first possibility should be categorically prohibited: it may be appropriate for politics to play a role in agency decision-making, but it should never play that role by undermining the process by which the agency uses expertise. The second possibility is also inappropriate: Again, politics may be a legitimate part of the ultimate decision, but to play that role it must be publicly acknowledged.

Both of these exemplars of politics hiding behind science are illegitimate. After all, the entire justification for letting political reasons intrude into regulatory policymaking is that such reasons are presumed to reflect the public opinion that elected the incumbent president. To continue with the *State Farm* hypothetical, if a political program to deregulate—or even a political program to assist the then-ailing auto industry—was driving the airbag regulation rescission, then that program should have been publicly acknowledged so it could have faced the test of public opinion. Again, politics has a legitimate role in regulation only because it is assumed to reflect the people's will. Accountability to that will is impossible if those political reasons are cloaked in a shroud of phony expertise-grounded justifications.[41] If a court suspects any such cloaking, it is justified in according heightened judicial review to the reasons the agency proffered.

As should be clear by now, this proposal uses the substance of the agency action and its stated reasoning as entry points into judicial review of the agency's internal procedures. Thus, it remains faithful to *Vermont Yankee* in the way that *State Farm* was faithful, by insisting on reasonable (and reasonably explained) agency action. To be sure, that insistence might well effectively require the agency to engage in certain procedures, but, as Justice White explained in *State Farm*, it does not entail courts directly requiring any particular procedures. This proposal also allows room for politically based decisions, as long as those political rationales are disclosed and the action is at least minimally reasonable.[42] But despite that genuflection toward politics, this approach still seeks to promote expertise-based agency action by requiring, so to speak, a "harder hard look" when the challenged action appears not fully supported by the agency's expertise.[43]

The Agency Record

One way to assist the review this chapter proposes entails courts requiring or encouraging agencies to include pre-decisional technical reports as part of the administrative record for judicial review. Chapter 6 very briefly mentioned this idea, in the context of offering ways to incentivize agencies to respect their internal fact-gathering expertise. This section elaborates on it.

First, a bit of explaining: When a plaintiff challenges an agency regulation, it is the agency's responsibility to submit to the court the record of the agency's decision. In cases governed by the APA's procedures for informal rulemaking—thus, in most cases—that record consists of the documents the agency relied on in reaching its decision. However, privileged documents are usually not considered to be part of the record and thus do not have to be submitted to the court. This creates a problem, given that documents used as part of the agency's internal deliberative process, such as drafts and other pre-decisional documents, fall within that generally accepted exemption from inclusion in the record.[44]

Exclusion of such pre-decisional documents from judicial review of agency action is justified partly on the theory that they are irrelevant to the court's task, which is to review the asserted justifications for the agency's action, not alternative justifications the agency never publicly adopted.[45] On this theory, the only version of a study or a report that matters is the final one that the agency actually relied on in making its decision. But scholars have convincingly argued that that final version provides an incomplete picture of what the court is tasked with reviewing—the agency's reasoning process that deposited it at that final endpoint.[46] Even more to the point, the type of judicial review suggested here—review that seeks to ensure that the agency's internal procedures promoted expert decision-making—requires understanding that internal deliberative process. That task in turn requires investigating what happened to the agency's expert-generated information before it took its final form.

An example may clarify this claim. In 2019, EPA experts wrote a draft report assessing the risks of certain particulate matter pollution (basically, soot), as part of a legally mandated review of an existing air pollution regulation. That draft stated that if the regulation were tightened a certain amount, annual deaths from soot pollution would fall from 45,000 to less than 33,000—a decrease of more than 25 percent. But it was just a draft. The final version of the report mentioned only that tightening the rule would reduce "health risks." Environmental advocates promised to make the omitted finding part of their challenge to the new rule, which failed to tighten the preexisting standard.[47]

The above example of an agency altering its own expert information came to light because the draft report was disclosed as part of a public peer review process. But even in that case, and certainly in others, requiring the agency to file such pre-decisional documents with the court as part of the administrative record could help courts retrace the agency's reasoning process, to ensure that its final result reflected an appropriate use of its in-house expertise. It would expose any political interference with agency experts' generation and presentation of technical information—the political interference with science the prior section described and decried. If, as may have been the case in the soot pollution example above, changes were made in those technical documents between the time they left the hands of the agency's technical experts and the time political officials signed off on them and cited them as support for their decision, there would be reason to wonder whether political interference with expertise was the culprit. In turn, there would be reason to suspect that any expertise-based justification for the rule was a sham. Such suspicion would thus trigger heightened judicial scrutiny of that justification. If changes were not made, but the regulation nevertheless reflected a conflict with the technical information, the agency would be forced to explain why politically inflected reasons justified the rule despite that conflict. As the prior section noted, failure to acknowledge that the decision rested on such political reasons would again trigger heightened scrutiny of the reasons the agency did in fact provide.[48]

A Caution

Courts are often asked to do more than they are capable of. To take just one example, some constitutional law scholars bemoan the Supreme Court's inability fully to implement *Brown v. Board of Education's*[49] school desegregation mandate, despite the great optimism that greeted *Brown*. They observe that whatever desegregation has occurred likely resulted less from judicial action and more from legislative activity: in particular, threatened cuts in federal education funding to districts that failed to desegregate.[50] By contrast, ingenious state government tactics and just plain stubborn resistance frustrated judicial desegregation orders for many years.

The same outsized ambition might also characterize judicial review of agency action. To be sure, many scholars insist that the development of hard look review in the 1970s accomplished substantial changes (whether positive or negative) in how administrative agencies operate. But agencies, like school officials, often have ways of avoiding the most significant limitations courts impose. For example, agencies enjoy considerable leeway to choose between implementing a statute by promulgating regulations implementing that law—this book's focus—or, alternatively, bringing enforcement actions alleging violations of the statute itself.[51] This leeway allows agencies, if they wish, to avoid stringent judicial review of rulemakings by proceeding instead via case-by-case adjudication.[52] Even if an agency wishes to promulgate a generally applicable statement rather than prosecuting a single party, it enjoys significant latitude to do so by promulgating a formally non-binding (but nevertheless likely influential) general policy document rather than a legally binding regulation. That regulatory option increases the odds that the agency can avoid judicial review even while reaping significant compliance from regulated parties who wish to stay out of the agency's crosshairs.[53]

Sometimes, agencies manage to avoid meaningful judicial review not, as described immediately above, by toggling between different modalities of acting,[54] but instead by exploiting the tensions inherent in the entire idea of judicial review. For example, in a notable 1981 DC Circuit case, the court held that ex parte communications between the EPA and the president concerning an important Clean Air Act rulemaking did not have to be included in the rulemaking docket the court could examine as part of its hard look review. The absence of those communications posed a real problem, given that hard look review requires the court to evaluate the reasons the agency actually had for taking the action it did—something it could not easily do without access to those confidential but likely critical communications.

Writing for the court, Chief Judge Patricia Wald, a notable administrative law expert, conceded that the lack of information about those private conversations meant that "[p]residential prodding" may have been the real but unstated reason for the agency's action, not the technocratic explanation the agency publicly provided. However, she concluded that constitutional considerations related to the president's Article II power to oversee the bureaucracy granted him the authority to communicate privately with his high-ranking officials.[55] Most rulemaking cases do not involve direct presidential intervention. But Judge Wald's recognition that courts may uphold regulations on rationales that do not reflect the agency's actual thought process stands as a reminder of judicial review's limits.[56]

This chapter's proposed reform of hard look review reflects analogous internal tensions. It would likely be a bad idea if courts, as part of hard look review, undertook to micromanage internal agency processes and structures. Recall the Supreme Court's 1978 *Vermont Yankee* decision rejecting lower courts' insistence that agencies provide more *outward*-facing procedures than the APA required. The Court warned that such aggressive judicial proceduralization of agency action not only lacked a legal basis, but would incentivize agencies to adopt the most elaborate procedures possible, in order to avoid having the rulemaking struck down.[57]

Judicial micromanagement of agencies' *internal* procedures and structures would present agencies with similarly confusing and intrusive signals about what they would need to do to avoid a loss in court. At best, agencies would respond in ways the Court worried about in *Vermont Yankee*—by acceding to every bureaucrat's (and indeed, every political appointee's) suggestion of a new study[58] and involving every potentially knowledgeable staffer in every deliberative meeting. At worst, agencies would face a judicial lottery, in which an aggressive panel of judges could single out one undisclosed document or sparsely attended meeting as a reason to accord the agency's reasoning stringent scrutiny. An aggressive form of the review this chapter suggests would essentially transform pre–*Vermont Yankee* courts' insistence on more robust *outward*-facing agency procedures into an even more intrusive, if concededly indirect, insistence on more robust *internal* agency procedures.

This does not defeat the case for this chapter's suggested approach to judicial review. (After all this discussion, let's hope not.) Again, such review must take care not to cross the line into micromanagement or to mechanically transplant information-development and participation norms from one regulatory context into another. Nevertheless, inquiries into expert information development and participation are critical to courts vindicating expertise when an agency utilizes it, and incentivizing an agency's use of its expertise when the agency is otherwise inclined to minimize it.

Still, the review this chapter proposes must remain sensitive to different contexts. Concrete rules are unhelpful, beyond the general principles of reasoned decision-making of the sort expressed in *State Farm*. But those principles are sound. Agency action cannot be understood as reasonable or well-reasoned if agency leadership ignores or suppresses experts' calls to develop and curate information. Similarly, agency action cannot be considered reasonable or well-reasoned if, in that action's crafting, the agency's experts are systematically excluded from the deliberation process. Only if these dysfunctions are avoided can we truly say that the agency head's final, solitary decision to adopt a particular policy is legitimate. Perhaps ironically, avoidance of those dysfunctions renders that final judgment legitimate even if it is made for largely political reasons, as long as those reasons are publicly expressed and the decision itself reflects minimal expertise-based rationality.[59]

A Final Thought

This chapter has proposed "procedure-reinforcing quasi-procedural" judicial review that seeks to encourage agencies to make full use of the expertise available to them. It concluded, immediately above, by conceding that such review will be imperfect and incomplete. This concession means that the goal of incentivizing agencies' use of expertise can only be fully achieved by attacking the problem on multiple fronts.

Judicial review is one such front. Another is presidents' self-control when imposing their political will on agencies, as chapter 5 urged. Yet another is careful selection of the right agency heads. As chapter 6 recounted, Professor Golden's study of the varied leadership styles of the different Reagan-era heads of the EPA established that a wide variety of policy goals can be achieved effectively and expertly if the agency's leadership treats its expert staff inclusively and respectfully.[60] Agencies themselves can also assist their own cause, if they adopt the structural and procedural norms and principles chapter 6 suggested. Indeed, even Congress can play a constructive role, even conceding its likely inability to provide more specific guidance to agencies, if it is nevertheless able to marshal the energy to conduct meaningful and methodical oversight of agency activities. There's enough work for everyone.

PART III

Information, Capacity, and Engagement

Chapters 8 through 10 close out the book by considering how agencies can best deploy their expertise, which part II situated within the federal government's institutions. Chapter 8 considers how agency experts should be able to create and disseminate scientific information relevant to their regulatory duties. It attempts to create a space for agencies' informational expertise within an overall agency structure in which politics and political leadership play a legitimate, but limited, role.

Chapter 9 considers the condition of the bureaucracy itself. It criticizes the outsourcing of regulatory work that has occurred over the last generation, and calls for returning much of that work to an expert, tenure-protected corps of career civil servants. It also examines bureaucrats' material working conditions, and calls for improvements, in order to ensure that the civil service can attract and maintain the quality workforce it needs to shoulder the work this chapter argues should be returned to it.

Chapter 10 examines how agencies can engage with the public. Improved public engagement is critical, not just to improving regulation itself, but to improving the public's understanding of and appreciation for the work agencies do. Only with that understanding and appreciation can the public come once again to trust regulatory expertise.

8

Protecting Informational Integrity

Depending on the source you refer to, the term "information age" has been around since at least 1960.[1] Regardless of its longevity, today it is a commonplace that society runs on information. In the twenty-first century, whoever controls what people read and hear is at least as influential as anyone who controls weapons or factories. Probably more.

Regulation also runs on information. As important as values and value choices are to regulatory decision-making, the fact remains that any competent regulatory system depends on the generation and presentation of, and deliberation over, vast quantities of complex information. Conversely, a regulatory system that is not structured to generate accurate information and facilitate careful deliberation about it is a system built to fail. This reality justifies this chapter's distinct treatment of the information issue, even though some of the issues it discusses were broached, in different contexts, in chapters 6 and 7. Information merits a dedicated discussion.

Competent expertise-based regulation requires several conditions for the treatment of information. First, information-based analysis must play a leading role in making regulatory policy. Chapter 6 explained that role, while chapter 7 discussed how courts could incentivize agencies to allow informed expert opinion to play it. Second, agency experts must enjoy the greatest latitude possible to generate and disseminate information. This chapter discusses those issues. Finally, agencies must cultivate and maintain the expertise that allows them to develop such information. Chapter 9 discusses that issue. This chapter considers information itself—its generation, but also its distortion and suppression.

An Overview of the Issue

One way to get a handle on the varied aspects of this issue is to begin with a broad assessment of how agencies treat information. In 2018, several scholars published the results of a survey of scientific staff in six federal agencies: the Environmental Protection Agency (EPA), the National Oceanic and Atmospheric Administration (NOAA), the Centers for Disease Control and Prevention (CDC), the Food and Drug Administration (FDA), and several sub-agencies within the Department of Interior (DOI): the Fish and Wildlife Service (FWS), the US Geological Survey (USGS), and the National Park Service (NPS). The survey measured responses to several questions relevant to the role of information in the respondent's agency's decision-making process.[2]

The results were troubling. One survey question offered fourteen possible responses to a query about the largest barrier within the agency to scientifically based decision-making. Some responses spoke to technical or legal obstacles, such as the complexity of the issue or the uncertainty of the agency's jurisdiction. However, the top five barriers selected were the "absence of leadership with needed scientific expertise," "influence of political appointees in your agency or department," "influence of the White House," "limited staff capacity," and "delay in leadership making a decision." Some of these selections should already ring bells: Chapter 5 spoke to presidential influence over agencies, while chapter 6 discussed the influence of non-expert, politically appointed agency leadership. Others—staff capacity and the leadership implications of relying heavily on political appointees—are treated in the next chapter.

For now, focus on what these survey responses mean for information development and processing. Consider the issue of political influence. Eighty-three percent of the EPA respondents, 58 percent of the respondents at the DOI agencies, and nearly 50 percent of the respondents in the other agencies agreed with the statement that consideration of political interests hindered science-based (i.e., information-based) decision-making. For the three agencies for which comparative data from 2015 were available (the FWS, CDC, and FDA), more respondents agreed with statements about inappropriate political influence in 2018 than they had three years before. Moreover, only a minority of EPA respondents disagreed with the statement that they had been excluded from discussions or decisions related to their work in which they would normally have expected to be included. In other words, only a minority of EPA respondents pushed back on the suggestion that they had been inappropriately excluded from such discussions or decisions.[3]

The survey had more bad news for the development of information-based expertise, revealing that censorship is a particularly salient focus for concerns about political interference. Consider the survey's results about experts' work on climate change. Nearly one-third of EPA respondents and more than one-quarter of DOI respondents agreed that they had either omitted the term "climate change" from their work or avoided working on that topic altogether. For two of the three agencies for which comparative 2015 data were available (the FWS, EPA, and FDA), the 2018 survey revealed that a larger percentage than in 2015 disagreed with the statement that they felt they could voice concerns about the agency's mission-driven work. (That is, in 2018, larger percentages than before felt that they could not voice such concerns.)[4]

The 2018 survey asked the respondents about their agencies' compliance with their scientific integrity policies. Those policies, which individual agencies instituted in response to an Obama administration executive order in 2009, specify the standards and norms the agency aspires to satisfy in order to ensure the integrity of its data-gathering and analysis. While respondents reported high levels of compliance with their agencies' policies, the scholars analyzing the results suggested that those positive responses referred to career staffer compliance. Open-ended survey comments suggested that that compliance did not carry over to the agency's political leadership.[5]

Political influence has always hovered over the bureaucracy's scientific work. In 1953, President Eisenhower's Secretary of Commerce fired the head of the National Bureau of Standards after the NBS head concluded that an additive marketed as prolonging battery life did not work, leading the Postal Service to ban mail advertising of the product. (He was reinstated after a public outcry.) By the end of his time in office, President Lyndon Johnson was vetting prospective members of the President's Science Advisory Committee (PSAC) for acceptable views about the Vietnam War. President Nixon simply eliminated the PSAC when its members came out against the proposed Supersonic Transport plane he championed. President Carter had a report on future natural gas supplies suppressed when it suggested a rosier supply picture than the one he was presenting to the nation in order to get his energy plan adopted. He also had the report's author removed from his position running an inter-agency task force.[6] Since at least the Reagan administration, the phenomena earlier chapters discussed—strengthened White House controls over agency action, the increased focus on selecting agency leaders based on political loyalty, and the larger numbers of political appointees in agency leadership positions—have institutionalized and strengthened this political influence.

Recall how the 2018 survey revealed aspects of that influence. Respondents identified political interference as a prominent concern, ranking it higher than others that might naturally come to mind when considering problems bureaucracies encounter when confronting difficult regulatory issues. Self-censorship—that is, the phenomenon of experts avoiding particular topics (or even particular descriptions of regulatory problems, such as "climate change")—was a significant phenomenon in agencies that dealt with hot-button issues. In the wake of the COVID-19 pandemic, we can add the CDC to the list of agencies that have encountered pressure not to raise certain issues.[7] Exclusion from decision-making was something else that respondents felt in all the surveyed agencies, as was the general sense that their expertise was not valued. Similarly, budget cuts were identified as a major factor.[8] Indeed, in that 2018 survey, published only a month after the pandemic shuttered American society, CDC staffers presciently (and tragically) "cited potential budget cuts and resource constraints around infectious diseases and international cooperation as limiting their ability to do their jobs."[9]

These findings reveal the issues that influence the role of information in expert decision-making. To what extent do agencies possess the raw capacity to generate the information expert regulation requires today? What dysfunctions afflict the process by which agency experts develop information? Is that information distorted by political leadership, based on political motivations? How is information disseminated—and how is it suppressed—both inside and outside the agency? How is it used in the decision-making process at the agency?

The first of these questions—raw capacity—is addressed in the next chapter, which offers prescriptions for rebuilding the federal bureaucracy. The last of these questions—the structuring of an agency decision-making process that properly accounts for expert information—was addressed in chapter 6. This chapter focuses on the middle questions, dealing with the generation of information, the preservation of its integrity, and its public dissemination. They focus closely on information itself, rather than the agency's proper use of it (discussed in chapter 6) or capacity to generate it (discussed in chapter 9).

These three issues—information generation, distortion, and dissemination—are critical if we want agency decision-making to rest on a foundation of knowledge and expertise. As if to bear this out, one week after taking office President Biden created a task force to review the effectiveness of the agency scientific integrity policies mentioned earlier. Its mandate? To "consider[] whether existing Federal scientific-integrity policies prevent improper political interference in the conduct of scientific research and the collection of scientific or technological data; [and] prevent the suppression or distortion of scientific or technological findings, data, information, conclusions, or technical results."[10] In other words, this chapter's topics: ensuring appropriate policies governing the generation, non-distortion, and free dissemination of expert information relevant to regulation.

This chapter began by observing that information is power. In short, it will investigate the extent to which experts should have power.

Developing Information

Despite its importance, information development might still seem to present a straightforward issue: Regardless of any need to allow a space for politics, one might intuit that, at the very least, experts should be free to generate raw information by conducting the appropriate scientific work. But a moment's reflection reveals this intuition to be too simple. Regulatory initiatives may depend on information-gathering and scientific investigation, but recall from chapter 6 that the decision to embark on a particular initiative (and thus implicitly to deemphasize others) is fundamentally an exercise in priority- and agenda-setting. For that reason, political leaders must play at least some role early in that process.[11] Even after deciding to embark on a particular project, the framing of the issues the experts are charged with studying is itself appropriately susceptible to political influence.[12] For example, deciding, first, to focus EPA's energies on soot pollution, and then second, to do so from the perspective of preventing respiratory illness rather than mitigating climate change, constitute partially political decisions, not exclusively scientific ones.

This is not to say that an agency's political leadership enjoys carte blanche to make those decisions. Statutes may impose deadlines or other "hammers" for certain actions that thereby demand prioritization on the agency's agenda, and thus the prioritization of scientific investigation. Moreover, recall from chapter 7 that once the leadership decides to prioritize a regulatory issue, the legal requirement that agency action not be "arbitrary" or "capricious" requires it to examine the issue's most important aspects. Such an examination would normally require the agency to develop particular information. For example, it would surely be arbitrary and capricious for an agency to strengthen an environmental rule without considering the environmental benefits the strengthened regulation might generate.

Still, political leaders have a variety of ways to interfere with information-gathering. In 2017, the Department of the Interior ordered the National Academy of Sciences to stop work on a nearly completed $1 million project DOI had commissioned during the Obama administration to study the health effects of mountaintop removal mining. Political influence was suspected, and a DOI inspector general, unable to discern a legitimate reason to stop the study after disbursing nearly half the $1 million, concluded that the amount disbursed had been "wasted."[13] The project was never completed. That same year, the Department of Energy canceled a ten-year, $100 million climate change research project that was already in its third year.[14] More recently, attention has focused on cancellations of COVID-19–related research projects, at least in one case because of political pressure arising from discovery of the identity of the project's Chinese research partner.[15]

Beyond mechanisms as blunt as simply canceling research projects, political leaders also have more structural methods of interfering with information development. Probably the most obvious is simply to starve the agency of the resources that allow its experts to develop information competently. Chapter 9 discusses the destruction of agencies' human capacity. But other such structural mechanisms also exist. Consider the EPA's so-called Science Transparency Rule, finalized in the last days of the Trump administration.[16] That rule restricted the EPA's ability to base regulatory decisions or "develop[] influential scientific information" on data failing replicability criteria. While seemingly a benign, "good science" measure (who could oppose downplaying data that can't be replicated?), environmental advocates heatedly attacked the rule. They observed that much data on which environmental health studies are based come freighted with agreements pledging the data's confidentiality (for example, because it contained personal medical information), making replication difficult. The rule limited EPA scientists' ability to rely on those studies, thus making it harder for them to build data-driven arguments justifying regulation.

Regulations like the Science Transparency Rule impair agencies' access to otherwise-valid scientific data. Such regulations thus degrade agencies' ability to generate new information by building on that existing, reputable data.[17] Suspicion about the Science Transparency Rule grows when one realizes that it permitted only the agency head—a political appointee—the authority to grant exemptions. This detail highlights a theme running throughout the question of agencies and scientific information—and, indeed, throughout this book's attempt to distinguish between legitimate political direction of administrative action and illegitimate intrusions on agency expertise. Simply put, there is almost no legitimate reason to place in the hands of the agency's political leadership the control over when relevant data otherwise ineligible for full incorporation into the agency's own scientific work can in fact be included.

To be sure, if one squints, one can perceive a sliver of a justification for giving the agency's political leadership the authority to make exemptions: If a particular regulatory initiative is a high political priority, the leadership should perhaps have the authority to make such an exemption. But that is not how the Rule's exemption power was phrased. Instead, the Rule provided *expertise-grounded* criteria for the agency head to consider when deciding whether to make an exemption.[18] Bestowing exemption-granting authority on the politically appointed agency head, while directing her to consider scientific, not political, factors constitutes a classic case of giving the agency's politicians control over scientific decisions. It taints what purports to be a "good science" rule with the stigma of political manipulation of science. That taint is worsened when one realizes that, by requiring the agency head to cite a technical justification for the exemption, the Rule hides from public view the political calculations that are likely motivating her.[19]

Ultimately, a federal judge struck down the Science Transparency Rule for failing the APA's procedural requirements. Unsurprisingly, the incoming Biden administration did not appeal the loss.[20] Nevertheless, examples like this illustrate the ability of an agency's political leadership to impair the agency's ability to generate information. Unfortunately, it is only an illustrative example of a more common phenomenon.[21] Such examples reveal the potential for controlling the most basic of information functions—its creation.

The Political Blue Pencil

Perhaps the most distressing element of presidents' and political appointees' attacks on expertise is the temptation, often succumbed to, to alter the information experts create. First Amendment law considers it a particularly egregious affront to be compelled to speak, as opposed to "merely" being silenced.[22] Conceptually, having one's information doctored to say something other than what one intended to say is similarly offensive.[23] But beyond the offense to the scientist lies the offense to the public and, indeed, to the entire process of expertise-based decision-making. If we cannot trust that administrative decision-making rests on accurate information, conveyed accurately to Congress, the community of relevant external experts, and the general public, we cannot say that regulatory outcomes are truly based in the best expertise our society can manage. Nor can we expect the public to have faith in that expertise.

Sadly, such interference—or, to speak gently, "blue pencil" editing—occurs regularly.[24] Over the last two decades, climate change research has been a prominent victim. Most infamously, James Hansen, a NASA scientist who has long warned about human-caused climate change, created a political firestorm when, speaking to Congress in 2007, he disavowed parts of his own written testimony that he charged had been edited, over his objection, by White House staff. He repeated to Congress something he had said the year before: "In my more than three decades in government, I have never seen anything approaching the degree to which information flow from scientists to the public has been screened and controlled as it has now."[25] Hansen's concern about the scope of that interference echoed a 2006 survey of climate scientists scattered across five federal agencies. In that survey, 73 percent reported what they considered inappropriate interference in their work, and 43 percent reported experiencing actual edits or changes to their work that changed their findings' scientific meaning.[26]

Nor is this politically driven distortion limited to Republican administrations. During the Obama administration, an EPA report on the effects of hydraulic fracking on drinking water was edited to allay concerns about those effects, apparently after inter-agency meetings that included White House staff. One former EPA employee stated his belief that the changes were made at the behest of the oil and gas industry. Ultimately, the EPA's Science Advisory Board concluded that the agency lacked adequate evidence to make those reassuring statements, and a corrected report was issued.[27]

Once again, the Trump administration's handling of the COVID-19 pandemic provides more recent examples of earlier, troubling phenomena. In September 2020, the administration came under fire for interfering with the CDC's Morbidity and Mortality Weekly Report, a previously sacrosanct presentation of public health data. Political appointees at the Department of Health and Human Services criticized particular weekly issues for allegedly casting the administration's pandemic response in a bad light, and sought control over their content. Political meddling also led the CDC to publicly advise that only symptomatic persons should get tested, despite evidence that asymptomatic spread was likely—advice the CDC later walked back.[28] Around the same time, reports appeared that the CDC had softened draft reports recommending workplace alterations to curb the virus's spread in meat-packing facilities. One workers' rights advocate described the changes as "really unprecedented," and continued, "Reports were always based on experts and scientists' findings about how to mitigate whatever hazard they were facing. This is clearly a case of the science being rewritten to appease political interests."[29]

The effects of such interference are unsurprising, although no less troubling for their predictability. By distorting information ostensibly generated by agency experts, the responsible political officials skewed debate by presenting flawed data, analysis, and conclusions that nevertheless carry the patina of scientific expertise. The public thus loses the benefit of relevant expert information when evaluating government conduct, forming political opinions, and making personal choices that depend on that information (such as whether to favor fracking, get tested for COVID-19, or work in a meatpacking plant). Such distortion also damages the credibility of expertise-based decision-making, in one of two ways. First, if the distorting conduct remains hidden, the resulting criticism of the flawed agency information calls government expertise into question. Alternatively, if the distortion is exposed, the entire concept of expertise-based regulation falls into disrepute as "all politics," thus damaging claims that government expertise merits respect and trust.[30]

These distortions also impair congressional oversight. The 2007 episode involving White House editing of James Hansen's congressional testimony on climate change illustrates the problem. Congressional oversight—a constitutionally authorized function—becomes impossible if Congress receives distorted information from agency experts. Hansen himself was sufficiently prestigious to successfully expose the White House's distortion. But the Hansen incident was not the only one.[31]

Beyond external constituencies, such distortions also harm the internal administrative process. One can easily understand how they demoralize agency experts, even to the point of triggering brain drains out of agencies to private institutions where research is better respected.[32] They also impair effective internal decision-making because of the obvious difficulties that arise when an agency confronts distorted information even before the start of regulatory deliberations where politics may play an appropriate role.

That last point may be obvious, but an example may still help. Consider the EPA's chemical risk assessment initiative. In the 1980s, EPA scientists decided that several of the agency's regulatory obligations would be well-served by creating a centralized database of chemical risk assessments that agency scientists, scattered both geographically and across EPA's program offices, had developed. As a group of scholars studying this initiative observed, the data that process generated were "pre-regulatory," in the sense that that information simply spoke to the technical properties of the chemicals in question and did not suggest particular regulatory decisions. Nevertheless, OIRA staff inserted into the data comments that were subsequently described as altering the meaning of the scientific findings EPA scientists had reached.[33] This incident was not the only example of such pre-deliberative tinkering with the raw materials that would eventually feed regulatory deliberations.[34]

Why would political officials take the trouble to interfere with internal information even before it was used in regulatory deliberations? Two prominent scholars reflected on that question in the context of chemical risk assessments similar to those the prior paragraph discussed. They noted the wide variability in results generated by different scientific modeling methods, and identified the tempting target that variability offered politically motivated agency leaders:

> From the standpoint of a deregulatory president swimming against both legal and political tides, . . . an analytical tool [i.e., modeling] that provides so much scientific leeway and, at the same time, appears technical and esoteric offers a clear pathway for reversing [regulatory] course. A political appointee can slip behind the technocratic curtain and tweak model inputs, assumptions, outputs, and interpretations in ways that withstand public and even scientific scrutiny, but are in fact nothing more than raw politics and ends-oriented decisionmaking.[35]

This language is a bit abstract, so map it onto examples that have already been mentioned. A political official desiring to ensure that certain chemicals are not highly regulated would surely be tempted to interfere with scientists' assessments of those chemicals' toxicity, especially if the tampering could be hidden under the guise of technically complex chemistry or biology. Similarly, recall the OSHA workplace regulation example from chapter 2, and how the calculation of the regulation's benefits in terms of the injury costs it saved varied wildly depending on something as esoteric-sounding as the discount rate the regulator selected. In that example, too, a regulator interested in defeating (or promoting) that regulation would be sorely tempted to cook the cost-benefit analysis books by tweaking such an objective-sounding input. Perhaps ironically, then, the sheer variability of some scientific assessments makes it even more important that responsibility for making such assessments rests with scientists, not politicians interested in forcing a particular outcome.

To repeat a point this book has often made, we can concede that politics has a legitimate role in regulatory decision-making. We can also concede that that role includes authority over what agency experts study. As discussed in the next section, that role also includes, at least to some

degree, control over who receives the information agency experts generate, and when. But if a boundary exists between expertise and politics,
one of its demarcations must protect the integrity of the information
experts generate. Simply put, nothing justifies the politically motivated
blue pencil.

Suppression

Beyond information distortion lies information suppression—an agency's
prevention of any meaningful dissemination of expert-generated information. Suppression is a serious problem. While previous administrations
have engaged in this practice,[36] here again the Trump administration
appears to have occupied a class by itself. One scholar described its tactics
in terms that reveal the various ways such suppression can occur, observing that the Trump administration "barred agency officials, including
scientists, from publishing their work, presenting at conferences or in
congressional hearings, and otherwise disseminating information that
the Administration prefers never be publicly accessible."[37]

The complex, iterative process by which agency experts (like other
scientists) generate and use information means that the concept of suppression is related to, but nevertheless distinct from, the phenomena
this chapter has already discussed. For example, preventing an agency
scientist from presenting findings to other experts constitutes a clear
case of suppression. But it also removes the would-be listeners' ability
to critique those findings and thus assist the original scientist, as well as
the listeners' own ability to generate additional information grounded
on that scientist's findings. This occurred, for example, in the Trump administration when EPA experts were denied access to a NHTSA analysis
relevant to auto fuel economy standards, even though the two agencies
shared legal responsibility for that regulatory program. That information
embargo prevented EPA experts from pointing out the glaring errors
in NHTSA's analysis and suggesting improvements.[38] Some suppressive
activities may also have the effect of distorting the information that is
disclosed—for example, creative redactions not only suppress the re-
dacted information but distort the disclosed material.

The variety of ways in which agencies can suppress information, the
different justifications for suppression, and the different impacts sup-

pression can have naturally trigger different responses. Consider just a few examples. Government-held information may be classified or contain proprietary or other confidential information, or reflect one of the other policy reasons generally acknowledged as justifying refusals to disclose it.[39] Congressional oversight and policymaking responsibilities may demand agency disclosure of information to Congress when more general disclosure may be appropriately limited. Recall, for example, the closed briefing federal officials held for senators on COVID-19 in late January 2020. Even assuming there was reason to shut the public out of that briefing, there surely would have been no reason to deny Congress the information the administration had about the brewing pandemic. Similarly, NHTSA's refusal to share its fuel economy findings with EPA appears unjustifiable, if for no other reason than Congress had given both agencies shared authority over that regulatory program.[40]

This sampling of examples yields several tentative conclusions about the range of appropriate government suppression. First, preventing disclosure of information to Congress raises difficult questions about the tension between its oversight authority and presidential claims of executive privilege. In recent decades, presidents have asserted broad claims of executive privilege to prevent even agency scientists from testifying about their work.[41] Often, the prospect of protracted litigation and political stalemate prompts both sides to reach compromises outside of the judicial process.[42] Nevertheless, as chapter 6 suggested, withholding from Congress expert scientific information relevant to its oversight role should at least raise red flags, given Congress's role in overseeing how agencies implement the responsibilities Congress itself gave them. The executive-congressional balance may well yield a different result if the information sought pertains to the agency's politically inflected regulatory deliberations. Of course, this distinction raises again the difficult line-drawing issues, discussed in chapter 6, between information-gathering and regulatory deliberation.

Disclosure to the public raises distinct issues. We can distinguish between disclosure to what we might call the professional public—that is, the community of scientists with whom agency experts are in professional dialogue—and the general public. Obviously, there is no realistic way to formally segregate those two audiences. Nevertheless, government officials could try to limit the forms by which and venues where agency experts reach out to the public, and thus the likely audience for any permitted disclosure.[43]

There is little justification for limiting professional exchanges, which, as part of the general peer review process, allow the further development of information and also assist agency scientists by providing expert critiques of their work. These benefits assuredly outweigh what little public confusion might arise from allowing scientific presentations of technical work at professional conferences, universities, and similar venues. Such presentations certainly may reveal deficiencies in the government's research on important and controversial issues. They may also embarrass political officials whose policy views are in tension with their own staff's research and increase pressure on them to adjust those views to better accord with that research. But embarrassment and pressure are not legitimate reasons to allow agencies' political leaders to restrict such professional interactions. Echoing a similar point made earlier, suppression of agency-generated information is less justifiable the more that information relates to scientific findings, as opposed to regulatory deliberations that the agency may legitimately wish to keep confidential.

Limits on the work of external advisory boards raise particular concerns. Whether ad hoc, institutionalized, or even required by statute, these boards are normally comprised of prestigious scientists from outside the government, experts in the relevant field, who provide high-level scientific advice to agencies. They can thus play important roles in improving the quality of agencies' scientific work. Unfortunately, agency heads and White House officials have impaired those boards' work by restricting their staffing or operation: politicizing or otherwise limiting eligibility for appointment, delaying meetings, or simply disbanding them. Such actions do not technically suppress the dissemination of government information. But they generate the same effects, by removing a useful audience that has the potential to improve agency information development.[44]

Information disclosure to the general public presents different issues. Such disclosure—via public appearances and interviews and writings in non-specialist media—presumably adds relatively little to the formal technical expertness of an agency's information or analysis. Even that seemingly obvious statement needs to be qualified, though, first by recognizing that the distinction between laypersons and professionals is not crystal clear,[45] and second, by acknowledging laypersons' expertise.[46] Nevertheless, disclosures of pre-decisional deliberative documents, such as an early draft of a technical report, run at least some risk of skewing public attitudes about regulatory issues.[47] These justifications potentially validate at least some limitations on such disclosures.

Still, compelling reasons push against broad government power to restrict experts' communication with the American public. That public is, after all, the sovereign to which agencies are accountable. Short of specific and articulable concerns, the general idea that the public will misunderstand the place of science in the regulatory process seems unconvincing as an all-purpose justification for muzzling public disclosures.[48] To be sure, government's credibility can suffer if it discloses certain information, or offers information-based advice, that turns out to be wrong. For example, it's undeniable that the confusion during the COVID-19 pandemic's early weeks about whether asymptomatic persons should wear masks gave the government's public health apparatus a black eye. On the other hand, nobody would have expected the government to simply say nothing on that question, even if it explained that refusal by citing its lack of certainty.

We can recognize that every situation is different, and that there might conceivably be a case for suppressing information that raised the potential for chaos—for example, information suggesting that citizens should flee any city where the COVID-19 virus was detected. But beyond such extremely unusual situations, accurate but accessible presentations of experts' scientific data, when accompanied by cautions about the changeability of the agency's analysis and the many factors that go into regulatory decision-making and advice-giving, reflect an appropriate standard of government interaction with the public. Indeed, it can improve the public's comprehension of the regulatory process. As chapter 10 will explore, that sort of communication can also improve the public's trust in the process.

Agencies can suppress public access to information even more blatantly. Today, agency websites are a critical, easily accessible source of information about an agency's actions and the regulatory issues it confronts. Beyond the periodic housecleaning any website needs in order to be usable, it should be unsurprising that different administrations will feature different content on a given agency website, in line with that administration's priorities. Nevertheless, some website alterations cross the line. For example, after 2017, references to climate change were largely removed from federal government websites, as were links to related information resources.[49] The Department of Agriculture removed reports about inspections of businesses suspected of abusing animals.[50]

Removing reports from a website or references to a particular issue, or even removing a term entirely (such as "climate change") has an insidious effect: Casual researchers may conclude that the problem is not a serious one, or, in the case of rewording phenomena such as "climate change," may be prompted to reframe the issue. It may seem hyperbolic for a book about regulatory procedure to cite George Orwell's insight from 1984 that changing the meaning of words or even the words we use to describe a phenomenon has the effect of molding thought. But the concern is real.

The issues surveyed above are real and serious. Their variety suggests a corresponding variety of responses. Some are straightforward. For example, advocates for open government have urged the federal government to improve its web archiving practices, to ensure the continued availability of information incumbent administrations have chosen to remove from agencies' current websites.[51] Other suggestions are similarly straightforward, but involve changing the power relationships within agencies and thus implicate more fraught concerns. For example, scholars have suggested that agencies' public affairs officials—the persons responsible for approving agency experts' media and other public appearances—should themselves be career civil servants rather than political appointees.[52] Still others are potentially quite fundamental, such as the suggestion, discussed in chapter 6, that firewalls be constructed between an agency's political leadership and its technical experts, and chapter 7's suggestion that the administrative record for judicial review include preliminary scientific analyses. The problem of informational integrity is variegated. So too must be the responses.

Conclusion: Informational Integrity's Importance and Role

In conclusion, consider some basic takeaways about the importance of the integrity of agencies' expert information. First, information generation is foundational. A competent regulatory process simply cannot get off the ground without experts' freedom to generate information once the political leadership sets the appropriate parameters for the scientific inquiry. Second, distortion impacts the credibility of the information agencies generate. It sows cynicism about agencies as repositories of unbiased, expert opinion on regulatory issues.

Third, suppression is similarly problematic. Agency experts' inability to present research and findings as part of professional give-and-take deprives them of an important tool that improves scientific work. Suppression may be similarly problematic when it impacts the general public's access to information. Such suppression prevents meaningful engagement between agency experts and the citizenry in whose name those experts regulate. It also restricts experts' access to citizens' knowledge that may improve that regulation and reduces opportunities for the public to develop trust in expert regulation.

But before agency experts can perform that engagement—or, indeed, any of the other informational functions this chapter has discussed—they must possess adequate capacity. Chapter 9 examines the importance of strengthening and protecting the career civil service bureaucracy. Chapter 10 then considers what that engagement should look like.

9

Nurturing and Protecting the Bureaucracy

Chapter 8 examined threats to agency experts' generation and dissemination of high-quality scientific information. But beyond those threats lies a more foundational one: the prospect that we will find ourselves lacking competent and empowered experts capable of producing that information and performing the other tasks critical to effective regulation. Wendy Wagner, a prominent scholar of the interface between science and policy, states the issue bluntly: "An agency's expertise is only as good as the quality of its scientific staff."[1] But assembling and maintaining a high-quality scientific staff is only part of the staffing challenge. Beyond considering how to rebuild an expert bureaucracy, this chapter also examines how to protect both its personnel and their expertise, not only in their information-generating and disseminating functions but also their skill in the art of regulating—what we have called their regulatory expertise.

After briefly recounting the rise of the modern federal civil service, this chapter spends substantial time discussing the movement, over the last generation, to outsource important aspects of the regulatory process to private sector contractors. Outsourcing may seem a fundamentally benign (or at least value-neutral) practice that is best left to wonks studying the intricacies of federal procurement practices. It is neither. While government outsourcing is a fact of life, when taken too far it can seriously damage the quality of government regulation and, indirectly but equally seriously, the health of the government's regulatory apparatus.

After examining the outsourcing issue, this chapter then considers the more quotidian, but no less critical, issues more directly affecting the material health of the federal bureaucracy as an institution: issues of compensation and working conditions. Both the chapter's consideration of outsourcing and its discussion of the bureaucracy's material well-being raise issues that are critical to this book's focus on expertise. Simply put, a bureaucracy that is restricted from doing what it was built to do cannot function as a font of institutional expertise. Nor can a bureaucracy that is fundamentally unwell. Unfortunately, the federal bureaucracy today is both.

In examining these questions, this chapter continues the book's broader narrative. After part I laid out the historical background, part II discussed how to improve the institutional framework within which the bureaucracy operates—that is, its relationship to congressional legislation (chapter 4), White House influence (chapter 5), its own political leadership (chapter 6), and reviewing courts (chapter 7). Part III centers on the bureaucracy itself. Chapter 8 considered how the bureaucracy should be able to deal with information, the lifeblood of effective regulation. This chapter considers the bureaucracy's health. Chapter 10 returns to the issue with which this book started: the decline in the public's trust in federal regulatory expertise. There we examine how agencies can deploy their capacity to increase public trust in regulation. But before agencies can deploy that capacity, they need to rebuild it. That's what this chapter examines.

The Road to the Modern Civil Service

Rebuilding presumes decline. In the case of the federal bureaucracy, that decline, both real and perceived, has proceeded apace since at least the 1970s. To examine what sort of rebuilding is required, it is appropriate to examine how the bureaucracy was built, and how it deteriorated.

The nation's earliest experience with regulation relied on private actors, acting on private motivations. There was criminal law, but crime victims and constables played important roles in apprehending and prosecuting perpetrators, with the constables seeking private compensation for the return of stolen property. There was taxation, but tax collectors were often private persons who kept a share of what they collected. As long as we don't ask too much of the analogy, in a very rough sense one could describe this sort of regulatory infrastructure as featuring an outsourced workforce.[2]

Still, at least by the Founding, competent government—including competent public administration—had arisen as a topic of discussion among American political leaders.[3] Over time, and especially during the first half of the nineteenth century, the government began providing more and more services—and imposing more and more regulation—via its own employees. Professional police forces began replacing private sheriffs, and the increasing regulation that attended an industrializing society was guided more and more by persons directly employed by the government—at first, mainly by state governments until the federal government became a significant economic regulator toward the end of the nineteenth century.

But these government officials, whether state or federal, were not bureaucrats in the modern sense. Throughout most of the nineteenth century, government regulation was performed by government employees hired not because of their competence but rather because of their political loyalty. This so-called patronage system, in which political leaders rewarded followers with government jobs, appeared early in American politics, but became especially prominent at the federal level with the election of President Andrew Jackson in 1828. It was also known as the "spoils system," reflecting the blunt statement, made by one of Jackson's supporters, that "to the victor belong the spoils."[4]

Arguably, the spoils system was well-designed for its time—a democratizing era witnessing the birth of modern American political parties. With an expanding electorate and campaigns that relied more and more on mass mobilization, it became increasingly important for victorious politicians to reward their followers. Allocating to followers coveted government offices, such as tax collector, harbormaster, or postmaster, allowed politicians to ensure that the recipients of such spoils remained followers and loyal party workers. After all, if the other party won the next election, those officeholders would be out of a job.[5]

But patronage was not a way to ensure effective provision of government services. If the only qualification for a government position was political loyalty, then there was no reason to think that government services would be provided efficiently.[6] Instead, one might think that those officeholders would be more interested in doing political work for their patrons, and even using the power of their offices to further their patrons' political interests. Moreover, the political basis for officeholding meant that holders of patronage positions departed if their patron lost the election. The resulting constant turnover did not bode well for steady administration performed by experienced officials who had developed expertise in their field. By mid-century, calls for a professional bureaucracy were circulating at both the state and federal levels. Those calls became irresistible after President James Garfield was assassinated in 1881 by a delusional seeker of a federal patronage office.

In 1883, Congress enacted the Pendleton Act, which established the federal civil service we know today. While it originally did not apply to many federal workers, that statute's establishment of a merit-based system for securing and holding government jobs began a process of professionalizing the federal workforce that continued well into the twentieth century. So did the Act's limitations on politicians recommending persons for civil service jobs and, conversely, its restrictions on civil servants engaging in political activity.

Still, despite the growth of federal regulation in the generation bracketed by the enactment of the Interstate Commerce Act in 1887 and the onset of the Great Depression in 1929, the federal bureaucracy remained relatively small. It was only with the New Deal and then the demands of World War II that federal employment skyrocketed. While the number of federal employees fell with the demobilization of vast numbers of soldiers after 1945 and again after the end of the Korean War in 1953, the number remained high, reflecting the staying power of the New Deal and the attendant need for federal employees to administer it.[7]

Throughout the 1960s and into the 1970s, federal spending increased beyond earlier levels, reflecting expenditures for both the Vietnam War and the Great Society programs championed by President Lyndon Johnson. Between 1960 and 1975, federal spending nearly doubled. But the federal workforce did not keep pace; rather, during those same fifteen years the number of federal employees increased less than 20 percent, from 1.8 million to 2.1 million.[8] That divergence between dollars spent and headcount is noteworthy. But even more extraordinary is what happened next: Over the following three decades (that is, by 2005), federal spending had doubled again, but the federal employee headcount had *fallen* back to the 1.8 million number that prevailed in 1960.[9]

How did that happen?

The Cracks Start to Show

By the late 1960s, forces began to coalesce that would threaten the status of the federal bureaucracy. President Richard Nixon harbored an innate suspicion of the federal workforce, believing—not fully incorrectly—that civil servants were inherently sympathetic to Democratic initiatives such as those launched as part of Johnson's Great Society. After initially experimenting with a more traditional cabinet- and agency-based management system, Nixon began building a shadow bureaucracy in the White House itself, abandoning that effort only at the start of his abortive second term.[10]

Around the same time, intellectual forces began to coalesce against the traditional civil service bureaucracy. Recall from chapter 1 that by the early 1970s, conservative business leaders, perhaps inspired by Lewis Powell's famous 1971 memo (also discussed in that chapter), had begun funding think tanks and law firms advocating for market-oriented solutions to national problems. One such solution was simply to regulate less. Calls for deregulation of particular industries increased throughout the 1970s, leading a Democratic administration under President Jimmy Carter to deregulate the commercial airline and trucking industries.

But simple deregulation was not enough. As President Reagan discovered, Americans like many types of regulation. For example, despite electing him and keeping him relatively popular throughout much of his presidency, Americans also consistently expressed their preferences for robust environmental regulation and entitlement programs.[11] Thus, the post–Great Society conservative regulatory agenda partially pivoted away from out-and-out repeals of such programs and toward devolving regulatory authority to the states. While such devolution did not necessarily mean less regulation, it did mean more decentralized regulatory decision-making. Many conservatives thought that move would lead to better, more responsive regulation—and quite possibly regulation that would be substantively more conservative, if it was taken out of the hands of perceived "liberal bureaucrats" in Washington. Such devolution also fit the Reagan administration's anti-(federal) bureaucrat rhetoric, which chapter 2 also described.[12]

By the early years of the Reagan administration, the puzzle pieces had appeared: a substantive preference for deregulation, a distrust of the federal bureaucracy, and a search for alternative regulators who might be more inclined to favor the incumbent administration's policy preferences. All that was needed was for someone to assemble the pieces into a picture.

The Need to Rebuild Starts with the Reason for the Erosion

Those pieces came together with the evolving thinking about outsourcing federal regulatory work to private contractors. Starting in the 1970s, free market advocates began arguing that such outsourcing would lead to more efficient regulation. They emphasized the asserted contrast between a nimble, profit-oriented private sector and a lumbering federal civil service that was more concerned with protecting its perks and increasing its size than regulating effectively.[13]

To be sure, government had always relied on private entities to get its work done. Recall the colonial criminal law and tax collection examples mentioned earlier. More recognizable types also developed. For example, at least as early as 1819, Congress authorized the government to contract out for steamship carriage of mail—a perfectly sensible move given the likely small mail cargoes not warranting a fleet of postal service vessels.[14] For distinct but related reasons about efficiency, it made similar good sense that it never grew the food that it served in its cafeterias (although, until the 1950s, it did manufacture the dentures Veterans Administration dentists supplied to their patients[15]). Instead, it purchased that food (and eventually, those dentures) from private suppliers—that is, it outsourced that supply. Eventually, it outsourced the cafeteria service itself.

But serving food to the regulators who patronize the agency cafeteria is not itself regulating—rather, it is ancillary to the regulatory process, a convenience for the bureaucrats who do the actual work of government. Of course, the line between regulatory services ("the actual work of government") and ancillary services is not always as clear as the distinction between drafting a regulation and providing lunch to the drafting team. In 1966, the Johnson administration issued OMB Circular A-76, which required the government to conduct public/private competitions when considering whether to outsource commercial goods and services.[16] Importantly, that circular exempted what it called "inherently governmental functions" from the outsourcing option. But that exemption just restated the difficult problem of distinguishing between regulation drafters and cafeteria clerks. As one prominent scholar observed, the category of "inherently governmental functions," even as clarified by an accompanying explanation and a government-provided illustrative list, "is hardly self-explanatory."[17]

This chapter will return to Circular A-76. For now, regardless of the vagueness of both its "inherently governmental functions" formula and the regulatory/ancillary distinction this book offers as an intuitive shorthand, by the 1980s agencies had begun relying on private entities to perform tasks closely tied to unmistakably regulatory processes.[18] Contractors were drafting and enforcing regulations and performing analogous government-sounding functions. Indeed, in a case of outsourcing-within-outsourcing, contractors were evaluating how effectively federal grantees (contractors in their own way) were using federal grant dollars to provide social services.[19]

Recall from chapter 3 that by the 1990s, contracting out for regulatory services was becoming more widespread, as part of the Clinton administration's Reinventing Government initiative and its more general "New Democrat" focus on harnessing the private sector to achieve public goals. Proponents of that initiative urged that government "steer" and let others "row," arguing that the result would be a leaner yet more effective government.[20] Such outsourcing of regulatory and near-regulatory functions held great appeal. It allowed government programs to continue operating while also allowing politicians to boast of reduced civil service headcounts as proof they were careful stewards of the public fisc and not captives to New Deal–style bureaucrat-heavy regulatory philosophy.[21] Indeed, during the Clinton years the formal civil service headcount declined by 400,000.[22] It is in this context that we can fully understand his 1996 boast that "the era of big government is over."[23]

Except it wasn't. Clinton made his statement as the post–Cold War "peace dividend" was working its way through the federal system, but by 2002 the number of contractors was rising again, reaching over 7.5 million in 2005 after falling to less than 4.5 million in 1999.[24] This increase likely resulted in large part from post–9/11 national security initiatives, most notably the massive federal spending incurred in Afghanistan and Iraq. The wind-down of those wars may well cause contracting numbers to fall. But just as important as the raw numbers is the fact that the increased work the federal government needed done was performed primarily by contractors, not civil servants. In that sense, not only is the era of big government not over, its composition has shifted away from traditional civil servants and toward private contractors. Nor is this shift due purely to the unique nature of post–9/11 expenditures, which might have called for temporary work best performed by temporary contractors. For example, between 1990 and 2002 alone, the ratio of contractors and grantees to civil servants rose from approximately 3.5:1 to over 4:1.[25]

The Effects of Outsourcing

The growth of outsourcing has had several problematic effects. First, as John DiIulio argues, it has harmed the perception and reality of bureaucrats' performance by foisting onto them an unmanageable supervisory responsibility. With more contractors performing larger and more critical roles in ever-increasing government programs, the corps of civil servants tasked with supervising contractors becomes overwhelmed. What follows is predictable: inadequate oversight that leads to regulatory failures.[26]

A state that has taken outsourcing to an extreme provides a telling case study of that dynamic. In 2014, Texas canceled Xerox's contract to run the state's Medicaid dental program after a federal audit determined that the state had paid more for Medicaid dental claims than the nine other most populous states *combined*, with Xerox's one dentist allegedly rubber-stamping thousands of claims per month. A member of the Texas Legislature accused the state of insufficient supervision of the contractor.[27] That's an unsurprising allegation, considering that the debacle occurred in the middle of Texas's sweeping initiative to privatize as much of the state's workforce as possible, with the amount it spent on contractors quadrupling between 2005 and 2013.[28] To repeat the formula: Increasing reliance on contractors, combined with reductions in civil service staffing, yields insufficient oversight and, in turn, regulatory disasters.[29]

One might think that such failures, if laid at contractors' doorsteps, would simply lead government to limit use of contractors more generally or, at the very least, reduce reliance on those that fail. But this response fails to account for the political clout large contractors individually and collectively exercise over Congress. That clout allows them to lobby Congress to ensure continued access to government contracting business.[30] The result is yet another variant of the regulatory capture that, as chapter 7 explained, triggered stricter judicial scrutiny of agency action in the 1970s. Ironically, though, this version of the capture story arises from a phenomenon—outsourcing—that seeks, at least ostensibly, to prevent the regulatory dysfunction supposedly created by civil servants' own self-interested conduct.

Still, it remains true that individual contractors have only a contingent relationship with their agency partners. Like Texas in the Medicaid example, the government can always fire the contractor.[31] But that reality creates yet another problematic dynamic: that regulatory policy will be distorted by skewed information and recommendations provided by contractors seeking to please their employers and thus continue (and perhaps broaden) their contracting relationship.

This possibility highlights one of the critical benefits that flows from civil servants' job protections: the fact that such security makes it easier for them to speak uncomfortable truths to their superiors. Anyone familiar with faculty governance and academic freedom in a university will intuitively understand how tenure protections enable such truth-telling, at least in an institution staffed with competent faculty who take their governance and research duties seriously.[32] For readers who prefer earthier language, consider what Michael Lewis said in his 2021 book about individual epidemiological experts who banded together to try to force the government to act more swiftly early in the COVID-19 pandemic: "To fire a competent civil servant is a pain in the ass."[33] Ideally, with that difficulty comes the provision of frank advice.

By contrast, if one squints one can see in today's contractor the faint outlines of the nineteenth-century spoilsman—a person endowed with government authority but incentivized to please his politician-boss. If today's spoilsman is less overtly political, he is by no means less self-interested. Rather, he and his Jacksonian ancestors are both incentivized to do what the boss wants, whether turning out favorable votes or providing the regulatory analysis the agency head wants to receive. Two authors captured the comparison nicely, referring to the modern government contracting regime as "pinstripe patronage."[34]

But, as the last paragraph implies, the policy distortion that can arise from outsourced regulatory analysis extends beyond the contractor seeking to please the agency official who signs the contractor's work order renewal. The distortion also runs in the other direction: from agency to contractor. It is quite possible to imagine the official in this scenario selecting a particular contractor exactly because the contractor is known to harbor a preexisting bias in favor of the official's preferred policy. The contractor's help in vindicating that policy can be critical. In a system like ours, where regulatory decisions satisfy or fail judicial review based on the analytical record the agency compiles, the ability to select those tasked with that compilation helps agency leadership craft a record favorable to their ultimate desired outcomes. Thus, not only does the contractor want to please the agency's leadership, but the agency's leadership has incentives to look for contractors who aim to please.[35]

Moreover, an agency's use of contractors might effectively bind the agency going forward. Jon Michaels provides straightforward examples of such binding, such as a city contracting with private waste collectors to haul garbage in environmentally harmful ways, with the contract binding future administrations to those undesirable methods unless the successor administration chooses to breach the contract and pay the penalty.[36] Consider an even more egregious example. In late 2020, it came to light that the Department of Homeland Security had contracted with states and, even more extraordinarily, a union of DHS employees, to not make certain changes to immigration enforcement policy for a period of time extending into the then-incoming Biden administration.[37] The Trump administration's willingness to contract away government's regulatory prerogatives reveals the extent of the risk that an aggressive agency might use agreements with regulatory partners to bind its successors to its desired regulatory policy. It thus becomes all the more important to limit such abuses by limiting the government's ability to contract out for regulatory services.[38]

There's a final cost to outsourcing, perhaps its most basic. As a corps of experienced, presumptively life-tenured professionals, civil servants possess a body of expertise to which the government can always turn. But if they are denied the opportunity to perform their core functions because those functions have been outsourced, that expertise will wither. People will leave, and those who stay will lose the institutional muscle memory that constituted part of the reason for providing them job security to begin with. As a longtime student of the federal bureaucracy wrote, "the outsourcing of management functions that are best performed in house undermines government performance in two ways: By utilizing second-best performers and by weakening or atrophying government's power to perform these functions in the future. Government managers cease to exist when they are not put to good use."[39]

The Proper Scope for Outsourcing

In light of the arguments presented above, it should not be surprising that prominent scholars of the bureaucracy have reached a negative verdict on the federal government's increased use of contractors. Paul Verkuil has chronicled not just the policy disasters that have flowed from increased state and federal reliance on contractors, but also the resulting perverse political incentives that have decreased government efficiency. John DiIulio has identified similar dysfunctions, while also emphasizing the inability of overworked federal civil servants to perform the "steering" function that President Clinton envisioned when he embraced outsourcing. Jon Michaels has found outsourcing to threaten our system of separated powers.[40]

Despite these critiques, it is surely the case that some outsourcing is appropriate. Returning to our preliminary discussion of this question, nobody thinks it is critical that the federal government operate its own cafeterias or even that it necessarily could operate them more efficiently than a contractor. (Maybe it could, or maybe not.) Thus, since some outsourcing is likely appropriate and other outsourcing not, the task becomes distinguishing appropriate from inappropriate outsourcing—that is, demarcating outsourcing's appropriate scope.

When thinking about that task, it helps to recall the distinction between regulatory and ancillary services, a distinction illustrated by our earlier one between drafting a regulation and serving food in the agency cafeteria. That distinction echoes the one drawn in the OMB Circular also mentioned earlier, Circular A-76, that prohibited the outsourcing of "inherently governmental functions." Circular A-76 draws a distinction that is conceptually clear: Sovereign functions—in our case, the actual process of using discretion to promulgate binding regulatory law—

should remain the responsibility of government employees. By contrast, what one might call ancillary or support functions—feeding the civil servants who make those sovereign decisions or supplying them with paper clips—can be outsourced.

This distinction is not enough to answer the hard questions, but it does at least some work. Lest anyone think that it reflects a straw person argument, since government would never contract out the actual sovereign function of deciding what binding law should look like, consider that tens of thousands of federal contracting dollars have gone to a private company named "Rulemaking Services." If one thinks that too much is being made of that name, consider that those dollars have gone to the performance of tasks including "Regulatory Studies" and "Policy Review/Development Services."[41] If one still insists that such contracts simply cannot be for "policy . . . services" that are particularly significant, consider that one of the Obama administration's signature regulatory initiatives—the climate change–fighting Clean Power Plan—has been described as largely crafted by lobbyists who then presented it to the EPA and briefed its leadership.[42] And if one thinks that the latter example must be an outlier, consider that, as early as 1989, a senator exclaimed that EPA "relies on contractors to do everything from rule-writing to rule enforcement." Indeed, a newspaper report from that same year quoted a Senate report as complaining that the Department of Energy was using 100,000 contract employees while boasting only 16,000 civil servants, and despairing that the former were performing "virtually all [of the agency's] basic functions."[43] When thinking about which functions can be outsourced and which can't, it's impossible to be too extreme in imagining the possibilities modern experience has offered.

Despite the conceptual clarity of the distinction between providing lunch and providing regulations, when it comes to the appropriate scope for outsourcing, the devil remains in the details. Even when considering obvious sovereign actions such as promulgating regulations, we must acknowledge that private parties regularly lobby administrative agencies to take one action or another. In doing so, they offer their own detailed policy prescriptions, either as part of the public comment process or in off-the-record meetings that occur before a rulemaking is commenced (and, indeed, that largely remain legal even after it starts). Of course, one expects (or at least hopes) that agencies will do their own work on proposed regulations. But even that expectation becomes blurred when private parties furnish a detailed model to the agency, which then adopts that work as its own. (Recall the Clean Power example from the previous paragraph.) Paul Verkuil gets to the nub of the question: In these situations, he writes:

> The contractor is not asked to perform a government function directly (whether "inherent" or not), but for help in making the decision. If the contractor does all the work to prepare a decision, has the decision line itself been crossed? When an official rubber stamps a contractor's recommendation, who is performing the government function?[44]

Indeed, who? And where is that "decision line"?

Sovereignty and Expertise

The answer may turn on the value we are seeking to vindicate. Verkuil's 2007 book, tellingly titled *Outsourcing Sovereignty*, focuses on the problem of government outsourcing its fundamental sovereign duty to govern. The problem Verkuil describes is a foundational one in American government. Indeed, it is foundational enough to take on a constitutional dimension, as reflected in his discussion of how the public-private divide in American law filters through constitutional doctrines such as the state action doctrine, due process, and the restriction on the delegation of lawmaking power to private entities.[45] To the extent one is concerned, as he is, about the outsourcing of sovereign government power, it is indeed appropriate to worry about those fundamental constitutional issues. But such high-level questions ultimately seep down into ground-level phenomena, such as contractors writing the explanations and defenses of regulations that agencies are required to publish in the *Federal Register*. Those actions also implicate sovereignty: As Verkuil notes, those explanations and defenses constitute "the intellectual underpinnings" of the law the agency is making.[46]

Verkuil and others are right to worry about the outsourcing of such fundamentally sovereign decisions as what a regulation should say and how it should be justified to the public and a reviewing court. But our subject is slightly different. We are concerned, not with the outsourcing of *sovereignty*, but the outsourcing of *expertise*. The two concepts are distinct. It is at least possible for an agency to retain sovereign control, by retaining control over the final decision whether to promulgate a regulation, even while outsourcing expertise-based functions, such as developing the information and analysis that support the regulation.

Indeed, government outsources expertise-based functions all the time. If you open the *Federal Register* and read an agency's explanation for its decision to promulgate a particular regulation, you will likely encounter studies done by non-governmental entities—corporate laboratories, university scholars, think tanks, and similar institutions. The agency's scientific contribution to rulemaking often takes the form of assessing and drawing conclusions from that preexisting science. It could hardly be otherwise: Forcing agencies to reproduce every bit (or byte) of information generated by a reputable external source would slow their regulatory pace to a crawl.[47]

This fact of life requires us to recognize that some expertise-based functions will inevitably be outsourced, thus raising the question of *how much* outsourcing is appropriate. This contrasts with the *sovereignty*-outsourcing question, where one can plausibly argue that *any* outsourcing is problematic.[48] Despite this conceptual difference between the sovereignty-outsourcing and expertise-outsourcing questions, insights into the former may still help us answer the latter. Help comes from the government's explanation of Circular A-76, the document demarcating outsourceable and non-outsourceable functions. That explanatory document describes as non-outsourceable "functions that require the exercise of discretion in applying Federal Government authority or the making of value judgments in making decisions for the Federal Government."[49] Ignore the endings of both of those phrases ("applying Federal Government authority" and "making decisions for the Federal Government"). Those endings speak to the actual exercise of sovereign power— "*applying* . . . Government authority" and "*making decisions* for the . . . Government."

Instead, focus on the characteristics of those sovereign acts—the fact that they involve "the exercise of discretion" and "the making of value judgments." Those phrases help us determine the appropriate limitation on outsourcing agency expertise. Agencies "exercise . . . discretion" and "mak[e] . . . value judgments" when they deliberate on how to balance scientific findings with policy and political concerns. That deliberation relies heavily on the regulatory expertise the introduction characterized as residing uniquely within agencies: "expertise in reconciling and accounting for conflicting evidence and arguments, disciplinary perspectives, political demands, and legal commands."[50]

Agencies exercise such discretion and make such value judgments—that is, they use their regulatory expertise—in a variety of different contexts. As suggested above, they do so when they deliberate on how to integrate scientific knowledge with political and other factors in the course of reaching a regulatory decision. But they also use regulatory expertise when they develop that scientific knowledge. As chapter 8 explained, gathering and analyzing information—test data, comments to a rulemaking, or even a contractor's assessment of previous studies—is not a purely technocratic enterprise.[51] Assumptions—often fraught ones—about sampling, extrapolations, discount rates, time horizons, and a whole host of other issues run through such data-gathering and analysis. As one example, recall from chapter 6 the Trump-era US Geological Survey mandate that USGS studies not consider climate change impacts beyond the year 2040. That mandate was universally understood as politically motivated to produce less pessimistic conclusions about climate change's effects, but was nevertheless cast as a simple modeling assumption.[52]

Thus, both deliberation on scientific data and the gathering of that data itself require the sort of regulatory expertise that rests with agencies. But contractors perform those functions all the time: They generate raw information, analyze it, and even draft the statements justifying proposed regulations that are based on it. Assume that at least some of this outsourcing is necessary as a practical matter. Assume further that performing such functions will inevitably entail judgment calls and uses of discretion. How can that outsourcing be allowed if it reflects the use of expertise that rests within the agency?

Perhaps the key to this puzzle lies in insisting that experts within the agency have a meaningful chance to evaluate the outsourced work, and to present it in an evaluated or analyzed form to the agency's political leadership. In other words, such outsourcing might be appropriate if the final step in that particular process—whether information-gathering or subsequent regulatory analysis—is performed by agency experts. To put it yet a third way: Outside contractors may perform functions that entail the use of expertise, but agency staff themselves must be the ones to perform the final stage of the given function.

This approach uses the language in the document explaining Circular A-76's "inherently governmental functions" formula to cast light on the outsourcing of both sovereignty and expertise. Recall that Circular A-76 explains that sovereignty consists of "making decisions" for the federal government and "applying" governmental authority. But it then goes on to suggest that the process of making those decisions and applying that authority—i.e., the process of exercising sovereignty—entails "exercis[ing] discretion" and "making . . . value judgments." This proposal argues that those exercises of discretion and making of value judgments provide the critical expertise-based input into the agency's ultimate exercise of sovereignty.

Stepping back and thinking about it from 30,000 feet, this proposal fits our basic understanding of why agency action is legitimate in our system. This proposal rests on the claim that exercises of sovereignty by administrative agencies ("making decisions" and "applying Federal Government authority") are legitimate because they flow from the agency's regulatory expertise (in its "exercise of discretion") or its political legitimacy (in its "making of value judgments"). While the A-76 explanatory document may not have intended to draw a connection between sovereign decisions and inputs into those decisions, it nevertheless described the first (sovereign action) as flowing from the second (expertise or political legitimacy). Hence, the conduct that is non-outsourceable: "the exercise of discretion [expertise] in applying Federal Government authority [sovereignty]" or "the making of value judgments [politics] in making decisions for the Federal Government [sovereignty]."

This approach provides an answer, albeit an indirect one, to the "how much outsourcing of expertise is too much?" question, by insisting that agency experts always be able to bring their own unique expertise to bear before an agency wields its formal sovereign power.[53] It recognizes the reality of outsourcing: As a practical matter, private entities will provide agencies with information and analysis, which will inevitably be colored by value judgments and assumptions that cannot be described as purely technocratic. Thus, private entities will do some deliberating. But this approach ensures that the function of adding regulatory expertise to the decisional process remains within the agency, by requiring that agency experts evaluate the work done by private contractors.

What would this proposal mean in practice? In a phrase: meaningful participation by in-house experts on every issue on which they possess expertise. That idea should sound familiar—chapter 6 urged those same participation rights for experts when it suggested reforms to agencies' internal decisional procedures. But now consider another facet of that proposal: how it affects the roles bureaucrats play. As John DiIulio and others have observed, the lack of such participation, and thus the complete delegation of the function in question to contractors, reduces civil service experts to managing the regulatory work of others, rather than performing that work themselves.[54] That is different work: As anyone who has ever been a manager can attest, managing someone else's performance of a task is manifestly not the same thing as performing the task itself.

Leave aside the fact that the in-house experts we are talking about are not necessarily trained in that managerial work, and thus may do it poorly. As one scholar observes, agency engineers may be good at engineering, but that doesn't make them good at supervising engineering contractors.[55] But assume away that (potentially serious) problem. Instead, focus on the more fundamental issue: Reducing agency experts to managing contractors' work means that those experts will no longer perform such work themselves. To continue the example, reducing an agency's engineers to supervising private contractor engineers means that those agency personnel eventually will stop doing engineering.[56]

Later, this chapter will discuss the implications of that fact for the attractiveness of federal civil service work. For now, reflect on the even more basic problem that agency experts are no longer utilizing their expertise. That in-house expertise is critical and unique—recall, again, that an agency engineer isn't *just* an engineer, but rather, an engineer who has learned how to work as a team with lawyers and meteorologists and political leaders and everyone else inside the agency to help craft effective regulations. (That's our idea of regulatory expertise, from the introduction.) Relegating that unique expertise to the agency's long-term storage closet cannot be a good thing for any system that cares about expert regulation. Left unused for too long, that expertise will atrophy.[57]

To avoid that outcome, once we concede that contractors will do some of the work it becomes critical that agency experts exercise meaningful substantive review of it. That does not mean redoing the work from scratch; there would be little sense in requiring that. Nor does it even mean performing an intensive check on the substance of every piece of every contractor's work. For example, a contractor's summary of rulemaking comments may not require the same level of in-house review as the assumptions underlying a key technical document a contractor created.

Instead, this approach requires that agency staff experts be empowered to apply to contractors' work product the unique regulatory expertise those experts possess. This grant of authority to agency staff of course will require them to make judgment calls; if one wants to "go meta," agency experts will have to use their expertise to determine when they should apply that expertise to the information contractors provide them.

Of course, that is an ambiguous set of marching orders for agency leaders, career agency experts, and contractors themselves. But such ambiguity is inherent in the outsourcing issue. Indeed, very similar ambiguity surfaces in regulations that attempt to clarify Circular A-76's concept of sovereign functions, as expressed in the circular's phrase, "inherently governmental functions." Those regulations recognize that "certain services and actions that are not considered to be inherently governmental functions may approach being in that category because of the nature of the function, the manner in which the contractor performs the contract, or the manner in which the Government administers contractor performance." That language is not particularly clarifying, but at least it acknowledges that some non-sovereign functions "approach" the exercise of sovereignty. Tellingly, one of the examples these regulations provide of such sovereignty-adjacent functions is "Services that involve or relate to the development of regulations."[58]

At the end of the day, all this detail simply confirms our intuition. There really is something about rulemaking that makes it different than providing lunch in the agency cafeteria. However, that "something" doesn't convert into sovereign functions all "services that involve or relate to the development of regulations." But maybe some of those services come close to sovereign functions, depending on "the nature of the function, the manner in which the contractor performs the contract, or the manner in which the Government administers contractor performance."[59] If that's not sufficiently precise for total satisfaction, that's what regulatory expertise is for.

What a Bureaucracy Needs

What does an adequately resourced agency need to perform the functions this chapter has described as non-outsourceable? Two things. First, it needs authority: the internal agency structure and legal tools that would allow agency experts to make appropriate use of the information and analysis they and contractors generate. Chapters 5 and 6 outlined the agency decisional structures that would empower agency experts. Those chapters and chapter 7 (discussing judicial review) offered suggestions for altering agencies' legal landscape to incentivize the creation of such structures.

Second, an adequately resourced agency needs capacity—the on-the-ground material resources, including human resources but also time and supporting infrastructure, to exercise that authority effectively. Adequate capacity requires resources of both sufficient quality and quantity. Regarding quality: As an important government report on outsourcing, known as the Bell Report, stated six decades ago, "[t]here must be sufficient technical competence within the Government so that outside technical advice does not become *de facto* technical decision-making."[60] Consider that statement. Without "sufficient technical competence," the report warns, external generators of "technical advice" gain the de facto authority to make the final decisions, simply because nobody within the agency has the knowledge to question that advice. Thus, high-quality capacity—"sufficient technical competence"—becomes a necessary condition for the exercise of actual decisional authority.

But quality is not enough. The Bell Report's insistence on "*sufficient* technical competence" also implies an adequate *quantum* of the expertise necessary to develop the information and analysis that agency policymakers need to perform their sovereign decision-making functions. The need for a sufficiently large corps of expert civil servants sounds obvious: An agency so understaffed that it does not know what its contractors are doing, let alone being able to review their work product, is not an agency that can perform its decision-making and decision-assisting tasks. But the need for sufficient expertise goes beyond the obvious. Expertise deficits can also trigger a spiraling decline. Consider government purchasing agents, and what happened when the Clinton administration's National Performance Review decided that they were expendable:

> As one means to increase government efficiency, the National Performance Review tried to streamline the procurement process. The government laid off many acquisition personnel because the government viewed them as simply "shoppers," who could be replaced with "actual" government workers using a charge card. However, with these drastic cuts to personnel, agencies found themselves in the middle of a vicious cycle: decreased staff levels resulted in increased need to obtain services necessary to complete their missions through contracting. However, agencies also employed undertrained smaller procurement workforces that were unable to handle the enormous growth of contracts—particularly service contracts, which are more complex than supply contracts. This forced agencies to contract out some of their acquisition functions. Thus, the more contracts they created, the more contractors they needed to administer these contracts, leading to still more contracts.[61]

This dynamic may remind some readers of Disney's *The Sorcerer's Apprentice*, where Mickey Mouse, as the apprentice, tried to shortcut his cauldron-filling task by commanding a broom to do the work, but found himself unable to control the rapidly multiplying brooms that created a watery disaster. Pity the civil servants who find themselves in the same position, with ever-increasing numbers of contractors falling more and more out of their control and the prospect of doing any substantive work themselves becoming more and more distant. This chapter already noted how turning experts into contract overseers atrophies their substantive expertise. With an assist from Mickey, the discussion immediately above explains the process by which that dynamic worsens.

Rebuilding the Bureaucracy

The identification of authority and capacity as key requirements for an effective bureaucracy reveals the urgency of rebuilding the civil service. Too many observers from too many perspectives have faulted the bureaucracy on both of these criteria. With regard to capacity, those observers have concluded that the federal government currently attempts to do too much with too few actual civil servants. The dynamic is clear, and troubling: In-house capacity shortages prompt increased use of contractors, who in turn are inadequately supervised by the experts (untrained in contract management) whose short-handedness caused the need for increased outsourcing to begin with. At the same time, those supervisory responsibilities distract agency experts from the substantive work in which they were hired to develop expertise.

Two obvious fixes present themselves. Either government needs to stop doing and providing an enormous amount of what it currently does and provides, or it needs to be rebuilt to accommodate those demands. As President Reagan discovered, the first fix is a political non-starter.[62] That leaves rebuilding.

How much rebuilding? John DiIulio, an academic who was deeply involved with the George W. Bush administration, urged in 2014 that the federal government commit to adding a net 50,000 civil servants per year for twenty years, with the goal of creating by 2035 a bureaucracy a million persons larger than it currently is.[63] This book does not purport to set a numerical goal. But, as the figures quoted earlier in this chapter make clear, it is surely problematic for a vastly more complicated government, spending multiples more money and implementing many more programs than it did sixty years ago, to employ approximately the same number of civil servants as in 1960. That discrepancy cannot be fully justified by technological advances or "working smarter"—consider how much of that lost headcount has not really been lost at all, but instead has merely migrated into suboptimal contract labor.[64]

But the rebuilding task is about more than numbers, and more than earlier chapters' proposals to give agency experts more authority in key decisional processes. It also requires improving the quality of the workforce. Part of that goal would be achieved simply by moving some contracted work back in-house. Sixty years ago, the Bell Report observed that high-quality professionals would be more likely to choose government employment if it promised the more cutting-edge tasks that entice competent would-be civil servants.[65] Reducing reliance on contractors would thus likely make the civil service more attractive. Indeed, this effect would be especially strong if the functions that were returned to a beefed-up corps of civil servants were exactly those that should have been returned for another reason—because they require the deliberation and use of discretion that render them inherently governmental, or at least close to it. This chapter has already explained how outsourcing creates vicious circles. Rebalancing the work assigned to contractors and civil servants can create virtuous ones.

So can enhancing the attractiveness of the civil service career path. For at least a decade and a half, commentators have bemoaned a brain drain from the federal civil service, with many persons leaving who would normally be ascending to positions of authority.[66] Related to that phenomenon is yet another factor that merits attention—the increasing presence of political appointees within agencies. Chapter 5's discussion of the White House–agency relationship set forth the basic problem: the explosion of political appointee slots in agencies, from less than 300 in 1960 to more than 3,600 by 2016—in a civil service that, to repeat, is essentially the same size as it was in 1960.

Chapter 5 also identified some of the problems that explosion has caused for agencies: poor performance by the agencies those appointees lead, those appointees' tendency to rely too heavily on contractors, and, perhaps ironically, agency drift and confusion due to delays in naming political appointees, obtaining Senate confirmation for those whose positions require it, and finding replacements when, as often happens, they leave for greener pastures. As it relates to the civil service itself, the presence of an excess of political appointees surely makes it harder for excellent staffers to rise to the top, thus contributing to career frustrations that likely drive much of the observed brain drain.[67]

Rebuilding the bureaucracy means more than recalibrating the balance of agencies' leadership corps away from political appointees and toward career civil servants. It also requires improving working conditions for the civil servants working below leadership levels. Those conditions have been problematic for decades. Again the 1962 Bell Report was prescient, noting, in the context of what we would now call high-tech research positions, that private entities with which the government contracted for such research often provided "a superior working environment . . .—better salaries, better facilities, better administrative support."[68] Forty years later, in 2003, the second Volker Report on the civil service, speaking of civil servants more generally, explained the exodus from public service and difficulty in attracting new staffers by citing "dismal working conditions," "invasions of personal privacy" growing out of intrusive background checks and similar requirements, and "the substantial difference" between public and private sector salaries.[69]

The results of such conditions should not come as a shock. Hiring limits and the generally perceived poorer quality of working conditions mean that the civil service is aging. A 2019 report revealed that there are five times more federal workers over sixty years old than under thirty years old, with those in that younger cohort comprising less than 6 percent of the federal workforce.[70] Much of the reason for this imbalance is that the civil service is seen today as an unattractive place to begin or make a career. On top of the factors discussed above, the multiple government shutdowns that have occurred over the last several years, each of which presents anew the question of whether and when civil servants will be paid, and the Trump administration's rhetorical attacks on the so-called Deep State, render this unattractiveness even less surprising.[71] Whether the Biden administration's early hints of a revival of aggressive federal regulation, and suggestions that younger voters favor such regulation, lead to a renewed interest in government service is a fascinating question.

Recommendations

Reforming the civil service—from creating hiring slots to improving its working conditions to assigning it meaningful substantive work— constitutes a massive topic, a full discussion of which would entail its own book. Keeping *this* book focused on the creation of conditions under which expertise-based administrative decision-making can flourish justifies focusing on several basic recommendations, while recognizing that many others may also assist the larger project of improving the quality of the civil service and the regulation it produces.

First, and perhaps most basically, civil servants must be given the authority to use their expertise, even when significant work is outsourced to contractors. Failing to give agency experts the authority to do the work they were hired to do would render superfluous any increase in their numbers or improvement in their material working conditions.

Second, and flowing from the first, the federal government—and the American people—must commit to reinforcing its current corps of civil servants by adding to their numbers. Increasing headcount by itself is not enough. But enough students of the issue from enough perspectives—from Paul Verkuil to John DiIulio to Paul Volker—have concluded that the current headcount is simply inadequate.

Third, the role of political appointees should be scaled back. The problems caused by over-reliance on political appointees were detailed in chapter 5, which explained the harm those appointees caused to agencies' ability to achieve their goals. This chapter added further concerns about political appointees when it briefly recounted the damage such over-reliance causes to the civil service itself. These concerns justify reducing the allowable number of such appointments.

Fourth, salaries and working conditions must become competitive with similar positions outside of government. This does not necessarily entail making pay commensurate with that offered by for-profit corporations, given the other benefits of public service, such as tenure protection, pension benefits, and the satisfaction of working in the public service. But when the pay scale is inferior to that offered even by the not-for-profit private sector, reform may be appropriate. As a witness for the Second Volker Commission put it, the federal government may not be able to compete on salary with dot-coms, but should be able to complete with dot-edus and dot-orgs.[72] The same could be said about working conditions.

Fifth, in exchange for these steps, accountability must matter. This entails reforms both to job tenure protections and post-hiring compensation structures, such as raises and bonuses. This resulting system should remain consistent with the principle of tenure protection and the additional principle, codified into law, of "equal pay for work of equal value."[73] Nevertheless, students of the civil service have concluded that both accountability and pay-based rewards for superior work are consistent with the basic principles of the system established by the Pendleton Act of 1883 and reaffirmed in the last major set of reforms to the civil service system, in 1978.[74]

Finally, while agency leaders must apply the merit system and other principles underlying the civil service, they should have the authority to do so flexibly, in ways responsive to their agencies' particular needs.[75] As observers have noted, the wide variety of functions played by different agencies means that application of those basic principles must necessarily vary.[76] For example, agencies such as NASA and the CDC, which employ large numbers of highly trained professionals occupying essentially niche positions, will presumably apply the "equal pay for work for equal value" principle differently than an agency such as DHS, with its large workforce of airport screeners performing identical work.[77] Nevertheless, those principles provide the foundation for a professional, expertise-based, and public service–oriented civil service.

Many other principles could legitimately be included in this list of basic guideposts for rebuilding a bureaucracy of experts. Obviously, ensuring that hiring strategies reflect market trends is critical.[78] So is reforming the Senior Executive Service (SES), which the 1978 civil service reform law established in the hope of creating a corps of elite senior civil servants capable of navigating the boundary between political appointees and civil service staffers.[79] Certainly, given this chapter's focus on outsourcing, one could also justifiably include additional ideas for determining whether and how to outsource government functions. Exclusion of these and other topics should not be understood to suggest their unimportance.

Nevertheless, the principles identified above are particularly critical. When given proper resources and a proper decisional role within the bureaucracy, expert civil servants utilized, managed, compensated, and protected in the ways described above can help rebuild government's capacity for expert decision-making. That rebuilt capacity will make expertise-based regulation both a reality and a phenomenon recognized and appreciated by the public. With luck, public recognition of that expertise may in turn make it easier to win public approval of measures bringing the civil service up to full strength in all senses of that term. Such measures can create a virtuous circle of improving bureaucratic performance and in turn public trust.

10

Rebuilding Trust

Part II of this book offered ways to strengthen the authority of agency experts, by altering the institutional relationships affecting agencies and their personnel. Chapters 8 and 9 complemented that effort by offering ways to strengthen career experts' information autonomy, decisional authority, and raw capacity. This chapter reveals those efforts' payoffs, by examining how empowered and strengthened agency expertise can engage with the American people. Chapter 9 ended by suggesting that improved agency engagement with the people in whose name it regulates can improve the public's trust in both agencies and their regulation. In turn, that increased trust promises to trigger a virtuous circle, in which improved trust increases public willingness to support those authority- and capacity-strengthening incentives, which will further improve agency performance and hence further increase public trust.

But increased trust is also its own goal. Distrust in government is corrosive to any democracy. Distrust in expert regulation is particularly worrisome because it generates a perception that the nation's government is simply incapable of keeping its promises (think of its botched rollout of the federal healthcare website in 2013) and even keeping Americans safe (think of its responses to Hurricane Katrina in 2005 and the COVID-19 pandemic in 2020). The resulting cynicism and disengagement constitute mortal threats to democratic self-government.

Distrust in expertise is particularly worrisome also because expertise already raises uncomfortable questions about democracy. It is possible to square expertise with democratic self-governance—indeed, this chapter ends by sketching out just such a path. But lack of trust in expert regulation makes that harmonization impossible, not just by encouraging public disengagement but also by increasing the attractiveness of even more politicization of the regulatory process as the only fix to an otherwise-failed system. To the extent such politicization translates into presidential control, a failure of trust in expertise threatens not just effective regulation but also the separated and checking powers that create the conditions for democracy.[1]

Trust, then, is critical—not just to the thriving of expert regulation, but to the thriving of a democratic system that is capable of responding to the myriad regulatory challenges the nation faces.

The Components of Trust

What does such trust require? While obviously a very broad question, we can map out some ideas. To start, trust of course requires some level of confidence in the basic competence of government actors.[2] Recall from chapter 3 that one recent study concluded that the public's trust in an agency turned more on its perception of the agency's expertise than its perception of either the agency's regulatory capacity or its staff's commitment to the agency's mission.[3] That finding, if it holds up, suggests that persuading the public that the agency is in fact staffed with experts will go some distance toward creating public confidence in its outputs.[4]

That persuasion job requires work, both in creating the reality of an expertise-rich bureaucracy but also in demonstrating that expertise to the public. Sometimes that demonstration takes care of itself: Every time FEMA responds effectively to a disaster, the public's confidence in the agency likely rises. But effective regulation often remains hidden. It's easy to forget, but in an average day in America no commercial airliners crash, no accidental food poisoning event sickens hundreds of people, and the economy is not rocked by a systemic failure that the government failed to foresee. As an old adage goes, it is not a news story when a plane lands safely. Nor does it become one because FAA regulations made that possible.

Perhaps non-crashing planes (and stock markets) are low bars. But the basic point percolates to the surface: In an average day in America, government regulation, by the FAA, the Department of Agriculture, the SEC, and every other agency, soldiers on silently and, in most cases, effectively. The hidden nature of much regulation requires affirmative effort by agencies to demonstrate their expertise—not for the show of it, but, again, to build public trust and support.

But we can say more. In a democracy, legitimacy and in turn trust must flow, at least in part, from a sense that as a substantive matter the majority's will is being carried out. Whatever might be the intrinsic legitimacy-generating value of voting and other rituals of self-government, that value would likely be significantly reduced if those rituals consistently failed to yield substantive results that election outcomes would normally suggest. In other words, to paraphrase the start of the chapter on presidential control (chapter 5), elections really should have consequences. This idea arguably justifies a strengthened non-delegation doctrine, which its advocates argue ensures a tighter connection between democratically elected representatives and the detailed policies government actually implements. That does not mean that a strengthened non-delegation doctrine is a requirement of democratic legitimacy; there may be other ways to ensure that the public's will is being carried out. But the non-delegation doctrine is one way to do that, if we assume away problems about whether that doctrine is workable or otherwise a good idea. Recall that chapter 4 called into question that workability and advisability.

The democratic accountability idea might also justify the last generation's trend toward presidential administration. Chapter 5 critiqued that trend. Most relevantly for current purposes, there is reason to wonder whether presidential involvement in regulatory rulemaking truly reflects the majority's political preferences. Certainly, for example, President Reagan's deregulatory nudges to the bureaucracy did not necessarily reflect the majority's preferences for continued robust environmental and entitlement programs.[5] More generally, as chapter 5 explained, the nature of both presidential and OIRA review raises questions about their effectiveness in methodically transmitting the electorate's preferences to agencies.

Given these critiques, this chapter will offer other suggestions for ensuring that agency action is democratically responsive. But just as important as responsiveness to winners is responsiveness to those who lost at the ballot box. The fact of losing should not mean that that side's interests should count for nothing in the political (or regulatory) calculus. A political system should not be considered legitimate if an identifiable minority consistently loses elections and as a result finds its interests consistently ignored. This realization poses hard questions for the perceived legitimacy of government action, including agency action. It requires a brief digression into theory.

Two very different theories attempt to account for this problem, both at the political and the regulatory levels. One theory—"pluralism"— holds that minority interests can be accounted for by creating a process in which all groups can bargain with each other, such that no group is consistently and completely shut out of power. Another— "republicanism"—maintains that the holders of political power should act based on their best understanding of what the public interest requires. Both theories attempt to prevent what James Madison called "the tyranny of the majority"—the first by creating a constantly shifting set of majority coalitions, and the second by transcending the very concepts of majority and minority interests in the search for a broader "public" interest.[6]

At the level of constitutional law, Madison and the other framers attempted to prevent that tyranny by incorporating both pluralist and republican insights.[7] As to the first, the structure the framers created—a federal system of separated powers in which the national government encompasses a large land area—was designed to minimize the power of one self-interested faction—even one comprising a majority—from oppressing the rest of the polity. But this pluralist system of differing power centers was also a republican one, since power was held not by the people directly but rather by elected officials who, it was hoped, would rise above faction and concern themselves with the public interest by deliberating together and reaching consensus.[8]

The structure of American regulatory law points in these same two directions. Innovations in administrative law, from the APA itself to the more robust procedures judges imposed on agencies during the 1970s and increased access to judicial review, sought to ensure full participation by all interested groups, as the pluralist model proposes. At the same time, theorists of regulatory law also point toward republican values of public-interested deliberation. As this book has explained, those values require that the public exercise influence over regulatory decisions, but also that those decisions satisfy a potentially rigorous judicial test for reasonable pursuit of the public interest.[9] As this chapter later explains, some legitimacy-enhancing steps agencies can take involve a combination of both increased (and more effective) public participation and the sort of deliberation embraced by republican theorists.

This digression into political theory reveals that legitimacy (and the trust that it implies) flows from more than ensuring that substantive outcomes track majority preferences. Instead, it can flow from the existence of a deliberative process that considers the interests that we all share together—the public interest. It can also flow from a pluralist process in which all groups are able to participate meaningfully.[10] Either way, agency action earns legitimacy because it results from an open and public decisional process of some sort.[11]

As a practical matter, both republican deliberation on the public interest and pluralist participation require accessibility and participation. Most federal officeholders, of course, work far from their constituents. But even they take opportunities both to meet constituents and present themselves and their programs to the people, in person or via media of all types. In the other direction, constituents enjoy the right to communicate with their representatives. While it is an open question how much influence such constituent communication has on them, especially in an era where more and more politics is nationalized, any congressperson who strays too far from constituent wishes does so at her peril. Presumably, such communications make those wishes clear.

Regulators lack the same relationship with the citizenry. Since bureaucrats are unelected, they lack politicians' felt obligation to meet and communicate with citizens. On the other hand, as previous chapters have explained, the APA mandates a process by which any person interested in an agency rulemaking may comment on a proposed rule. Much of what follows will consider ways to improve on the meaningfulness of that right to comment. More generally, it will also consider ways to improve on agencies' interactions with citizens and citizens' access to agencies and the work they do.

Competence and responsiveness to majoritarian preferences, but within a meaningfully accessible process that sincerely attempts to promote the public interest: These are the building blocks of a structure in which the public can develop trust in the bureaucracy. Earlier chapters addressed the first of these criteria, when they made the case for an adequately resourced bureaucracy that is empowered to influence agency decision-making. This chapter considers the remaining three: responsiveness, accessibility, and deliberation.

Getting to Know You

A basic challenge confronting agencies' attempts to build public trust is the need for agencies to become familiar with the public and its preferences, and for the public to become familiar with agencies and their work. Of course, most Americans know at least something about agencies and their activities—at the very least, they know enough to have opinions about them.[12] But very few Americans know agencies in the sense of being able to interact with them in meaningful ways, at least when the interaction takes the form of something other than an agency's singling out of an individual for action—say, the Social Security Administration's denial of a claimant's application for disability benefits or the IRS's auditing of a tax return. In contrast to such particularized interactions, when an agency acts more generally—for example, commencing a rulemaking process—the average citizen's ability to engage meaningfully with the agency, and thus the agency's ability to learn about public preferences—is limited.

This is not because the law is formally unfriendly to citizen-agency interaction. To the contrary, the APA's rulemaking procedures—rightly lauded as "one of the greatest inventions of modern government"[13]—allow direct public input on a proposed rule, via a commenting process that is at least ostensibly streamlined and informal. In recent years, the Internet has further simplified the actual mechanics of the commenting process. Finding a particular rulemaking is now easier than ever: In addition to searching an agency's own website, a citizen can simply search www.regulations.gov for any pending rulemaking on a particular topic. Once there, commenting is as easy as clicking on the "submit a comment" button, and either attaching a file or just typing in the comment box.

These innovations raised the prospect of a much more accessible rulemaking process. The new ease in learning about a given rulemaking is particularly important. Whereas before, gaining that knowledge usually required either being "in the know" or otherwise perusing a print or online version of the daily *Federal Register*, with regulations.gov all one has to do is enter search terms in the appropriate window and view the results. And of course, submitting a comment used to require mailing (or, later, faxing) it; today, it's done with a click of a mouse.

The information on regulations.gov also promised to improve commenting itself, and thus the quality of citizen participation. First, the ability to access the agency's own supporting materials in its electronic rulemaking docket allowed commentors to submit more informed comments. Beyond even that important benefit lay the promise of a dialogue among commenters. If identifying a pending rulemaking and (to a lesser degree) submitting a comment posed challenges in the pre-Internet era, engaging with other comments posed a nearly insuperable barrier. Comments were kept in a docket in a room at the agency's headquarters in Washington. They were accessible there, but finding them (obviously) required being in Washington (or hiring someone who was) and taking the time to monitor comments as they arrived.

Today, comments are made available online, thus allowing commentors to respond to others' comments (and, of course, for those responses to elicit replies in turn). This availability promised a true dialogue among interested parties, in which persons read and responded to each other's comments. Among the many favorable hoped-for results: better rules, resulting from agencies' ability to leverage the online rulemaking dialogue; better public participation, both in terms of sheer quantity but also the quality of the exchanges; and more trust in government.[14]

Unfortunately, this ease of access and of (more richly) communicating did not change much. As a 2013 study by the Administrative Conference of the United States concluded, "the move online has not produced a fundamental shift in the nature of notice-and-comment rulemaking. The process remains quite recognizable."[15]

Why? In brief: access means different things. The online revolution succeeded in making it easy for citizens to locate pending rulemakings, review the agency's supporting documents and others' comments, and submit responsive comments. But it did not make proposed rules or their factual and policy backgrounds any less complex—and thus, any less accessible, in the sense of being comprehensible.[16] Nor did it provide more comprehensible guidance to citizens about those factual and policy issues. Nor, of course, did the Internet change the actual substantive steps of the rulemaking process. Finally, as discussed shortly below, it also did not change the type and style of the comments that would have the most impact.

Undoubtedly, the Internet did change some things. By making comments easier to submit, it enabled the phenomenon of mass commenting—that is, rulemakings featuring exceptionally large numbers of comments, or what one scholar called "torrents of e-mail."[17] The poster child for this phenomenon was the FCC rulemaking that considered whether to rescind its previous decision mandating net neutrality. During the second phase of the FCC's consideration of that issue, more than 21 million comments were received. Lest anyone consider that number an unqualified victory for participatory governance, consider that only 6 percent of those comments were unique—94 percent of the comments were submitted multiple times. That's not necessarily a bad thing, if all those citizens were persuaded by an advocacy group's argument and copied and pasted the suggested comments into the regulations.gov comment box. Unfortunately, on several different occasions, more than 75,000 comments were received at precisely the same moment. In addition, more than half the comments received came from email addresses that were, for one reason or another, suspect.[18] Finally, in May 2021, New York's Attorney General announced that a coalition of internet service providers had funded an effort that sent nine million fake comments to the FCC under the names of unsuspecting (and unconsenting) individuals.[19]

The net neutrality example reveals several issues. The phenomenon of mass commenting, in which large numbers of the same or nearly the same comment are submitted, raises fundamental questions about the nature of the rulemaking process—is it essentially a plebiscite, in which every comment counts (especially if there are a lot of them), or is it a scientific and policy inquiry, in which only reasoned comments matter? Or is it a little of both, depending on the nature of the issue and the nature of the comments?[20] The net neutrality example also raises a more obvious question about whether the Internet's technological capabilities render rulemaking susceptible not only to the virtues of more informed and dialogic participation but also to the evils of manipulation. The net neutrality example suggests that they do.

Those risks are serious. But leave them to the side. Concentrate instead on the more relevant question for this book's purpose: What can technology do to advance, not just the ability of already sophisticated commentors to do even more with their comments, but the accessibility and comprehensibility of the regulatory process, and thus its openness to meaningful citizen input? The point is to make it easier for Americans to participate meaningfully in the regulatory process—not just by making participation a matter of clicking a mouse, but also by making it easier to say something helpful. Facilitating such informed access would help everyday Americans get to know regulation, the process for doing it, and the choices it requires. It would also help agencies understand what Americans really think about a proposed rule.

Thus, regulatory innovations should aspire to more than simply making agency action more technologically accessible to citizens. Rather, they should incentivize citizens to engage with agencies as those agencies deliberate. The difference between these goals matters. As two authors note in their important report on this issue, referring to the film *Field of Dreams*, simply building it (a more accessible process) is no guarantee that they (the citizenry) will come (participate).[21]

That more ambitious goal is important. Encouraging Americans to engage meaningfully with the regulatory process is not just a good thing in itself. Rather, more to the point of this book, such engagement is critical in order for citizens to come to trust the bureaucracy's expertise. Hundreds of years ago, a king's subjects might have had a mystical faith or trust in his ability to protect them, even though they never saw him and certainly never had a chance to urge their own opinions on him. Not so in a twenty-first century democracy.[22]

Bringing Americans Along

The challenge, then, goes beyond increasing Americans' information about pending regulatory matters, to include helping them make sense of those matters, providing them meaningful forums for expressing their views about them, and encouraging them to do so.[23] Certainly, increasing their information is critical; going back to the days when citizens had to find a federal government reading room so they could read the *Federal Register*'s paper edition and then expecting them to submit a useful comment without the benefit of the agency's background information is a formula for frustration and disengagement. But for most Americans on most issues, it is not enough to present them with that information in the form of hyperlinks on regulations.gov and to make commenting as easy as a mouse click. To truly engage the American people in a way that makes Americans feel like the process is theirs—and thus worthy of their trust—requires more.

To be sure, technology can help. In the years since the 2013 ACUS report provided a mixed review of its impact on the rulemaking process,[24] technology has progressed even further. Most notably, social media has become more ubiquitous in Americans' lives. With that development comes the potential for more than a process in which commentors can know what the agency and other commentors are thinking about an issue. Instead, the rise of social media raises the prospect of broad-based conversations about regulatory issues.

Of course, social media already hosts broadly based conversations about public issues. Much of the result is ugly, as illustrated by the paradoxically simultaneous degradation of political discourse and Americans' retreat into our own epistemic bubbles, as chapter 3 examined. That experience teaches that any useful social media conversation about regulatory policy must be a moderated one. Agency moderation can take many useful forms that capitalize on social media's broad reach. Agencies can use social media to push out to the public information about regulatory initiatives, rather than simply passively sitting back and waiting for citizens to log on to regulations.gov and search for rulemakings.[25] They can also use it to explain the basics of the rulemaking process, and clarify the parameters of both the regulatory questions the rulemaking poses and the information the agency is seeking.[26] These points are important: Effective participation in regulation requires an understanding of the relevant legal and policy backdrop, so participants can understand what is and what is not at stake in a rulemaking. For example, a citizen's comment that criticized a statutory policy would have little impact on an agency's consideration of a regulation that simply sought to apply that policy. Agency boundary-setting can keep the conversation on track.

Still, the sort of education this type of moderation implies poses serious challenges for agencies. The regulatory issues an agency confronts in a rulemaking can be extraordinarily intricate, requiring an understanding of both complex scientific data and interlocking statutory provisions and existing regulations whose meanings, backstories, policy implications, and interrelationships may be known to insiders but not at all obvious to the general public.

Of course, none of this is always and necessarily true. One interesting example out of many was the Department of Transportation's (DOT's) 2011 rulemaking proposing a regulation banning use of electronic cigarettes on aircraft.[27] On the one hand, the rulemaking centered on scientific analysis of the health effects of second-hand e-cigarette vapor. Still, the basic question that rulemaking posed—should use of e-cigarettes be allowed on airplanes—was within most Americans' grasp. More fundamentally, a regulation that aims at non-technical benefits—e.g., equity or comfort or aesthetics—raises questions especially appropriate for citizen input. Not every aspect of every rulemaking requires a PhD in Chemistry or a Master's in Public Policy.

But an even deeper challenge lurks in educating the general public about effective commenting. Scholars have identified a style of effective commenting—impersonal, analytical, data-based, and reasoned—that is often lacking in citizen comments, which tend to focus more on the commentor's personal and contextualized experience, often unsupported by data. To illustrate this difference, consider the following portion of a comment, made on regulations.gov in response to DOT's proposed e-cigarettes on aircraft rule:

> As an electronic vapor product user for over a year, I should report that because of my use of these products, I have been able to eliminate a 30+ year habit of smoking regular cigarettes. My health has improved immeasurably. . . . I should point out that not once has anyone exposed to my use of these products complained of my use of them. Anecdotal to be sure, but there is near consensus among my peers.[28]

Anecdotal, indeed, as the commentor concedes. Unfortunately, this is just the sort of comment that, exactly because of its anecdotal and personal nature, likely gets little serious consideration at the agency. That is the case at least when, as with the e-cigarettes rule, the relevant issues are scientific (here, the health effects of second-hand e-cigarette vapors). Instead, what likely get the agency's attention are comments like one submitted in the e-cigarettes rulemaking from a consumer group and an anti-regulation institute that regularly participates in rulemakings. That comment cited court cases, made legal arguments, critiqued the agency's studies by offering studies of its own, and was organized in a logical, point-by-point structure that resembled a legal brief.[29]

Indeed, the second comment's resemblance to a legal brief likely caught the agency's attention exactly because it included arguments that were easy to imagine as supporting a court challenge to the regulation. That resemblance gave the agency reason to suspect that its authors were willing and able to bring such a challenge if the final rule displeased them. Indeed, a Washington lawyer's article providing practical advice to commentors explained that a prime reason for commenting was to lay a foundation for a legal challenge.[30] It may overstate the case, but the logic of that advice holds that if a would-be citizen-commentor has no interest or capability to mount a serious court challenge to an eventual regulation, then her comment is less likely to be taken seriously.

In light of what a group of scholars called the "community of practice"[31] that has developed between agencies and sophisticated repeat players in the rulemaking process, individual citizens shoulder a double burden when they seek to participate. It's not just that they often lack knowledge of the technical issues implicating the rulemaking— the scientific, legal, and policy backdrops. Rather, they also lack an understanding of how the process "really works"—that is, the styles of argumentation most likely to sway an agency. Of course, these two deficiencies go hand in hand: the way the process "really works" entails argumentation about science, law, and policy that lies beyond most Americans' knowledge and skill. But, as suggested by the end of the last paragraph, the connection extends even farther than that: If it's true that agencies pay attention to comments that suggest the capability of mounting an effective legal challenge, then average Americans' inability to pose a plausible threat of effective litigation against the agency provides yet an additional reason their comments will not carry equal weight with rulemakers.[32]

One can question this analysis, both as an empirical and as a normative matter. In other words, one can question whether average Americans' comments really do count for very little, and one can also question whether they *should* count for very little. But the analysis clearly holds at least to some degree. Nor does it necessarily cast rulemakers in a bad light. Rather, one can understand why even a sincere, public-spirited rulemaker would in fact give greater weight to comments consistent with the "community of practice." After all, the rulemaker is also part of that community; thus, she's likely to believe that such comments really are objectively more useful and relevant. So is the judge who would be asked to determine whether a regulation reflects a reasonable use of the agency's expert judgment—expertise that, at least on scientific issues, is, again, grounded in that community's discourse.

Thus, the deck seems stacked against effective citizen participation, and in turn, against the agency's final product gaining credibility and therefore trust from the public. The picture reveals highly complex regulatory questions, addressed by a process that while ostensibly open to the public nevertheless depends on communication norms most citizens don't share, and subject to judicial review by and at the behest of inside players well-versed in both those norms and the underlying technical analysis. Creating an easier user interface on regulations.gov is not enough to change any of this.[33]

Broadening "the Process"

The answer—or at least one answer—lies in broadening the rulemaking process to include more robust opportunities for citizen participation. As the above discussion explained, the APA's comment process, while ostensibly informal and streamlined and thus already amenable to broad participation, is significantly less accessible to most Americans than to sophisticated and well-resourced repeat players. What we need instead is a recognition that public participation in the rulemaking process can consist of more than participation in the APA-mandated comment procedure. To be sure, agencies have taken modest steps in that direction. For example, a rulemaking's life cycle often features not just the APA-contemplated Notice of Proposed Rulemaking (NPRM) that presents a regulation's proposed text and invites comment, but also an Advance NPRM (ANPRM), which announces the agency's interest in or tentative ideas about a rulemaking, and invites earlier-stage, more foundational comments.

Agency deliberation about a possible rule begins much further back than even the process that directly precedes the issuance of an ANPRM.

The authors of the earlier-mentioned 2018 report on public engagement in rulemaking stress the importance of the agency's assembling of its regulatory plans for the year, as part of its legally required creation of the agency's annual regulatory agenda.[34] They point out that those earlier stages of agency deliberation provide opportunities for public participation that, exactly because of their preliminary nature, may be more amenable to effective participation by the general public. At those earlier stages, nothing—or at least not as much—is set in stone, and thus the agency's thinking is not as bound up in detailed and complex scientific and legal issues.

One can understand those earlier-stage decisions as reflecting an agency's use of a particular type of discretion—not just (or mainly) discretion over how to interpret complex data, but rather, discretion over more value-inflected judgments about which regulatory issues to prioritize. Exactly because these agenda-setting decisions are relatively more value-laden, they may legitimately (a key word) be subjected to meaningful public scrutiny. While even they should not turn on the result of a de facto plebiscite—for example, selecting a regulatory priority based on the number of positive comments it receives—citizen preferences can appropriately play a significant role in making them.

At this point, we can drill down a bit. If a plebiscite is not the right model for evaluating public input into even these value-laden decisions, what is? Several possibilities emerge. One very promising family of ideas turns on the concept of a facilitated discussion among citizens. The idea here is that the agency convenes a group of citizens and facilitates a discussion among them—in this case, about the regulatory priorities the agency should adopt. The authors of the 2018 ACUS report identify a number of variants on this idea, from "listening sessions" to focus groups and similar vehicles. Their details and the differences among them need not concern us. Rather, the important points are these. First, the discussion occurs at early stages, before the focus becomes dominated by complex questions of science, law, and policy that tend to diminish the potential for meaningful public participation. Second, the agency seeks out a broad variety of participants, perhaps even explicitly favoring persons who normally would not participate in the regulatory process. Finally, the conversations are guided and facilitated by representatives of the agency, with the agency's role including both education of the participants about the background issues and actual facilitation of the conversation.[35]

Focusing on public participation at these early stages, through vehicles like these, brings several benefits. First, it emphasizes participation at stages where public input can be most useful. By the time a complex regulatory issue reaches the proposed rule phase, any remaining regulatory latitude has likely become constrained within a range of options that require deep technical knowledge to understand, let alone influence. By contrast, issues at the agenda-setting and similarly early phases may turn more on political or social preferences, issues on which the general public may have relatively more to contribute. Deciding whether passenger health requires banning e-cigarettes on aircraft may require technical knowledge. Deciding whether DOT should prioritize regulating airlines' baggage loss policies or tarmac delays is something on which passengers can have useful input.

Second, and relatedly, public influence over agenda-setting appropriately reflects the political nature of that exercise. If agency action reflects a tension between politics and expertise, agenda-setting, with its focus on deciding how to use scarce regulatory resources, speaks more to politically grounded value choices and less to apolitical expertise, even if expertise may inform those value choices. Thus, agenda-setting is more appropriately influenced by a group (the public) whose claim to participation rights rests on democratic control rather than its scientific knowledge. Indeed, to the extent citizen participation aspires to do more than generate ideas, a variant of such facilitated discussions—a citizen-jury—can provide the means for the type of informed, deliberative, public-regarding recommendations for agency action—a republican administrative system—this chapter described at its outset.

Third, the format of this sort of public participation—as a discussion, rather than as comments funneled to a centralized agency decision-maker—is more appropriate to agenda-setting as opposed to resolving scientific questions. As anyone who's done it knows, setting an agenda—for example, a family deciding how to spend a vacation day—is a matter of discussion, deliberation, and compromise. By contrast, resolving scientific questions requires analyzing data, reviewing others' analyses, and reaching conclusions, whether about the right answer or, in cases of uncertainty, the parameters for the right answer. That latter process is simply less susceptible to effective completion via a process that features the sort of guided discussions set forth above. Moreover, an agenda-setting discussion may be more amenable to the type of agency guidance described above. By contrast, such guidance might trigger suspicions in a process that seeks to choose between different technical and policy analyses.

Getting Creative

Once we understand that agencies can seek out different forms of participation at different stages of the regulatory process, the way opens for them to act creatively in affirmatively cultivating meaningful public input. At that point, technology can reenter the picture. In addition to allowing citizens easier communication with agencies, technology also allows agencies to employ innovative ways of soliciting earlier-stage public participation that don't necessarily have to comply with the strictures of the APA's rulemaking process.

Consider an example. During the Obama administration, the Consumer Financial Protection Bureau (CFPB) wanted to improve mortgage loan disclosure forms to help home purchasers better understand the loans they were contemplating. The Bureau used Twitter and Facebook to push announcements about its initiative. It then posted alternative forms on its website, and asked interested persons to identify aspects they liked and disliked and to identify information that those forms omitted that should be included. The CFPB's initiative did more than simply use social media to announce a conventional rulemaking. By posting actual mock-ups of forms, interested persons could see more than just a regulation's text. They saw instead the regulation's proposed result—a look at a future world that included that regulation. One of that approach's many benefits is that it presented the regulatory issue in a way that made it far more accessible to average Americans—persons who would be deeply impacted by the forms drafted in response to the agency's regulation, but who might not otherwise be interested in or able to comment on a proposed rule that simply recited regulatory text.[36]

But innovative public engagement doesn't always require advanced technology. In-person (or online) focus groups can be used at even earlier stages of the rulemaking process. For example, NHTSA, the auto safety agency, has used focus groups to learn about drivers' understanding of auto safety measures as part of its decision-making on how best to inform consumers of autos' relative safety. This is in many ways an ideal use of public participation, since the relevant knowledge—about drivers' awareness of and appreciation for particular safety technologies—resides within the public itself.[37] At the same time, such use of public knowledge can make clear to the American people that the agency is interested in seeking out the public's views and that it also understands the importance of drivers' roles in auto safety. The connection thus created between the agency and the public can only help improve the agency's image, and thus begin a virtuous circle in which trust in the agency creates more engagement, which in turn generates more trust.[38]

Step back from these examples now and focus on deliberative entities such as citizen juries. Such entities aspire to involve the public in a meaningful way in the regulatory process while avoiding the formalities and straightjackets of the normal rulemaking process. Recall that that latter process risks devolving into one in which uninformed individuals, isolated from other persons who might have different perspectives, provide nothing more than anecdotal responses to a regulatory question, via a format that, while ostensibly informal, nevertheless forces citizen input into rigidly defined channels. By contrast, the hope for citizen-juries and similar vehicles is that citizens, when provided valid information and asked to deliberate with others without the channeling provided by a proposed regulation or even a proposed regulatory approach, will provide reasoned input that reflects, if imperfectly, what an informed and deliberative public opinion would conclude.

This aspiration hearkens back to the nation's founding period, when it was hoped that well-educated and virtuous elites would govern the nation and, when they did, would do so in the public interest rather than in the interest of what James Madison called "factions," and what we today would call interest groups. More romantically, it hearkens back to the ideal of the New England town meeting, where all the citizens of a (presumably small) town would gather, debate the issues confronting the town, and, it was hoped, vote based on their conception of the town's general interests.[39]

Leave aside the analogies for now; in the next section we will return to comparisons with the Madisonian structure. Instead, contrast a de facto referendum on a given rule—for example, a mass-comment rule-making such as the one on net neutrality—with a procedure such as a citizen-jury. That latter procedure involves the public in a more meaningful and creative way, while retaining rulemaking's foundation in expertise. It thus creates the conditions in which the public becomes more trusting of agency expertise, exactly because that expertise is deployed to generate the democratic accountability that encourages citizens to extend that trust. In other words, it combines our seemingly opposite poles of democratic self-government and regulatory expertise.

It's a nice hope. Still, such procedures must be implemented correctly. Stories abound of citizen participation efforts that foundered because of suspicions that the experts were using the citizen process only as window-dressing to ratify a decision that was already made. For example, when the US Army attempted to get local community buy-in for its plans to construct facilities for incinerating chemical weapons, the citizen-staffed "Community Review Teams" it convened wrote reports that were due just a month before the completion of the army's legally required Environmental Impact Statement, which had taken four years to draft. The obvious suspicion? That the citizen-drafted reports were last-minute add-ons included just for show.[40]

Nor are these processes necessarily cheap; when done right, they may be time- and resource-intensive.[41] Conducting one requires crafting the questions the agency wants the jury to consider, preparing the background information, assembling and convening the jury, providing it technical and informational assistance, presiding over its deliberations, and distilling and digesting its conclusions—all of which take time and money. While not a citizen-jury, given its open-ended invitation to comment on the proposed disclosure forms, the CFPB's process of soliciting public input on different mortgage loan disclosure models required getting the word out to a large enough group of citizens, building a website that could accommodate the sort of granular reactions to different parts of the models the agency sought to obtain, and, again, digesting the information.

Still, steps like those should not be significantly more burdensome than conventional agency practices of gathering stakeholders for meetings or even hosting academic symposia. At the very least, they should be used when informed public participation can do the most good, in terms of increasing the quality of the resulting action but also improving the connection between citizens and regulatory actions. Thus, for example, citizen-juries may be especially useful when the issue requires some level of basic value judgment, such as the airline baggage loss/tarmac delay prioritization example mentioned earlier. Much more profoundly, they can also be useful when an agency approaches fraught questions not easily reducible to objective quantification, such as the value of a human life.[42]

For their part, initiatives like the CFPB's mortgage form regulation process and NHTSA's focus group about auto safety devices can be useful when the subject matter turns on citizen perceptions that cannot be easily obtained by blunter means, such as public opinion polling, that may not reflect informed and deliberative judgment. On such issues—unlike, say, regulations of economic arrangements primarily involving sophisticated parties—meaningful, guided public input beyond the participation guaranteed by the APA's notice-and-comment provisions could pay particularly high dividends in terms of citizen trust in regulatory expertise.

A Madisonian Process

Return now to our analogy between the processes sketched out above and the constitutional structure as James Madison explained and defended it. If we squint, we can see the outlines of that Madisonian structure in the innovative procedures this chapter has recounted and outlined.

Recall from early in this chapter that Madison advocated for a federal system, with a central government of continental scale subject to the checks and balances of three separate but interdependent branches. In urging that structure, he hoped to create a government that would be sufficiently strong to govern without being tyrannical. In particular, he hoped to prevent the accumulation of power in the hands of any self-interested group grounded on shared economic, social, or other interests—which he called a "faction." (Importantly, a "faction" could constitute a numerical majority—simply winning an election did not render such a group any less a "faction.")

Madison's insight was that splitting up governing power both vertically, through federalism, and horizontally, through the separation of

powers, would make it impossible for factions to gain political dominance. The geographic sprawl of the new nation would also prevent that
result, as he believed that the nation's continental scope would make
it even harder for candidates espousing factional interests to coalesce
into a national majority. Madison hoped that that structure, as well as
its basis in indirect popular representation in government, would produce government by selfless, well-educated, public-regarding elites who
would govern with the public interest foremost in their minds.[43]

The rise of political parties in the 1790s, as well as the difficulty of
structuring political offices in order to favor their occupation by elites,
cast immediate doubt on some of Madison's prescriptions.[44] But for our
purposes, what is more important is the foundation stone of Madison's
structure—the idea that a public interest exists and that its vindication
was the one legitimate goal of government.[45] Conceding the conceptual
and practical distance between James Madison's constitutional thinking
and our present-day regulatory system, one can still discern the outlines
of his thinking in the picture of agencies this chapter, and this book
more generally, has sought to paint.[46]

First, one can understand the federal bureaucracy as an institution
possessing distinctive knowledge and charged with promoting the public interest. Despite those characteristics, it remains susceptible to public
opinion, in the sense that public comment on rules mirrors public pressure on legislators,[47] the further sense that agencies remain indirectly
politically accountable to the people via their more directly accountable
political leadership, and the still more distant sense that the legislation
authorizing agency action emanates from the people's representatives.[48]

That concern for democratic accountability also influenced Madison's
thinking.[49] Madison envisioned a system in which law would be made
by the people's representatives, just as today statutory law enacted by
democratically chosen leaders sets the parameters for regulatory policy.
But our modern regulatory state's democratic commitment goes deeper.
The APA's provision for public participation in the process by which
most legally binding regulations are promulgated[50] reflects a rejection
of a purely technocratic vision in which unelected bureaucrats enjoy
freedom to regulate without having to seek public input.[51] Taking that
democratic commitment a step farther, the initiatives described earlier
in this chapter seek to ensure that public input is meaningful, even when

it comes from unsophisticated non-repeat players—that is, the mass of the citizenry.

Nevertheless, that popular input is not determinative—the CFPB still made the final decision about what the mortgage disclosure forms should look like, and agencies convening citizen-juries would similarly make the final decisions on the issues those juries discussed, even if the jury issued a recommendation. Even as further crafted into a public deliberation exercise, the rulemaking process need not devolve sovereign power to a subset of citizens, in the same sense that the lawmaking process Madison created was not a pure democracy. Rather, it is a process in which expert bureaucrats seeking to promote the public good incorporate the public's insights,[52] preferences,[53] and value judgments[54] into their decision-making. One can spot the family resemblance to Madison's ideal congresspersons, whose authority rested on popular control but who nevertheless possessed decision-making authority and were expected to wield it only after deliberating, rather than mechanically reflecting their constituents' preferences. In doing more than simply opening a comment window and passively receiving comments, even from average Americans for whom that process does not allow effective participation, initiatives like the ones this chapter has described allow for meaningful citizen input into the decisions that those agencies, just like Madison's Congress, retain the ultimate power to make.

That citizen input is indirect. But the same is true with the rest of the federal government, too. We are a republic, not a pure democracy: In most cases we elect legislators to make our laws, rather than making them ourselves.[55] Of course, we don't even elect our bureaucrats, so the distance between citizen and lawmaker is even greater when law emanates from the bureaucracy rather than Congress. But we can indirectly influence them, via agencies' political leadership and the public participation made possible by the APA and the initiatives this chapter has discussed. Those initiatives can create the conditions for republican regulation, just as Madison hoped that the combination of elections and public-spirited deliberation by officeholders would create republican legislation. Just as Madison hoped for government by democratically selected, public-spirited, knowledgeable leaders, we can hope for regulation by democratically accountable, public interest–promoting experts. If we can manage that, then we will have squared the circle political scientists have been attempting to square since at least the late nineteenth century. We will have succeeded in creating a public administration that we can call both democratic and expertise-based.

Back to Trust

Madisonian political theory may be interesting to academics, but what does it have to do with increasing public trust in the expertise of twenty-first-century administrative agencies? Plenty. Democratic accountability is an indispensable component of public trust in our regulatory system. Expertise alone is not enough; if it were, that trust would turn exclusively on regulatory successes and failures, and would thus ebb and flow with circumstances. More important, our democratic heritage rebels at the idea of unaccountable agencies setting the nation's regulatory course. Federal judges are similarly unelected, and often face legitimacy crises even when their self-described role and ostensible task purports to limit them to interpreting law, not making it. By contrast, administrative agencies explicitly and self-consciously make policy, a process that, as this book has explained, includes making politically fraught value judgments in implementing broadly worded statutes. The idea that such tasks would be performed by unelected officials asserting power based solely on their expertise would create a legitimacy crisis that dwarfs that faced by federal judges.

On the other hand, agencies *are* experts. Their legitimacy has always rested in part on that fact, and will continue to do so, as long as bureaucrats are unelected and regulatory problems are complex and incapable of full resolution by political actors making political choices. The challenge thus becomes filtering that expertise through democratic accountability. There are different ways to accomplish that filtering. Chapter 4 considered Congress as the proper vehicle. It concluded that neither forcing it to legislate more precisely (nor, as chapter 5 noted, relying on its informal oversight) made Congress a likely candidate for transmitting the public's values to agencies. At the other end of Pennsylvania Avenue, presidential influence over agencies can help. However, chapter 5 argued that the balance between presidential control and agency autonomy has become badly skewed in favor of the former. But that chapter nevertheless recognized an appropriate role for presidential control, via (limited) presidential power to place political appointees in agencies, White House–led coordination among agencies and between them and the White House itself, and simple informal pressure of the sort presidents always apply to agencies.

The initiatives this chapter has suggested complement those political branch controls over agencies, by helping agencies establish their own political legitimacy via their direct connection with the American people. But this type of democratic accountability is unique—and uniquely helpful—because it creates a connection between that accountability and agency expertise. By involving the American people in regulatory projects that are deeply informed by that expertise, agencies can introduce Americans to that expertise and involve them in the process of utilizing it. Concededly, that involvement may not take the form of technical discussions about regulatory details, given Americans' general inability to participate effectively in such discussions. But by providing input where it can be most helpful, Americans can nevertheless make a meaningful contribution to agencies' use of expertise.

That's where Madison comes in, now for the final time. As the prior section explained, Madison's system attempted to filter public-spirited and, indeed, expert deliberation through the electoral process. By providing for filtered democratic participation through elections (often indirect, as with the Senate (originally) and the presidency (ostensibly still the case[56])), Madison hoped to provide democratic accountability for the elite deliberations he hoped his system would generate. In other words, elite decision-making could become democratically accountable, and thus worthy of the public's trust. So too with our current situation. The initiatives this chapter has suggested are designed to ensure democratic accountability, not for the elite decision-making of Madison's time, but for the expert decision-making of our own. By creating accountability for that expertise, the hope is that they instill public trust in it.

In a world of pandemics and climate crises and dizzying technological change, that trust is needed more than ever.

Conclusion

The Return of the Elephant

This book—and the readers who have come along with it—have traveled a long distance. An appropriate ending for the journey is a glance back to its start. So return to the last section of the introduction, before the trip began in earnest. That section referred to the elephant in the room—the Trump administration's response to the COVID-19 pandemic. It cautioned that that experience—searing for so many Americans and seemingly emblematic of the issues of bureaucratic capacity and expertise—would not be the sole, or even the primary, focus of the book's analysis. Nevertheless, that experience is likely deeply relevant for many readers—for many of us, the pandemic will be the most memorable public experience of our lives. So consider how that experience speaks to what this book has discussed.

Presidential interference: Chapter 5 spent a lot of pages criticizing over-intrusive, politicized presidential interference in regulation. The experience of 2020 reflected this phenomenon in abundance. The president publicly and explicitly pushed back against his public health experts' warnings and advice. He installed his own White House COVID-19 advisor—someone who had no experience in infectious diseases. He called the pandemic a hoax.

Relations between political appointees and experts: When the story of the pandemic is written, much of it will focus on the relationship between agencies' expert staffs and their agency and White House political leaders. In *The Premonition*, Michael Lewis's book about the government's early pandemic response, he follows the Wolverines, a group of experts scattered throughout the federal and state health bureaucracies who had to meet and work informally to do the work they (correctly) thought they needed to do to learn about and combat the pandemic, despite their exclusion from meaningful participation in the official government response. The circumstances that necessitated their informal operation reflect the exact opposite of in-house agency experts methodically marshaled to confront a regulatory threat. It is hard to imagine a more explicit violation of the principles chapter 6 offered.

Ill-considered bureaucratic reorganizations: In *The Premonition*, Lewis also recounted the story of the National Security Council's pandemic preparedness task force being disbanded, with its members being dispersed throughout the bureaucracy or simply leaving the government entirely. Opinions differ on the significance of that decision. But it is surely the case that, as one commentator observed, "[a] basic rule of bureaucracy is that your structures reflect and reinforce your priorities."[1] Recall from chapter 6 Professor Golden's recounting of Anne Gorsuch, President Reagan's first EPA administrator, doing something similar to EPA's enforcement teams.[2] The motive for disbanding the pandemic team may not have been as malicious as Gorsuch's. But the result was the same: a degradation of bureaucratic capacity.

Judicial review: Throughout the pandemic, the Supreme Court dealt with several high-profile cases considering challenges to state and local government closing and capacity-limit orders, often brought by religious organizations claiming First Amendment rights to continue in-person services. While the Court's performance in these cases varied, at its worst it completely refused to recognize expertise-based arguments in favor of the restrictions. Much less did it incentivize such decision-making, as chapter 7 urged should be the appropriate goal of judicial review of agency action.[3]

Information control: Throughout the pandemic, the White House attempted to control and distort the information the CDC and other health agencies sought to push out to the American people. From advisories to the public about mitigation and safety measures to the CDC's *Morbidity and Mortality Weekly Report* aimed at public health professionals, agency information was controlled, distorted, and suppressed. That experience reveals the importance of chapter 8's insistence that agency informational integrity be protected.

Capacity cuts: Recall from chapter 8 the 2018 survey of scientists at six federal agencies, including the CDC. That survey, published in April 2020—a month after American society was shut down—included concerns expressed by CDC scientists that budget cuts and other resource constraints made it harder for them to engage in programs dealing with international cooperation and infectious disease tracking—work that was critical in the pandemic's earliest stages. As chapter 9 explained, such destruction of bureaucratic capacity can only lead to bad regulatory outcomes.

Ineffective interaction with the public: One cannot hold agency leadership blameless. In addition to other mistakes, the failure of the government's leading health institutions to engage frankly with the American people early in the pandemic did not help the situation. Their early flip-flops on mask-wearing and the CDC's confusing, if welcome, relaxation of mask-wearing recommendations in May 2021, before the onset of the Delta variant, reflect the sort of public engagement that seems almost calculated to inculcate the public distrust of administrative expertise chapter 10 addressed. Grant that it's hard for agencies to provide reliable information under circumstances of extreme and fast-changing scientific uncertainty. Failure to communicate the parameters of that uncertainty, and inadequate suggestions for how Americans could think about responding, did not help.

Chapters 5, 6, 7, 8, 9, and 10: They are all covered in this short recounting of our extended national tragedy. The fit is not perfect, to be sure. For example, the flawed conduct above mostly did not involve the federal administrative rulemaking this book has focused on. But the fact that that conduct implicated the same concerns this book has addressed suggests that this book's prescriptions are indeed generally applicable to all types of agency action, not just rulemaking. The larger point, though, is that the most tragic failure of bureaucratic expertise in our lifetimes—and the failure that will reverberate for so long with so many Americans—has clear connections to the problems this book has identified and for which it has suggested fixes.

We should do something about those problems. Next time it may be even worse.

ACKNOWLEDGMENTS

In 2012, Barack Obama found himself in hot water when, addressing small business owners and referring to their businesses, he said, "you didn't build that." The criticism was unfair, as any reader could have concluded from perusing the context surrounding that statement: He was explaining that an entire social and government web combined to allow businesses to grow and flourish. He could just as easily have repeated the African saying that "it takes a village to raise a child." But that got Hillary Clinton in trouble.

I didn't build this book. Instead, to mix metaphors (and politicians), it took a village. My enviable perch as a tenured law professor allowed me the sabbatical that gave me the time to write it. For that, I must thank Brooklyn Law School and its dean, Michael Cahill. Several other persons or groups of people also played special roles that deserve mentioning. My always indefatigable editor at NYU Press, Clara Platter, was supportive and enthusiastic about this project from the day I mentioned it to her. Lauren Jacobsen, Catherine Kim, Minna Kotkin, Jon Michaels, Richard Murphy, Zachary Price, Shalev Roisman, Bijal Shah, Lou Virelli, and Evan Zoldan all read one or more chapters of the draft, and offered extremely helpful comments within my truly unreasonable time constraints. Parker Brown, Shimon Friedlander, Ru Hochen, Derek Knight, Cody Laska, Thu Nguyen, Thomas Pearce, Maya Sparks, Jedediah Tift, and Michael Wozniak all provided wonderful research assistance. Kathleen Darvil of the Brooklyn Law School library was extraordinary in helping me track down obscure reports and monographs.

Two other larger groups require mention. First, the community of administrative law scholars. This book seeks to present and analyze, in a condensed and accessible form, the wisdom of many first-rate scholars of the American regulatory system. Their written work and their always-welcoming attitude over the course of my career have inspired and encouraged me.

Second, thanks are due to the students to whom I have taught administrative law over the past twenty-five years. Their enthusiasm and interest in the material have pushed me to become a better teacher and, in the process, a better scholar.

Finally, as always, my most profound thanks go to my husband, who during the course of this project yet again had to indulge my obsessiveness with finishing one more thought before dinner, night after night. I suspect he eventually took to calling me in to dinner five minutes before it was ready, knowing my likely response. Regardless, he kept me nourished, physically, intellectually, and emotionally over the course of writing this book during the pandemic winter and spring of 2021.

NOTES

INTRODUCTION

1 See, e.g., Mashaw and Harfst, "Regulation," 260–61 (noting similar confidence in the ability of regulators to regulate in ways leading to safer automobiles); ibid., 261 n.12 (citing references to the space program as part of that confidence).

2 See Halberstam, *Best and Brightest*.

3 See Rubenstein, "Supremacy," 1145–46 ("From the 1940s through the 1960s, administrative governance became widely accepted and normatively entrenched. . . . The script flipped in the 1970s. Public trust in government reached historic lows in reaction to the Watergate scandal, a struggling economy, and faltering regulatory programs. A widespread view was that the national government 'had given its best shot' but 'had failed.'").

4 Pew, *Public Trust*.

5 See Rogowski, "Administrative Presidency," 38–45.

6 See, e.g., Andreen, "Success."

7 See Thomas, "Maintaining," 168; ibid. (citing another scholar's similar suggestion).

8 Verkuil, *Valuing*, 26.

9 See American Water Works, "Survey." The same dynamic of distrust based on past experience appears to explain at least part of African Americans' lower trust in COVID-19 vaccines. See Kum, "Fueled."

10 See Saad, "U.S. Readiness."

11 US EPA, *Scientific Integrity*, 2 n.1.

12 See Lewis, *Fifth Risk*, 191–219.

13 Collins and Evans, *Rethinking Expertise*, 24–27 (discussing contributory expertise); ibid., 28–35 (discussing interactional expertise).

14 See, e.g., Eyal, *Crisis*, 34 ("Unlike 'contributory experts,' the possessors of interactional expertise lack practical competence in a given specialist domain. They don't know how to run the experiments. . . . What they can do, however, is *converse* about this specialist knowledge in a fully competent and interesting way.") (emphasis in original).

15 Collins and Evans, *Rethinking Expertise*, 24–25 (citing Dreyfus and Dreyfus, *Mind Over Machine*, 21–36).

16 Eyal, *Crisis*, 23–24.

17 Shapiro, "Failure," 1099. See also Fisher and Shapiro, *Administrative Competence*, 57 (referring to this type of expertise as "decision-making" expertise).

18 McGarity, *Reinventing*, 5.
19 Shapiro, "Failure," 1099.
20 See Fisher and Shapiro, *Administrative Competence*, 56 ("Interactional expertise is what turns different types of expertise into the expert capacity of an administrative institution.").
21 McGarity, *Reinventing*, 5–6.
22 Berman and Carter, "Policy Analysis," 3.
23 Douthat, "When You Can't Just 'Trust the Science.'"
24 Kagan, "Presidential Administration."
25 Indeed, scholars have observed that concerns about competent administration have surfaced since the nation's founding. See, e.g., Fisher and Shapiro, *Administrative Competence*, chapter 4. Because a deep dive into that longer-term history would require more space than this book can allot, and because the 1970s mark the most recent inflection point in this discussion, this book begins the story with that decade.

CHAPTER 1. THE GREAT TRANSITION

1 See Pew, *Public Trust*.
2 This statement is subject to the caveat that, at least into the 1960s, the Republican Party retained remnants of a pro–civil rights stance that favored federal power to ensure racial equality. See Schmidt, *The Sit-Ins*, 158.
3 See Nathan, *Administrative Presidency*, 48–49; 53–55.
4 See Pew, *Public Trust*.
5 See Layzer, *Open*, 48–49.
6 Compare ibid., 52 (describing the memo as "particularly influential") with Schmitt, "Legend" (questioning its impact).
7 See Layzer, *Open*, 48–49 (think tanks and journals). Between 1971 and 1978, the number of corporation and industry lobbying organizations in Washington increased from 175 to nearly 2,000. Ibid., 50 n.80. In 1971, Mobil Oil Corporation began buying space on the Op-Ed page of the *New York Times* for what eventually became their iconic advertising stating the company's position on public issues, a practice it later expanded to other major newspapers. See ibid., 50–51.
8 For example, polls taken in the mid-1970s continued to show strong support for environmental protections. See Gilroy and Shapiro, "Polls," 273. Even at the end of the decade, public support for environmental regulation remained high. See Layzer, *Open*, 80–81 (citing poll results from 1977–1980). But see ibid. (citing other polls that suggested eroding support for environmental regulation).
9 See Thompson, "First Sagebrush Rebellion."
10 See Layzer, *Open*, 66.
11 "Command and control" regulation is generally understood to refer to regulation that imposes standards or requirements, backed up by sanctions for failure to comply. See, e.g., Baldwin, "Regulation," in *Human Face*, 65.
12 See ibid., 59–60.

13 See ibid., 60–62.

14 See, e.g., Layzer, *Open*, 64–66.

15 See Stine, "Environmental Policy," in Fink and Graham, *Carter Presidency*, 191.

16 US President, "Improving."

17 See Percival, "Checks," 129–38 (Nixon program); ibid., 138–41 (Ford programs).

18 See Layzer, *Open*, 77.

19 See ibid., 76.

20 A prominent scholar of the federal bureaucracy, Paul Light, connected declining morale in the federal workforce with such statements. See Light, *Government Ill Executed*, 126 ("No one knows for sure how federal employees might have answered [Light's] surveys [about workplace morale] before Watergate and the steep fall in public trust in government. Yet, there is good reason to argue that the current disquiet can be traced back to the mid-1970s when members of Congress and presidents campaigned assiduously against the government they led.").

21 See, e.g., Reagan, "Speech to Hilldale College"; Perlstein, *Reaganland*, 865; Stiff, "Battle" (noting the anecdote's lack of factual basis).

22 One additional development merits a brief introduction before being deferred to a later chapter. During the 1970s, federal courts greatly expanded the procedures agencies had to satisfy before promulgating regulations. Justified as both an assurance of a legally adequate procedure in its own right, but also as an attempt to assure the substantive rationality of the resulting regulations, this procedural revolution converted the rulemaking process from a straightforward, streamlined process to one that considerably increased the cost and duration of rulemaking proceedings. Questions about the ultimate benefit of such proceduralization, and whether it even imposed inordinate resource and time costs on agencies at all, remain controversial. For current purposes, it is enough to say that subsequent charges of bureaucratic incompetence rested, at least in part, on bureaucratic torpor and indecision that at least some scholars have traced back to courts' ratcheting up of the procedures agencies were required to satisfy. Chapter 7, which deals with judicial review, considers these issues.

CHAPTER 2. POLITICAL, DOCTRINAL, AND BUREAUCRATIC CHANGES

1 Schlafly, *A Choice*. Phyllis Schlafly went on to become a prominent opponent of the women's rights movement in the 1970s, and played an important role in the defeat of the Equal Rights Amendment.

2 See Reagan, "Speech to Hilldale College."

3 See, e.g., Novak, *People's Welfare*.

4 See, e.g., Farber and Hemmersbaugh, "Shadow," 272 (noting that most environmental laws impose a feasibility standard).

5 To be sure, deregulation does not necessarily imply a lack of or deemphasis on expertise. For example, an agency may conclude, based on careful expert study, that deregulation of an industry may be the best way of reaching a particular social goal. Still, the Reagan-era deregulatory agenda pushed against what had

been agencies' general embrace of more intensively-controlling mechanisms of achieving such goals.

6 See Golden, *What Motivates* (suggesting, based on information-gathering from bureaucrats of that era, that most of them understood their roles as implementers of the administration's program and did their best to carry it out). Nevertheless, that study recounts the tensions that did arise between agencies' permanent staffs and their Reagan-appointed political leadership. Professor Golden's study is discussed in more detail later, in chapter 6.

7 See Reagan, *Inaugural Address*, 2 ("In this present crisis, government is not the solution to our problem; government is the problem.").

8 Ingraham, *Foundation*, 101.

9 See Miller, "Early Days," 95 (noting pre-Reagan regulatory review initiatives).

10 US President, "Federal Regulation."

11 See McGarity, *Reinventing*, 284.

12 U.S. Const. Art. II § 3.

13 See, e.g., Calabresi and Yoo, *The Unitary Executive.*

14 Independent agencies are those whose heads have been immunized from at-will presidential removal power. In other words, agencies are considered "independent" when the president is required to provide a reason, beyond simple policy disagreement, if he wishes to remove the head. Executive Order 12,291 exempted independent agencies from its regulatory review requirements. See US President, "Federal Regulation," § 1(d). Such agencies raise important separation of powers questions that are considered later in this chapter and in chapter 5.

15 See Fisher and Shapiro, *Administrative Competence*, 205–207 (discussing the rise of cost-benefit analysis).

16 Sassone and Schaffer, *Cost-Benefit Analysis*, 128.

17 See Livermore and Revesz, *Reviving*, 75.

18 One scholar has suggested empaneling citizen juries to make recommendations about such value-intensive quantification decisions. See Nou, "Regulating," 618. Chapter 10 discusses citizen-juries.

19 Courts have interpreted at least some laws as mandating a zero-risk regime. E.g., *Public Citizen v. Young*, 831 F.2d 1108 (D.C. Cir. 1987) (interpreting federal food additive law).

20 See Farber and Hemmersbaugh, "Shadow," 272.

21 See, e.g., Driesen, "Cost-Benefit."

22 "Dawes," *Oxford Guide*, 171.

23 See, e.g., Polsby, "Presidential Cabinet Making," 20 (concluding, on the eve of the Reagan years, that no president had pursued only one strategy of filling cabinet officers, but instead had combined elements of client-group interests, subject-matter specialties, and generalist experience).

24 Quoted in Nathan, *Administrative Presidency*, 28.

25 See Polsby, "Presidential Cabinet Making," 19.

26 See Nathan, *Administrative Presidency*, 29 (general observation); ibid., 30–33 (Nixon experience). See also Ingraham, *Foundation*, 96–100 (discussing Nixon and Carter experiences).

27 See Nathan, *Administrative Presidency*, 88–90 (importance of political vetting); ibid., 89 ("Reagan chose cabinet officers whose experiences and personality prepared them for a period of government service that above all would advance the purposes and program of his presidency.").

28 See Ingraham, *Foundation*, 99 (Carter administration); ibid., 101 (Reagan numbers); ibid., 100 (vetting of Reagan appointees).

29 See Golden, *What Motivates*, 121–126 (EPA "hit lists"); Berman and Carter, "Policy Analysis" (political vetting).

30 See Berman and Carter, "Policy Analysis."

31 It can also refer to less desirable social goods, for example, prison confinement: private prison populations have exploded over the last two decades. See Gotsch and Basti, "Capitalizing," 7 ("Between 2000 and 2016, the number of people incarcerated in private prison facilities increased 47 percent while the overall prison population increased 9 percent.").

32 Michaels, *Constitutional Coup*, 91–98.

33 Verkuil, *Valuing*, 15.

34 Milward, "Implications," 41–62 (cited in Ingraham, *Foundation*, 115–16). On the other hand, the qualified language used earlier in the paragraph ("something appears to have happened") reflects one scholar's conclusion that, until the mid-1980s, accurate information about the number of government contractors is very difficult to come by. See Light, *Government Ill Executed*, 194-195

35 See Comptroller General, *Recent*, 8; ibid., 8 n.1 (citing a 1980 report finding a similar reliance).

36 See Hollis-Brusky, "Helping Ideas," 201 (quoting the Reagan administration's Solicitor General as recounting that that administration "'fought on two fronts'": a political front focusing on deregulation and tax cuts that would starve government of resources, and "'the legal front'").

37 U.S. Const. Art. II §§ 1, 3.

38 The question whether the unitary executive theory contemplates presidential control over agency adjudications is an interesting one, but one that need not detain us. What matters for our purposes is the unwillingness, noted in the next two paragraphs of the text, of any White House to assert Article II authority to oversee adjudications. See Vermeule, "Conventions," 1211–14 (discussing this issue).

39 5 U.S.C. § 557(d).

40 Proposed Exec. Order Entitled 'Fed. Regulation,' 5 Op. O.L.C. 59 (1981).

41 See Hollis-Brusky, "Helping Ideas," 206.

42 Shane, "*Chevron* Deference," 691.

43 Independent agencies are further discussed in chapter 5.

44 467 U.S. 837 (1984).

45 The text uses the words "attempted to clarify" because, in subsequent years and decades, the Court hopelessly muddled the deference question. That difficulty need not occupy us because the Court, at least for now, has ostensibly remained faithful to the *Chevron* framework discussed in the text.

46 See Criddle, "*Chevron's* Consensus," 1273.

47 467 U.S., 865–66.

48 This justification raises questions about whether *Chevron* deference is appropriately accorded independent agencies, given the president's lesser control of them. See, e.g., May, "Defining" (considering this question).

49 To be sure, in later years, the Court sometimes did rely on the consistency of the agency's interpretation when applying *Chevron* and, indeed, when deciding whether *Chevron* even applied. But for our purposes, the important point is how *Chevron* itself considered these issues.

50 See, e.g., Meazell, "Presidential Control," 1778 ("[E]xpertise was viewed by supporters of the New Deal as the ultimate answer to politics. Thus, independent agencies—which burgeoned during the New Deal—were designed with the purpose of shielding expert decisionmakers from the shifting winds of politics.")

51 487 U.S. 654 (1988). Justice Kennedy, having just taken his seat on the Court, did not participate in *Morrison*.

52 The ambiguity lies with a 1936 case, *Carter v. Carter Coal*, 298 U.S. 238 (1936), that involved delegation of federal power to private entities, rather than administrative agencies. A careful reader might see a connection between such private delegations of governmental power and the outsourcing discussed earlier in this chapter and considered further in chapter 9.

53 Such constraints include presidential preferences, as expressed, for example, in the Reagan White House regulatory review executive order, and procedural requirements, such as those imposed by the Administrative Procedure Act, 5 U.S.C. § 551 et seq.

54 See *Marbury v. Madison*, 5 U.S. 137, 177 (1803) ("It is emphatically the province and duty of the judicial department to say what the law is.").

55 463 U.S. 29 (1983).

56 Ibid., 43.

57 463 U.S., 58 (Rehnquist, J., concurring in part and dissenting in part).

58 Ibid., 59 (Rehnquist, J., concurring in part and dissenting in part).

59 See Rosenberg, "Congress's Prerogative," 632 ("In [*Morrison* and a 1989 case], the Court expressed unequivocal approbation of a very far reaching, though not limitless, power in Congress over agency structure, location, and relationships *that may properly have as its principal object the desire to limit the President's influence over the development and implementation of administration policy.*") (emphasis added).

60 An important detail here is the question whether less presidential control over an agency simply means more control by the other political branch, Congress, as opposed to an increase in agency autonomy. Space limitations do not allow exploration of this question here, which is nevertheless an important factor when considering how these developments impact the latitude for agency expertise.

CHAPTER 3. POLITICIZATION CONSOLIDATED

1 See Criddle, "*Chevron*'s Consensus," 1273 n.3.

2 For more details about the George H. W. Bush administration's approach to the bureaucracy, see Percival, "Who's in Charge?," 2505–11.

3 See Pildes and Sunstein, "Reinventing," 6 (describing President Clinton's decision as "a dramatic and in many ways quite surprising step").

4 Regulatory agenda review refers to the requirement that an agency submit for White House review its regulatory plans for the upcoming year. The Reagan administration instituted this requirement in a separate executive order, issued in 1985, which, unlike the Clinton version, exempted independent agencies.

5 Kagan, "Presidential Administration."

6 See ibid., 2283–84.

7 US President, "Regulatory Planning and Review," Preamble.

8 Ibid., § 9.

9 See Kagan, "Presidential Administration," 2290 ("These directives . . . became . . . Clinton's primary means . . . of setting an administrative agenda that reflected and advanced his policy and political preferences.").

10 See ibid., 2302.

11 See chapter 8.

12 E.g., In re: Cheney, 406 F.3d 723 (D.C. Cir. 2005) (*en banc*) (rejecting claims that a White House energy task force violated the Federal Advisory Committee Act by conducting its business in secret).

13 E.g., US Department of Justice, *Investigation*.

14 See, e.g., Criddle, "Fiduciary Administration," 455 ("many critics argued that in Executive Order No. 13,422, Bush crossed the Rubicon dividing agency rulemaking discretion from presidential administration by formally supplanting administrators' statutory authority"). That order also removed that appointee from direct reporting responsibility to the agency head, thus further bypassing internal agency hierarchies. See ibid.

15 See, e.g., Watts, "Controlling," 694 (concluding that the requirement that this officer approve all agency rulemaking "le[d] to the further politicization of the rulemaking process").

16 See, e.g., White House Office of the Press Secretary, *Obama Administration*.

17 See Watts, "Controlling," 701–4 (comparison to Clinton); ibid., 703–4 (use of the Internet).

18 See ibid., 706–10; ibid., 708–709 (Sebelius's role); 709–10 (Obama's denial of responsibility).

19 See ibid., 704–5.

20 A January 2021 search of a database of legal scholarship for appearances of "Trump" in the same sentence as "unprecedented," limited to 2017 and beyond, resulted in more than 600 hits.

21 US President, "Reducing Regulation."

22 Institute for Policy Integrity, *Roundup*.

23 See Desikan, "150 Attacks."

24 Saiger, "Obama's Czars," 2583.

25 Walters, "Litigation-Fostered," 169 n.213.

26 Emerson and Michaels, "Abandoning."

27 Clinton, "Remarks," 144; id., 148.

28 See Light, *Government Ill Executed*, 171 n.17.

29 See Osborne and Gaebler, *Reinventing Government*, 25–48 (discussing those terms).

30 See Michaels, "War" ("Reagan's now legendary polemics against the federal bureaucracy were validated—and stripped of their partisan bluster—by Bill Clinton.").

31 See, e.g., Robinson et al., *Understanding*, 12.

32 Pew, *Public Trust*, 25.

33 See Light, *Government Ill Executed*, 159 (noting this irony).

34 See Rogowski, "Administrative Presidency," 31.

35 See ibid., 38–45. The study was performed by the researcher presenting vignettes to the survey participants explaining that a particular agency had experienced staffing changes that impacted either its capacity, expertise, or the ideology of its staff, and asking the participants to evaluate their confidence in that agency. See ibid., 33–38.

36 See ibid., 35 (reprinting the vignettes presented to the survey group).

37 Kim, "Role of Trust," 611.

38 Garrett et al., "Assessing," 232.

39 See generally, e.g., Hubbell, "Symbol-Maker"; Ingraham, *Foundation*, 101 (describing "strident antibureaucratic rhetoric" emanating from the administration).

40 Kilgore, "Starving."

41 Verkuil, *Valuing*, 17. One study suggested that presidential attacks do not impact public perceptions of the bureaucracy. See Yackee and Lowery, "Understanding Public Support." But the authors note the very tentative nature of that conclusion. Regardless, presidential undermining of bureaucratic capacity and expertise may indirectly impact public attitudes, as discussed in the text.

42 Reagan, *Speaking*, 392.

43 See Magill, "Revolution."

44 See, e.g., *Whitman v. American Trucking Ass'n*, 531 U.S. 457 (2001).

45 *Morrison v. Olson*, 487 U.S. 654 (1988).

46 519 U.S. 452 (1997).

47 Independent agencies may also be more susceptible to influence by Congress.

48 For an example of how that deference could cut in different directions as relevant to expertise, compare Barmore, "*Auer*," 844–45 ("Given that policy choices account for a substantial part of the work that *Auer* does, a shift to [a less deferential standard] would entail major costs to the political accountability of agency decision-making.") with Clarke, "Uneasy Case," 180 (observing that by the time of

Auer in 1997, the justification for *Auer* deference had shifted toward recognition of agency expertise).

49 *Free Enterprise Fund v. Public Co. Accounting Oversight Board*, 561 U.S. 477 (2010); *Seila Law, LLC v. Consumer Fin. Protection Bureau*, 140 S.Ct. 2183 (2020).

50 See, e.g., *Seila Law*, 2192 (describing a Rehnquist-era precedent, *Morrison v. Olson*, 487 U.S. 654 (1988), as one of two "exceptions to the President's unrestricted removal power").

51 See, e.g., *Free Enterprise Fund*, 499 ("No one doubts Congress's power to create a vast and varied federal bureaucracy. But where, in all this, is the role for oversight by an elected President? . . . One can have a government that functions without being ruled by functionaries, and a government that benefits from expertise without being ruled by experts. Our Constitution was adopted to enable the people to govern themselves, through their elected leaders.") (paragraph break omitted).

52 *Kisor v. Wilkie*, 139 S.Ct. 2400 (2019).

53 The surprise flows from the fact that recent Republican appointments to the Court have often professed fealty to the views of Justice Antonin Scalia, who was *Chevron*'s greatest defender on the Court.

54 See, e.g., Nichols, *Death*.

55 See ibid.

56 See, e.g., Nelkin, "Political Impact," 37 ("The complexity of public decisions seems to require highly specialized and esoteric knowledge, and those who control this knowledge have considerable power. Yet democratic ideology suggests that people must be able to influence policy decisions that affect their lives.").

57 Lippman, *Phantom*, 57–58.

58 See Eyal, *Crisis*, 82–84.

59 See de Beaumont Foundation, "Changing." To be sure, the focus group also expressed views consistent with a willingness to trust certain experts. In particular, several members found persuasive the fact that the vast majority of doctors offered the vaccine took it. See ibid.

60 *Reno v. ACLU*, 521 U.S. 844 (1997).

61 See Rosenwald, "Mount Rushmore," 32.

62 See Berry and Sobieraj, "Understanding," 765.

63 See Rosenwald, "Mount Rushmore," 6.

64 See Berry and Sobieraj, "Understanding," 763–764.

65 See, e.g., Barker and Knight, "Political Talk Radio."

66 See Berry and Sobieraj, "Understanding," 763.

67 Nichols, *Death*, 147–148. See also Eyal, *Crisis*, 48 (citing declining trust in "science" among conservative Americans over time).

68 Nichols, *Death*, 147.

69 See Pariser, *Filter Bubble*; Sunstein, *Going to Extremes*.

70 Some commentators argue that the filter bubble concept is seriously exaggerated. See, e.g., Bruns, *Are Filter Bubbles Real?*

71 See Robinson et al., *Understanding*, 38–41 (identifying value convergence, along with perceptions of competence, as a determinant of public trust in agencies).

72 See ibid., 18 ("Trust is often particularly important for environmental policy, which frequently involves complex issues that are poorly understood by the public. Consequently, the public must trust the government to regulate in the best manner.").

73 See Mounk, "Undemocratic Dilemma," 100.

CHAPTER 4. A CALL TO CONGRESS

1 See, e.g., Mortenson and Bagley, "Delegation," 296–300.

2 See Locke, *Second Treatise*, 363 ("The power of the Legislative being derived from the People by a positive voluntary Grant and Institution, can be no other, than what that positive Grant conveyed, which being only to make Laws, and not to make Legislators, the Legislative can have no power to transfer their Authority of making Laws, and place it in other hands.").

3 Compare Wurman, "Non-delegation" (finding a historical foundation for the doctrine) with Mortenson and Bagley, "Delegation" (not finding one).

4 See Posner and Vermeule, "Interring."

5 See, e.g., Mashaw, "Prodelegation."

6 See Lowi, *End*; Schoenbrod, *Power*.

7 See Scalia, "Legislative Veto," 21 ("with very few exceptions, all of the decisions made by the executive branch could be made instead by Congress itself (in which event they would be 'legislative') and have become 'executive' functions only because Congress has chosen to commit them to the second branch").

8 *J. W. Hampton Co. v. United States*, 276 U.S. 394, 409 (1928).

9 See *Yakus v. United States*, 321 U.S. 414, 426 (1944).

10 This example is from the provision of the Clean Air Act that was challenged in *Whitman v. American Trucking Ass'n*, 531 U.S. 457 (2001). See 42 U.S.C. § 7409(b) (1).

11 *A.L.A. Schechter Poultry Co. v. United States*, 295 U.S. 495 (1935); *Panama Refining Co. v. Ryan*, 293 U.S. 388 (1935).

12 One possible exception is the Bituminous Coal Conservation Act of 1935, struck down in *Carter v. Carter Coal*, 298 U.S. 238 (1936). The provision arguably struck down on non-delegation grounds created a structure in which mine owners were empowered to set legally binding prices for coal. One could read the case to hold that the delegation of legislative authority to private groups violated the non-delegation doctrine. But it could be read as resting on other grounds. See Volokh, "New Private-Regulation," 973–80 (suggesting a due process grounding).

13 *National Broadcasting Corp. v. US*, 319 U.S. 190 (1943); *American Power & Light v. SEC*, 329 U.S. 90 (1946). By contrast, the non-delegation principle continues to be vibrant in many states. See Iuliano and Whittington, "Non-delegation Doctrine."

14 *Gundy v. United States*, 139 S.Ct. 2116 (2019). Beyond the seven justices' votes discussed in the text, Justice Alito concurred in the plurality's judgment upholding

the law but expressed a willingness to reconsider the Court's current deferential stance on non-delegation questions. The ninth justice, Justice Kavanaugh, did not participate in the case, although in a subsequent case he suggested that he too would be willing to reconsider the current doctrine. Thus, there are currently five justices open to a reconsideration, with Justice Barrett, the newest justice, not yet having had a chance to speak on the issue as a justice.

15 More conceptually, one might also object that this sort of limitation on agency discretion "misunderstands the nature of administrative competence" by inappropriately limiting agencies' ability to use their expertise, as that term is more broadly understood. Fisher and Shapiro, *Administrative Competence*, 28.

16 See, e.g., Stewart, "Beyond Delegation," 331–35.

17 Some scholars suggest that congresspersons in fact like ambiguous statutes, exactly because they allow consensus to be reached while giving interested parties the chance to influence how an agency interprets that language. See Nourse and Schachter, "Politics," 596–97.

18 See Chafetz, "Gridlock?" 52 (finding the origin of the major questions doctrine in a 1994 case, *MCI v. AT&T*, 512 U.S. 218 (1994)).

19 576 U.S. 473, 485–486 (2015) (citations, internal quotations, and paragraph break omitted).

20 Ibid., 491, 492.

21 Indeed, in *Chevron* the Court stated that deferential, Step 2 review—the kind of review the major questions doctrine refuses to employ—applies when, after applying "traditional tools of statutory construction," the court cannot find that Congress had an intention on the question in issue. Thus, in a major questions case, a court would have to conclude that those "traditional tools" failed to reveal congressional intent, but would then still press forward to interpret the statute itself without deferring to the agency. Given that, by hypothesis, the "traditional tools" courts use to interpret a statute had come up dry, there's no reason to think courts retain any comparative expertise over agencies in the subsequent search for statutory meaning.

22 See Sunstein, "Two 'Major Questions' Doctrines."

23 See *Whitman v. American Trucking Ass'n*, 531 U.S. 457, 475 (2001) ("It is true enough that the degree of agency discretion that is acceptable [as a non-delegation matter] varies according to the scope of the power congressionally conferred."). See also *United States Telecomm. Assn v. Federal Comm. Comm'n*, 855 F.3d 381, 419 (D.C. Cir. 2017) (Kavanaugh, J., dissenting) ("Th[e] major rules doctrine (usually called the major questions doctrine) is grounded in two overlapping and reinforcing presumptions: (i) a separation of powers-based presumption against the delegation of major lawmaking authority from Congress to the Executive Branch and (ii) a presumption that Congress intends to make major policy decisions itself, not leave those decisions to agencies.") (citation omitted).

24 See, e.g., Levinson, "Foreword," 71.

25 See *Motor Vehicle Mfrs Ass'n v. State Farm Mut. Ins. Co.*, 463 U.S. 29, 41–42 (1983).

26 One prominent scholar, writing in 1987, suggested that the result of such judicial insistence on specificity would be Congress farming out (literally, internally delegating) the task of crafting more specific standards to committees, with little review by the full House or Senate. Stewart, "Beyond Delegation," 331–32. Whether today's increased polarization would allow even that suboptimal result is an open question.

27 This book's focus on administrative expertise, and this chapter's focus on ways Congress might be forced to make the political decisions that today are often made by agencies, makes it relatively less important to focus on informal oversight Congress may exercise over agencies. Even scholars writing in recent years have noted the difficulty of reaching firm conclusions about such oversight, but at least some scholars have questioned Congress's effectiveness in overseeing agencies' work, and whether such oversight truly reflects the public's political preferences. See Clinton et al., "Influencing," 389–92 (difficulty); Kagan, "Presidential Administration," 2256–60 (effectiveness and responsiveness).

CHAPTER 5. CURBING POLITICAL CONTROL

1 See Golden, *What Motivates*, 6 (stating that "the administrative presidency is distinguished by its use of this [ideological] appointments strategy at all levels of the organization . . . not only at the cabinet level but also . . . as far down into the bowels of the agency as the law will allow").

2 Of course, the elephant in this sentence is the assumption that elections are in fact conducted fairly and competently. A myriad of fundamental issues—some structurally ingrained in the Constitution, such as the Electoral College, and others not but just as fundamental, such as the persistence of racial discrimination in voting and the role of money in influencing electoral results—cause significant distortions in electoral results. This book brackets this major problem. More subtly, scholars question whether electoral choices in fact reflect policy preferences, as opposed to the public's estimation of economic conditions and the president's personal performance. See, e.g., Erikson and Wlezien, "Forecasting." Of course, none of this is even to mention more blatant attacks on fair elections, as were witnessed during and after the election of 2020.

3 Wilson, *Study*, 210 (1887) (arguing that administration should "lie outside the proper sphere of politics"); quoted in Mashaw, *Reasoned Administration*, 146 n.9.

4 See Mashaw, *Reasoned Administration*, 146 (describing the idea that administration and politics could be rigidly separated as "a cartoon of the Progressive vision"); ibid. ("Progressives did not necessarily believe that administration was a value-free enterprise. Their interest was in protecting the pursuit of public ends from partisanship, incompetence, and corruption."); Fisher and Shapiro, *Administrative Competence*, 139 ("Wilson . . . argued that the civil service would take its marching orders from the president and Congress, which linked public administration to democratically adopted legislation, political oversight, and the electoral process. The aim was to reduce, if not to eliminate, the role of crude politics in

the implementation of those policies, not to separate public administration from politics.").

5 U.S. Const. Art. II, §3.

6 See Mashaw, *Reasoned Administration*, 146–47 ("Administration in the American constitutional scheme has no independent constitutional basis. Administration is an artifact of—and subservient to—the political actors in Congress, who create and fund it and the President who appoints high-level personnel and has the constitutional duty to oversee implementation.").

7 Chapter 4 discusses congressional supervision via congressional grants of more limited authority. Other mechanisms of congressional oversight have been criticized as episodic and ineffective. See, e.g., Kagan, "Presidential Administration," 2256–60. For example, much congressional oversight has often been characterized as led by particularly interested congressmembers or committees, thus reducing any broader democratic accountability. See, e.g., Pierce and Shapiro, "Political and Judicial," 1207–9.

8 See Shane, "*Chevron* Deference," 691.

9 Shapiro, "Failure," 1099.

10 One can also understand a call for an autonomous bureaucratic voice in regulation as based in constitutional concerns. Jon Michaels, for example, defends that autonomous voice as a part of a system of de facto separated powers. See generally Michaels, *Constitutional Coup*.

11 The procedural fairness justification is particularly powerful when presidential control is set against administrative autonomy in the context of administrative adjudications. The statutorily and constitutionally required procedures agencies must follow when they adjudicate, and the deeply problematic prospect of presidential interference in adjudications justifies agency independence from presidential interference when agencies adjudicate. Indeed, as if recognizing the procedural fairness imperative, presidential regulatory review executive orders have regularly excluded agency adjudications from the White House review mandate.

But procedure impacts rulemaking, also. Scholars have suggested that, even in rulemaking, the statutorily required procedures agencies must follow mean that agencies "gather more public input and receive more public scrutiny, both of which tend to ensure that they will better assess public preferences." Bressman and Vandenburgh, "Inside," 83.

12 No doubt other mechanisms of presidential control exist—for example, White House influence on an agency's budget has been recognized as a tool for presidential influence. See, e.g., Pasachoff, "President's Budget." For space reasons, this book focuses on explicit regulatory influence, as with White House regulatory review and control over the personnel that play leading roles within agencies.

13 Review of this sort can impact public perceptions of agency action. For example, in 1976, the EPA Administrator, when asked about the result of any clash between the White House and the agency on a regulatory matter, was reported to have

insisted that the agency would prevail, "in part to protect what he sees as the 'regulatory integrity' of the agency in the eyes of the public, the Congress, and other federal agencies." Bureau of National Affairs, "Office of Management," 696 (quoting the Administrator).

14 See US Department of Justice, "Memorandum from U.S. Department of Justice," 3, in *Role of OMB*, 488.

15 See, e.g., ibid., 488–89.

16 U.S. Const. Art. II §§ 3, 1.

17 See, e.g., Calabresi and Yoo, *The Unitary Executive*.

18 See U.S. Const. Art. I § 8, cl. 18 (authorizing Congress to enact "all Laws which shall be necessary and proper for carrying into Execution the . . . Powers [previously specified in Article I] and all other Powers vested by this Constitution in the Government of the United States, or in any Department or Officer thereof"); *Seila Law LLC v. Consumer Financial Protection Bureau*, 140 S.Ct. 2183, 2224 (2020) (Kagan, J., dissenting) (making this argument).

19 See Memorandum from U.S. Department of Justice, 4 ("Of course, the fact that the President has both constitutional and implied statutory authority to supervise decisionmaking by Executive Branch agencies does not delimit the extent of permissible supervision. It does suggest, however, that supervision is more readily justified when it does not purport wholly to displace, but only to guide and limit, discretion which Congress has allocated to a particular subordinate official.").

20 See US President, "Federal Regulation," §§ 2, 3(a), 3(f)(3), 5(b), 6(a), 7(c), 7(e), 7(g).

21 See, e.g., Percival, "Who's in Charge?," 2504 (discussing studies of OIRA's Reagan-era regulatory review practices that found evidence of OIRA seeking to delay the promulgation of regulations with which it disagreed).

22 See Percival, "Checks," 165 n.221.

23 See US President, "Regulatory Planning and Review," § 9 ("Nothing in this order shall be construed as displacing the agencies' authority or responsibilities, as authorized by law.").

24 See ibid., § 7.

25 See, e.g., Percival, "Who's in Charge?," 2504–5 (discussing *Environmental Defense Fund v. Thomas*, 627 F.Supp. 566 (D.D.C. 1986), in which the court found that OIRA had blocked EPA from promulgating a rule in time to meet a congressionally imposed deadline).

26 See US President, "Regulatory Planning and Review," §1(a) (Clinton order, specifying "equity"); US President, "Improving Regulation and Regulatory Review," §1(c) (Obama order, including "human dignity").

27 See *State v. BLM*, 286 F.Supp.3d 1054 (N.D. Cal. 2018) (finding the suspension to be arbitrary and capricious in part because it failed to provide a reasoned basis for reversing regulatory course).

28 See, e.g., Driesen, "Distributing," 9 ("The feasibility principle exemplified in [two Supreme Court cases construing regulatory statutes] generally requires strin-

gent regulation, but presumptively subjects this demand for stringency to two constraints. First, the principle authorizes government agencies to forego physically impossible environmental improvements. Second, the principle authorizes government agencies to forego constraints so costly that they cause widespread plant shutdowns.").

29 This is a long-standing phenomenon. See Percival, "Checks," 143 (citing a source identifying this problem as pre-dating the Carter administration).

30 See, e.g., Wagner, "A Place," 2055–56.

31 See Williams, *Mismanaging*, 94–97; ibid., 94 ("A long-standing complaint against analytic offices [such as OIRA] is that many of the bright, quantitatively oriented staff persons . . . have little or no understanding of or appreciation for organizational structure and procedure that are often critical factors in arriving at policy decisions.").

32 See Michaels, *Constitutional Coup*, 192 (describing it as "a major thumb on the scale at the last possible minute"); ibid., 193 (describing OIRA "swoop[ing] in and alter[ing] that which was already forged in the administrative arena"). To be clear, that moment isn't necessarily the very last one, as the executive orders in question mandate OIRA review at several stages of the rulemaking process, including the stage when a mere notice of proposed rulemaking is under consideration. Still, such notices are complex documents in themselves, thus arguably justifying Michaels's "last minute" description as applied to those preliminary, but still critical, documents. One might be tempted to cite the OSHA workplace exposure standard example, discussed earlier in this chapter, as an illustration of this last-minute dynamic, but the blame in that case appears to lay with OSHA submitting the regulation to OIRA only one day before the court-imposed deadline.

33 Bressman and Vandenbergh, "Inside," 70.

34 National Academy, *Presidential Management*, 38.

35 See, e.g., Nagareda, "*Ex parte*," 606–7.

36 See ibid., 608 (noting this effect).

37 Bressman and Vandenbergh, "Inside," 70.

38 See Blumstein, "Regulatory Review," 888.

39 See, e.g., Saiger, "Obama's Czars," 2588.

40 See Blumstein, "Regulatory Review," 889–893.

41 See Saiger, "Obama's Czars," 2584 (need to rein in agency heads); Blumstein, "Regulatory Review," 885–886.

42 See Steinzor, "The Case," 277.

43 See Nathan, *Administrative Presidency*, 28–29.

44 See Saiger, "Obama's Czars," 2592 (discussing scholars' views).

45 See Blumstein, "Regulatory Review," 885–86.

46 See generally Golden, *What Motivates*.

47 See Williams, *Mismanaging*, 13 (discussing one cabinet secretary's experience with such appointees).

48 See Bressman and Vandenburgh, "Inside," 70.

49 See Wagner, "A Place," 2051–52; ibid., 2052 n.163.
50 See generally, e.g., Steinzor, "The Case" (presenting the case for abolishing OIRA regulatory review); Emerson and Michaels, "Abandoning," 444–45 (calling for it to be curtailed); Bressman and Vandenbergh, "Inside," 91–98 (offering suggestions for its overhauling).
51 See Steinzor, "The Case," 277–78.
52 See Shapiro and Schroeder, "Beyond Cost-Benefit," 479–82.
53 US President, "Regulatory Planning."
54 See Katzen, "OIRA at Thirty," 110 ("[T]he end result [of such White House coordination] would be better coordinated and coherent regulatory actions, and ultimately better decisionmaking.").
55 See, e.g., Steinzor, "The Case," 279–81.
56 See Administrative Conference, *Improving Coordination*.
57 See ibid., 43–46 (discussing OMB's role in encouraging such coordination); ibid., 42–43 (providing examples of other White House offices that can also encourage it).
58 Scholars have also identified other coordination roles White House offices may be able to play, such as the control OMB (OIRA's parent office) has over agencies' budgets. See Pasachoff, "President's Budget," 2246–50. Going beyond OMB, another possibility for imposing White House control and coordination of cabinet offices is the concept of cabinet councils, subject-matter groupings of cabinet secretaries led by the president, assisted by White House staff. See Williams, *Mismanaging*, 75–76 (discussing the Reagan-era experience with such councils).
59 See Kagan, "Presidential Administration," 2282–84.
60 See, e.g., Bressman and Vandenbergh, "Inside," 66 (noting responses to a survey of EPA personnel, indicating these other actors were perceived as playing important roles in influencing EPA regulations).
61 Kagan, "Presidential Administration," 2319.
62 She was not the first to make that move: The 1981 DOJ memo validating Reagan's OIRA review order also relied on supposed implied statutory authorization.
63 The answer to the legal question does not change if White House pressure is privately, rather than publicly, imposed. For most rulemakings, neither the Constitution nor the APA prohibits ex parte communications from anyone. See, e.g., *Action for Children's Television v. Federal Communications Comm'n*, 564 F.2d 458, 474 n.28 (D.C. Cir. 1977). See also *Sierra Club v. Costle*, 657 F.2d 298, 405–407 (D.C. Cir. 1981) (recognizing constitutional authority for confidential presidential contacts with agencies in informal rulemakings).
64 This discussion omits the possibility of the president's staff directing agency heads to take particular actions, given the complex constitutional concerns that might arise if the president sought to delegate whatever directive power he had to his staff. While a fascinating question, analysis of that issue would take us far afield. See Saiger, "Obama's Czars," 2605–9 (discussing this issue).
65 See, e.g., Saiger, "Obama's Czars," 2588 (noting this argument).

66 See, e.g., Calabresi, "Normative Arguments," 58–70; ibid., 81–86.

67 Criddle, "Fiduciary Administration," 456–57.

68 See Kagan, "Presidential Administration," 2308; Farina, "Chief Executive," 185 ("sporadic and fortuitous"); ibid. (presidential time constraints). Indeed, even presidential interest in the more programmatic topic of agency agenda-setting has been described as episodic and more concerned with public relations than with systematic White House influence over agencies' regulatory plans. See Coglianese and Walters, "Agenda-Setting," 108.

69 See, e.g., Shane, *Madison's Nightmare*, 161.

70 See, e.g., Erikson and Wlezien, "Forecasting" (effect of economic conditions); Shane, *Madison's Nightmare*, 161 (same); Michaels, *Constitutional Coup*, 92–93 (Reagan).

71 Kagan, "Presidential Administration," 2308.

72 See Bressman and Vandenbergh, "Inside," 83; see also Saiger, "Obama's Czars," 2590 (suggesting this in particular about Obama's czars, given how he selected them).

73 See Bressman and Vandenbergh, "Inside," 83–84.

74 Ironically, the Interstate Commerce Commission, the agency generally regarded as the model for this type of agency, was originally structured with more political oversight. See Breger and Edles, *Independent Agencies*, 30–33.

75 See Kagan, "Presidential Administration," 2308–9.

76 See, e.g., ibid., 2278 n.124; ibid., 2288.

77 See, e.g., ibid., 2347.

78 See Vermeule, "Conventions," 1179–81.

79 See, e.g., Bressman and Vandenburgh, "Inside," 70 (concluding that "[e]ven if such [idiosyncratic or episodic White House attention to agency action] promotes accountability on a limited basis, the concern is that it may not promote rationality in a systematic way, as a model of agency decision-making should").

80 See, e.g., Shane, *Madison's Nightmare*, 164 ("the President's capacity to tell subordinate administrators what to do is far more likely to inhibit, rather than advance, robust intrabranch policy debate") (citing Luneberg, "Civic Republicanism," 403–4).

81 But see Saiger, "Obama's Czars," 2612 (broaching a version of this possibility).

82 See Pasachoff, "President's Budget."

83 Perhaps surprisingly, scholars have found little empirical evidence speaking to the actual effect of White House influence. See Coglianese and Walters, "Agenda-Setting," 109–10; ibid., 110 ("One major challenge [in studying the effect of external institutions on agencies' agenda-setting decisions] derives from the lack of clear counterfactuals, or what agencies' agendas would have looked like in the absence of one or more of those outside institutions.").

84 See Shane, *Madison's Nightmare*, 164 ("To achieve public interest-centered dialogue within the executive, it is important not to tighten the reins on subordinates excessively, but to provide incentives for administrators to speak freely and for the

President actually to listen to diverse voices despite the predictable dominance of his own.").

85 DeMuth and Ginsburg, "Rationalism," 906.

86 See Kagan, "Presidential Administration," 2342–46; id., 2341 (quoting Hamilton).

87 See Mashaw, "Recovering," 1304 (recounting attempts by presidents since Washington to influence the bureaucracy).

88 Kagan, "Presidential Administration," 2356 (concluding that the differing perspectives of presidents, White House staffers, agency heads, and agencies themselves "counsel hesitation both in acknowledging and asserting presidential authority in areas of administration in which professional knowledge has a particularly needed and significant function"). To be sure, her concession appears focused on situations requiring significant agency *technical* expertise. See ibid.

89 See National Commission, *Urgent Business*, 18 (numbers up to 2001); Piaker, *Help Wanted* (number in 2016).

90 See Ingraham, *Foundation*, 97–105.

91 See O'Connell, "Vacant Offices," 919–20.

92 See, e.g., O'Connell, "Actings," 707 n.512 (noting the additional confirmation delays faced by sub-agency head administrative positions).

93 See Williams, *Mismanaging*, 141.

94 See Hiatt, "For Biden."

95 See Lewis, "Testing."

96 Verkuil, *Outsourcing*, 166–168.

97 National Commission, *Urgent Business*, 20.

98 For example, the Republican campaign strategist Lee Atwater was reported to believe strongly that young campaign staffers should be rewarded with Schedule C political appointee positions. See Wheaton, "Obama." As if to illustrate the raw political patronage aspects of at least some of these appointments, one Schedule C appointee in the State Department who worked on the 2016 Trump campaign was arrested in connection with the January 6, 2021 insurrection at the Capitol. See Gerstein, "Trump Appointee."

99 See Shapiro and Wright, "Future," 577 ("The administrative presidency seeks to rein in bureaucratic discretion by centralizing decision-making in the White House and by sending vast numbers of political appointees into the agencies to monitor and control the bureaucrats.").

100 See Williams, *Mismanaging*, 13; ibid., 84–85 (describing Bell's account). Scholar Paul Light was quoted as saying about such appointees during the Reagan years that "[t]hey are ideologically committed. There is no allegiance to the department, but to the Oval Office or the conservative cause. No administration has penetrated so deeply." Ibid., 75 (quoting Light being quoted in Smith, *Power Game*, 303). See also ibid., 85 (quoting an interviewee who served on a congressional staff who noted the tendency of ideologically motivated officials within the Education Department "to give studies to their friends to 'prove' their ideological positions").

CHAPTER 6. RELATIONSHIPS WITHIN THE AGENCY

1 Kennedy, "Do This!," 61 (quoting Rudalevige, "Executive Orders," 157).

2 See Golden, *What Motivates*, 20–25. See also Niskanen, *Bureaucracy* (arguing that bureaucrats will over-regulate in order to build an empire).

3 See Golden, *What Motivates*, 20–25.

4 Lewis, *Fifth Risk*, 41 (emphasis in original).

5 See, e.g., Garand et al., "Bureaucrats," 182–83.

6 See Golden, *What Motivates*, 62–63.

7 See, e.g., Garand et al., "Bureaucrats," 183. Still, this study found the "socialization" model to be not as powerful as one in which bureaucrats have preexisting political views that motivate them to enter government service. See ibid., 200.

8 See Nathan, *Administrative Presidency*, 69–76 (noting President Reagan's focus on ideological compatibility when selecting his political appointees).

9 See, e.g., Golden, *What Motivates*, 73–74 (self-preservation conduct at FNS).

10 See, e.g., ibid., 49–50 (public servant conduct at NHTSA); Shapiro and Wright, "Future," 602 (reaching similar conclusions more generally).

11 See Hirschman, *Exit*.

12 See Golden, *What Motivates*, 91–92 (discussing internal policy debates at the CRD); ibid., 75 (discussing leaks at the FNS); ibid., 128–29 (discussing leaks at EPA). "Loyalty" would consist of remaining with or in the unsatisfactory institution or situation, hoping that matters would improve. See ibid., 18–19.

13 See, e.g., ibid., 52–54 (neglect at NHTSA).

14 Indeed, that meshing extended to agency leaders embracing externally imposed limits on the agency's autonomy. See, e.g., ibid., 119 (observing that the first Reagan-era head of the EPA welcomed White House regulatory review of her agency's proposed regulations).

15 See ibid., 121–22.

16 See ibid., 45–46 (pushing drafting duties upward); ibid., 69 (excluding career staffers).

17 See ibid., 137–46.

18 See ibid., 106 (CRD); ibid., 80 (NHTSA and FNS).

19 *Motor Veh. Mfrs. Ass'n v. State Farm Mut. Ins. Co.*, 463 U.S. 29 (1983).

20 See Golden, *What Motivates*, 49–50.

21 That discursive process creates better regulations not just because it incorporates the views of the agencies' experts, but also because it does so within a process that allows for questioning and debating of those views. That process thus ensures accountability for the decisions the agency ultimately makes and the reasons it gives for them. See Fisher and Shapiro, *Administrative Competence*, 93–95.

22 Golden, *What Motivates*, 23.

23 During the Reagan years, a common refrain among his allies was to "let Reagan be Reagan"—that is, allow him to be his authentic conservative self.

24 To be sure, this simple dichotomy between expert careerists and not-so-expert political appointees elides considerable complexity about particular types of ca-

reerist expertise. To use the NHTSA example, auto engineers may have expertise relevant to the agency's mission, but so might the agency's lawyers; whether one or the other becomes the dominant "careerist" position on an issue will turn on a variety of factors. For example, after NHTSA lost several important court cases in the 1970s, lawyers became ascendant in the agency's decisional process, and engineers faded into the background. See Mashaw and Harfst, "From Command," 181.

25 McGarity, "Internal Structure," 61.

26 See, e.g., ibid., 70–73 (describing that process); Wagner, "A Place," 2031 (discussing the framing issue). Indeed, Professor Wagner suggests that the initial framing decision should be made by policymakers. See ibid., 2062 ("Policymakers . . . should formulate the questions that technical analysts research, but the job of assembling and evaluating the quality of the evidence bearing on the question(s) is appropriately conducted by agency experts.").

27 See Golden, *What Motivates*, 70.

28 See Revkin, "Cheney's Office."

29 See, e.g., Dearen and Stobbe, "Trump Administration."

30 See Davenport and Landler, "Trump Administration."

31 See McGarity and Wagner, "Deregulation," 1785–1800.

32 Ibid., 1796.

33 See ibid., 1784.

34 See ibid., 1797.

35 McGarity and Wagner suggest ideas such as these, which are discussed at the end of this chapter.

36 See Wagner, "A Place," 2066.

37 Reilly-Diakun, "Addressing."

38 See Wagner, "Science Charade," 1618–1627 (providing examples of situations like these).

39 Reilly-Diakun, "Addressing," 223.

40 See ibid.

41 See Wagner, "Science Charade," 1654–73 (discussing these and other incentives agencies may have for scientizing policy).

42 Indeed, it is probably also the case that agency leaders simply will not always know how useful or problematic the information their researchers develop will turn out to be.

43 See, e.g., Reilly-Diakun, "Addressing," 222–24 (considering such suggestions). For a more general example of such guidelines that attempt to balance similarly nuanced considerations in the context of a similarly complex problem—separating an agency's adjudicative functions from other functions the agency plays—see *Separation of Functions*, 101 FERC 61,340 (2002).

44 See Goldman et al., "Perceived Losses," 13–14. Smaller but still significant percentages of experts from other agencies similarly disagreed with the statement. See ibid. This survey is further discussed in chapter 8.

45 See Golden, *What Motivates*, 121–26.

46 5 U.S.C. §2302(a)(2)(D).

47 Ibid.

48 See, e.g., *Daniels v. MSPB*, 832 F.3d 1049, 1054–1055 (9th Cir. 2016) ("An [agency official], who makes an erroneous decision, does not violate the law (or engage in gross mismanagement) any more than does a district judge who is subsequently reversed on appeal.").

49 See, e.g., 2 *Foreign Affairs Manual* 070 (Dissent Channel). See also Doremus, "Scientific," 1645 (discussing the State Department's dissent channel and its possible applicability to other agencies).

50 See Van Schooten and Schwellenbach, "Stifling."

51 See generally Francis, *Statutory*.

52 IGs can also investigate violations of dissent channels' non-retaliation protections. See generally Van Schooten and Schwellenbach, "Stifling."

53 US Dept of Interior Office of Inspector General, *Investigative Report*.

54 See Doremus, "Scientific," 1604–5. An option incorporating elements of both dissent channels and IGs entails establishment of what Professor Holly Doremus calls "scientific ombudsmen." These would be offices located outside of any existing agency, staffed by persons who understand the relationship between experts and policymakers, to whom agency staffers can take concerns about inappropriate political interference in agency operations. The difficulty here is with the powers such an office should wield. Professor Doremus suggests these offices have power to require the agency to review the complained-of conduct, pass such complaints along to Congress, or even draft reports that would become part of the administrative record a court would examine in a challenge to the infected rule. See ibid., 1645–46. These provocative suggestions raise difficult questions about workability (in particular, the suggestion that agencies be required to evaluate concerns made by ombudsmen) and usefulness (the suggestion that such concerns be passed along to congressional oversight committees). The judicial review possibility raises an interesting prospect. Chapter 7 examines the appropriate burden of explanation that courts should impose on agencies when a regulation is challenged as insufficiently grounded in regulatory expertise.

CHAPTER 7. JUDICIAL REVIEW

1 See *Roe v. Wade*, 410 U.S. 113 (1973).

2 See, e.g., *Webster v. Doe*, 486 U.S. 592 (1988) (considering a claim that the CIA director acted unconstitutionally when he terminated an analyst because of the analyst's sexual orientation).

3 The Constitution, in particular, the Fifth Amendment's Due Process Clause, also regulates agency procedures when the agency acts as an adjudicator. When the agency in question is a state agency, the Fourteenth Amendment's Due Process Clause steps into the shoes of the Fifth Amendment's analogous clause.

    Agencies also take many important regulatory steps that do not create binding law. For example, an agency may "merely" issue a document that expresses its view about how it will approach a particular regulatory question, without purporting to endow that approach with legally binding status. Such "guidance documents" may be quite important for regulated entities and the public, given the unmistakable signals they often send about an agency's attitude toward a given regulatory issue. Nevertheless, they are not formally law and the APA exempts them from any procedural requirements.

4 This chapter does not discuss fact-finding separately from policymaking. As the chapter will make clear, however, agency fact-finding is governed by the same standard as its overall policymaking function. Thus, in most cases of rulemaking, agency fact-finding, just like its policymaking, must not be arbitrary and capricious.

5 5 U.S.C. § 706(2)(A)–(D). Section 706 authorizes reviewing courts to take other actions as well, but the ones cited in the text comprise the lion's share of situations involving judicial review.

6 See, e.g., *Pacific States Box & Basket Co. v. White*, 296 U.S. 176 (1935). See also Mashaw, *Reasoned Administration*, 8 ("pre-New Deal administrative law had relatively thin rationality requirements"); Fisher and Shapiro, *Administrative Competence*, 159–61 (discussing the deference courts extended to agency decisions during this era).

7 See *Citizens to Preserve Overton Park v. Volpe*, 401 U.S. 402 (1971) (reviewability); *Association of Data Processing Serv. Orgs. v. Camp*, 397 U.S. 150 (1970) (broadening standing under the APA); *United States v. SCRAP*, 412 U.S. 669 (1973) (broadening standing under the Constitution); *Abbott Laboratories v. Gardner*, 387 U.S. 136 (1967) (timing). During this period courts also expanded the procedural rights persons enjoyed when agencies withdrew important government benefits. See *Goldberg v. Kelly*, 397 U.S. 254 (1970).

8 See generally Stewart, "Reformation."

9 435 U.S. 519 (1978).

10 See, e.g., Stewart, "*Vermont Yankee*," 1816–1818 (describing *Vermont Yankee* as "unsound" and "self-contradictory," and leveling other criticisms).

11 See, e.g., *United States v. Nova Scotia Food Products Corp.*, 568 F.2d 240 (2d Cir. 1977); *Portland Cement Ass'n v. Ruckelshaus*, 486 F.2d 375 (D.C. Cir. 1973).

12 See Fisher and Shapiro, *Administrative Competence*, 201.

13 *Int'l Harvester Co. v. Ruckelshaus*, 478 F.2d 615, 652 (D.C. Cir. 1973) (Bazelon, C.J., concurring).

14 See, e.g., Krotoszynski, "History," 999.

15 For a deeper discussion of the different questions arbitrary and capricious review asks, see generally Virelli, *Deconstructing*.

16 See Mashaw, *Reasoned Administration*, 111 ("Whether an administrator has given a reason that addresses a relevant consideration, been responsive to issues raised by participants, or collected a sufficient evidentiary base for reasoned judgment, depends upon how those issues are framed. And a reviewing court's vision of how the agency should have framed the questions for resolution is vir-

tually indistinguishable from a judgment about what is required for substantive reasonableness.").

17 463 U.S., 51.

18 The data showed that seat belt usage did in fact increase with the cars specially equipped with automatic seat belts (that is, seat belts that, when buckled, remain engaged indefinitely until a driver unbuckles them). But the agency concluded that that increased usage could not be extrapolated to the general public, because it was a relatively small increase and the sample group (purchasers of the specially equipped cars, who paid extra money for the automatic seat belt option) was presumably more safety-conscious than the general public. The Court rejected this reasoning, observing that automatic seat belts had the advantage of inertia—that is, they stayed buckled until the user affirmatively disengaged them. See 463 U.S., 54. The four-justice partial dissent found the agency's reasoning adequate to satisfy arbitrary and capricious review, even if it was "by no means a model." Ibid., 58 (Rehnquist, J., concurring in part and dissenting in part).

19 Scholars disagree about the meaning lawyers and agencies should accord *State Farm*. Adrian Vermeule concludes that *State Farm*'s stringent review is an outlier and that most Supreme Court and lower court scrutiny of agency policymaking is much more deferential. See Vermeule, *Law's Abnegation*, 157–60. Other scholars counter that, even assuming Vermeule is correct, *State Farm* essentially scares agencies into indulging in more intricate and costly reasoning exercises. See, e.g., Lieb, "Also, No," 271–72.

20 The term "ossification" dates to a 1992 article. McGarity, "Some Thoughts," 1419. See also Seidenfeld, "Long Shadow," 581 ("the review that has most often been accused of ossifying agency action is what most scholars would deem substantive review under the reasoned decisionmaking standard laid out in *State Farm*").

21 See Pierce, "Judicial Review," 72–75 (describing a case where poor agency performance was attributable to the agency's lack of funding); ibid., 88 ("If the courts adopt [a] rigid adherence to demanding administrative law doctrines . . . the judiciary will contribute significantly to both the reality and the perception of poor performance by underfunded agencies.").

22 See 463 U.S., 50–51.

23 See, e.g., *NLRB v. Wyman-Gordon Co.*, 394 U.S. 759, 779 (1969) (Douglas, J., dissenting) ("the survival of a questionable rule seems somewhat more likely when it is submerged in the facts of a given case") (internal quotation omitted); Pierce, "Two Problems," 301 ("[C]ourts are less demanding when they review agency policymaking undertaken through ad hoc adjudication of specific cases."); Mashaw and Harfst, "Legal Culture," 302–9 (explaining why NHTSA was so much more successful in its case-by-case automobile recall litigation than its rulemaking litigation).

24 See, e.g., Vermeule, *Law's Abnegation*, 157–60.

25 See, e.g., Sitaraman, "Foreign Hard Look," 505 n.70 (citing scholars taking this position).

26 For a somewhat related but distinct approach to judicial review, one that is focused on reinforcing not simply expertise but the author's vision of how agency action implements foundational ideas about the separation of powers, see Michaels, *Constitutional Coup*, 179–201.

27 For an analogous proposal, cast in broader, constitutional terms, see ibid., 182 ("Consider . . . a court that suspects civil servants weren't given their due in an administrative proceeding. . . . That court . . . may apply a particularly demanding version of arbitrariness review—or altogether withhold deference. Withholding or limiting deference punishes agencies that either never delved especially deeply into, among other things, the science, sociology, or economics of a given rule or disregarded those expert findings.").

28 Cf. *Sierra Club v. Costle*, 657 F.2d 298, 408 (D.C. Cir. 1981) ("[I]t is always possible that undisclosed Presidential prodding may direct an [administrative] outcome that is factually based on the record, but different from the outcome that would have obtained in the absence of Presidential involvement. In such a case, it would be true that the political process did affect the outcome in a way the courts could not police. But we do not believe that Congress intended that the courts convert informal rulemaking into a rarified technocratic process, unaffected by political considerations or the presence of Presidential power."). While *Sierra Club* dealt with presidential influence on rulemaking, the same principle—that political considerations necessarily play a role in administrative actions—applies to political considerations emanating from agency leaders themselves, rather than the president.

29 See Araiza, "In Praise."

30 *State Farm*, 463 U.S., 43 (internal quotations omitted).

31 See Golden, *What Motivates*, 50 ("Most interviewees were convinced that [the agency head] had acted unilaterally on this decision, disregarding staff advice. . . . The telling aspect of this episode is the comment that consistently followed the recounting of the episode, the gist of which was that if [the agency head] had let the careerists write the order rescinding the regulation, it would not have been dismissed by the Supreme Court as 'arbitrary and capricious.' . . . Careerists told me that if they had had the opportunity, that is, if they had not been excluded from the process, they would have used their expertise to write an effective rescission order, one complete with the type of evidence and arguments that could have withstood the Court's scrutiny.").

32 Garland, "Deregulation."

33 Ibid., 530 (describing *Vermont Yankee* as a decision about "purely procedural" requirements); ibid., 543–45 (citing the "quasi-procedural" aspects of *State Farm*); ibid., 545 (explaining the Court's rejection of the government's *Vermont Yankee* argument); ibid., 545–49 (citing *State Farm*'s "substantive" aspects).

34 Ibid., 530.

35 An additional problem with focusing judicial review directly on agency compliance with any such procedures is that the agency may violate some of these pro-

cedures without those defaults necessarily being problematic from an expertise perspective. For example, in March 2021, the EPA's Inspector General released a report documenting non-compliance with that agency's procedural guidelines for rulemaking. See US EPA, Office of the Inspector General, *EPA*. Some of those violations resulted from confusion about the process, lack of clarity about which officials could legally ignore some requirements, and data entry problems. See ibid., 16–17. Focusing judicial review on such failures, if those failures are relatively trivial or reflect inadvertent non-compliance with vaguely worded requirements, raises the risk of focusing judicial review on technical errors that say little about the effectiveness of the agency's use of its expertise. Moreover, a strict judicial focus on enforcing the letter of such procedural rules might lead courts to ignore more serious process issues that such rules do not formally address.

36 565 U.S. 42, 52 n.7 (2011).

37 Readers wishing to confirm the similarity of agencies' analyses in cases involving policymaking and the interpretation of ambiguous statutes should recall chapter 4's discussion of *King v. Burwell*, the Affordable Care Act tax credits case. In *King*, the Court, after refusing to accord *Chevron* deference to the agency because of the importance of the underlying issue, set about to interpret the statute itself. After conceding that the statute was ambiguous, it ultimately settled on an interpretation based on its reasoning about the policy impacts of the two alternative interpretations on the table. In other words, in performing its own statutory interpretation of an ambiguous statute, the Court did what agencies do when confronted with ambiguous statutes—it engaged in policy reasoning.

38 See 467 U.S., 865–66.

39 This happy equivalence may not last much longer. In recent years, individual justices on the Court have grown uncomfortable with *Chevron*. Thus, at some future point the Court may reject *Chevron* deference in favor of a judicial rule of no deference to the agency, even when it interprets an ambiguous statute. How such a lack of deference would fit next to *Chevron*'s own statement that such interpretations reflect policymaking, thus justifying judicial review that looks like arbitrary and capricious review, and how it would fit with *Judulang*'s insistence that *Chevron* deference review is indeed the same as arbitrary and capricious review, constitute fascinating topics that are best left to another day.

40 For example, a note in chapter 6 pointed out an agency's attempt to provide general guidelines governing similarly nuanced decisions about separating an agency's adjudicative function, and those who support it, from other functions the agency performs. See *Separation of Functions*, 101 FERC 61,340 (2002).

41 Indeed, beyond disserving agencies' democratic accountability, such cloaking also discredits expertise, by exposing the agency's phony expert analysis to critique.

42 Such "minimal reasonableness" is necessary, even when an agency forthrightly cites politics as the reason for its action, because a truly irrational agency action simply cannot be saved by an agency's blunt statement that "that's what we got elected to do." Rejecting such a statement as inadequate does not disserve

democracy. Beyond the more conceptual objection that democracy should be understood as more than the simple aggregation of voting results at a particular point in time (an objection discussed in chapter 10), the practical fact is that the law the agency is irrationally implementing was *also* the product of a democratic process—the legislative process. Ignoring that law, or applying it irrationally, disserves *that* democratic process. To state the point somewhat differently, the democratic legislative process, by commanding the agency to use its expertise, it-self limits the role of politics by requiring agency action that satisfies at least some minimal standard of expertise.

43 To be sure, a decision may be "fully supported" by agency expertise even when that expertise allows the agency head a range of possible ultimate choices. In other words, the requirement that expertise "fully support" the agency's decision does not necessarily mean that that expertise commands one and only one ulti-mate choice. On the other hand, presumably in most cases a requirement of such expertise does take certain options off the table.

44 See, e.g., *New York v. Salazar*, 701 F.Supp.2d 224, 236 (N.D.N.Y. 2010) (the "weight of authority holds that '[a] complete administrative record . . . does not include privileged materials, such as documents that fall within the deliberative process privilege.").

45 See, e.g., *Ad Hoc Metals Coalition v. Whitman*, 227 F. Supp. 2d 134, 143 (D.D.C. 2002) ("Judicial review of agency action should be based on an agency's stated justifications, not the predecisional process that led up to the final, articulated decision. . . . [A]gency actions are judged based on what was decided, not on what was considered.").

46 See, e.g., Wagner, "Science in Regulation," 116 ("In . . . a decision process [that ranges over years and 'multiple different analytic documents, notice and com-ment processes, and . . . scientific discourse over the scientific information'] the final decision document is simply the conclusion or ending. Without these earlier chapters, one is unlikely to be able to reconstruct the analysis that preceded it.").

47 See Davenport, "Trump's."

48 Of course, if the documents were not altered, and they supported the agency action, there would be no reason for the court to be suspicious, thus opening the way to more deferential judicial review.

49 347 U.S. 483 (1954).

50 See generally Rosenberg, *Hollow Hope*.

51 See *SEC v. Chenery Corp.*, 332 U.S. 194 (1947).

52 To be sure, policy decisions made via adjudications are also susceptible to hard look review. But, as this chapter noted earlier, adjudications allow agencies to cloak policy decisions in a veil of particularized facts, which may well frustrate full-bore hard look review.

53 See, e.g., Anthony, "Interpretive Rules," 1333–55 (describing how agencies use policy documents to avoid the possibility of judicial review).

54 See generally Magill, "Agency Choice," 1383 (discussing different modalities).
55 *Sierra Club v. Costle*, 657 F.2d 298, 408 (D.C. Cir. 1981) ("Presidential prodding"); ibid., 405–408 (Article II considerations).
56 See ibid., 408 ("[I]t is always possible that undisclosed Presidential prodding may direct an outcome that is factually based on the record, but different from the outcome that would have obtained in the absence of Presidential involvement. In such a case, it would be true that the political process did affect the outcome in a way the courts could not police. But we do not believe that Congress intended that the courts convert informal rulemaking into a rarified technocratic process, unaffected by political considerations or the presence of Presidential power.").
57 See 435 U.S., 546–47.
58 Indeed, Professor Golden identified demands for yet more study and information as one of the tools used by NHTSA's political leadership when it sought to delay regulations. See Golden, *What Motivates*, 46.
59 For an analogous proposal in the context of *presidential* political preferences, see Kagan, "Presidential Administration," 2377.
60 See Golden, *What Motivates*, 137–46.

CHAPTER 8. PROTECTING INFORMATIONAL INTEGRITY

1 See Merriam-Webster, "Information Age."
2 Goldman et al., "Perceived Losses." Chapter 6 briefly mentioned this study.
3 Ibid., 10 (first set of numbers), 16–17 (second set), 13–14 (third set).
4 Ibid., 14, 18. The FDA was the outlier agency on this question.
5 See ibid., 20.
6 See Berman and Carter, "Policy Analysis" (Eisenhower, Johnson, and Nixon episodes); Mintz, "Energy" (Carter episode).
7 See, e.g., Weiland, "'How the C.D.C.'" (recounting efforts by Trump administration officials to interfere with the CDC's research and information dissemination, including the agency's Morbidity and Mortality Weekly Report).
8 See Goldman et al., "Perceived Losses," 12–16 (exclusion, budget cuts, and overall sense of not being valued).
9 Ibid., 13.
10 US President, "Restoring Trust," § 2(b)(i).
11 See, e.g., McGarity, "Internal Structure," 70 (noting that EPA rules originate in a "program office" headed by a politically appointed assistant administrator and identifying that individual's role); ibid., 72 (noting the role played in initiating rules by a "steering committee" comprised of high-level representatives of political appointees); Wagner, "A Place," 2062.
12 See McGarity and Wagner, "Deregulation," 1793.
13 See Human Rights Watch, *Coal Mine* (political influence); Kendall, *Letter* (Inspector General statements).
14 See Sabin Center, "10 Year."
15 See Trager, "US Funder."

16 US EPA, "Strengthening Transparency."

17 Indeed, the final EPA rule further tightened its limitations on use of privately generated data, in a way that would have impacted the agency's other scientific outputs. See ibid. See also "Letter from 39 Research Organizations."

18 See US EPA, "Strengthening Transparency," 493.

19 Recall that chapter 7 called for closer judicial scrutiny of ostensibly expertise-based decisions that appeared to be actually grounded in unacknowledged political motivations. That same justification for doubting the agency's claimed expertise foundation surfaces in this situation as well.

20 *Envt'l Def. Fund v. Envt'l Prot. Agency*, 2021 WL 270246 (D. Mont. Jan. 27, 2021) (merits decision); *Envt'l Def. Fund v. Envt'l Prot. Agency*, 2021 WL 402824 (D. Mont. Feb. 1, 2021) (vacating the rule).

21 For example, the George W. Bush administration imposed centralized guidance on how agencies should conduct peer review, a move that many criticized as skewing peer review toward industry-funded peer reviewers. See Berman and Carter, "Policy Analysis," 12.

22 See *West Va. State Board of Educ. v. Barnette*, 319 U.S. 624, 633 (1943).

23 In First Amendment law, government compulsion of one of its scientists to say something she wishes not to say triggers two related but distinct doctrinal issues: limits on government's ability to compel speech and the speech rights of government employees. See Fisk and Chemerinsky, "Political Speech" (discussing these issues).

24 See, e.g., Doremus, "Scientific," 1604–1609 (providing examples).

25 Hansen, "Political Interference," 4.

26 Berman and Carter, "Policy Analysis," 11; Doremus, "Scientific," 1648 n.244 (identifying additional instances of similar interference and distortion).

27 See Wagner and McGarity, "Deregulation," 1741.

28 See Jaffe, "Media Reports."

29 See Rosenberg, "CDC" (quoting Deborah Berkowitz, a worker safety expert at the National Employment Law Project).

30 See Shapiro, Steinzor, and Shudz, "Regulatory Dysfunction," 13 ("White House involvement in the development of [technical EPA chemical profiles] is a power grab that discredits EPA's scientific experts").

31 See Doremus, "Scientific," 1611–12.

32 See, e.g., Weiland et al., "Political Appointees" (noting that CDC researchers considered resigning in the face of political interference). Consider also the statement of one respondent to a 2006 Union of Concerned Scientists survey, addressing the situation at the US Geological Survey:

> Regarding objectivity of USGS BRD GCR, to date we have had little scrutiny of our research I suspect largely out of lack of interest. However, as has been covered in the journal *Science* and others, biologists working especially with endangered species have not been so fortunate. But the review of all USGS research results including even mundane annual progress reports

is now subject to 'policy' review at two levels within USGS centers, and it is proposed for the same at the regional USGS level. . . . This process is, of course, cumbersome, does little if anything to help the quality of science, and is easily subject to increased checks on content. If I were staying within USGS research, this would be much [*sic*] concern to me. It, along with little or no research support within USGS, is the major source of poor morale. I am fortunate in being able to leave the Federal Government, and return to the university which I will be doing shortly. (Union of Concerned Scientists, *Federal Climate*)

To be sure, the likelihood and magnitude of this exodus dynamic turns on other factors as well. For example, Professor Golden's study of NHTSA suggested that automotive engineers within that agency tended to stay with it despite problematic aspects of the Reagan administration's leadership, because the economic difficulties then being experienced by the auto industry reduced the availability of comparable jobs outside the agency. See Golden, *What Motivates*, 51. Compare ibid., 96–98; ibid., 102 (noting more of a brain drain at the Department of Justice Civil Rights Division, with Professor Golden suggesting that the more robust market for lawyers helped make those attorneys more willing to leave as a result of disagreements with the agency's direction).

33 See Shapiro et al., "Regulatory Dysfunction," 12–13.

34 See, e.g., McGarity and Wagner, "Deregulation," 1729–33 (providing other examples).

35 See ibid., 1730.

36 See, e.g., Shapiro, "OMB," 1086–87 (noting attempts made by the George W. Bush administration to suppress dissemination of government scientific knowledge); Percival, "Checks," 137 (noting a Nixon administration OMB Circular "which required agencies to submit proposed testimony, reports, or legislation to OMB prior to their transmission to Congress").

37 Glicksman, "Shuttered Government," 602. See generally Webb et al., "When Politics."

38 See Meyer, "We Knew."

39 Many of those reasons are set forth in the exemptions from the disclosure requirement mandated by the Freedom of Information Act (FOIA), 5 U.S.C. § 552. While FOIA is certainly relevant to this chapter's general information disclosure discussion, its structure, based on private citizens' requests for information rather than proactive government disclosure of it, raises distinct issues.

40 See also Glicksman, "Shuttered Government," 611–14 (discussing the Trump administration's attempt to limit the circumstances under which the Endangered Species Act requires agencies to consult with wildlife protection agencies about ways proposed agency actions can be changed to limit damage to threatened species).

41 For examples of such claims, see Hsu and Johnson, "White House Refuses"; Werner, "White House Asserts."

42 See *Trump v. Mazars USA, LLP*, 140 S.Ct. 2019, 2029–31 (2020) (noting this history).

43 See, e.g., Friedman, "EPA Cancels" (describing an EPA cancellation of talks EPA personnel had planned on giving at a conference on the future of Narragansett Bay, apparently because of the likely mention of climate change).

44 See, e.g., McGarity and Wagner, "Deregulation," 1756–67 (describing recent abuses of the scientific advisory committee process).

45 See, e.g., Coglianese, "Weak Democracy," 117 ("The local sanitation engineer for the City of Milwaukee . . . will probably have useful insights about how new EPA drinking water standards should be implemented that might not be apparent to the American Water Works Association representatives in Washington, DC.").

46 See, e.g., Eyal, *Crisis*, 39–40 (discussing the contributions of "lay experts").

47 See *Russell v. Dep't. of the Air Force*, 682 F.2d 1045, 1048 (D.C. Cir. 1982).

48 This justification becomes even less compelling if, as chapter 7's discussion of judicial review proposes, courts require agencies to submit pre-decisional documents to the court when a plaintiff challenges an agency action. Of course, public disclosure that is contemporaneous with the agency's deliberative process—that is, disclosure that occurs while the agency is still deliberating on the issue that information addresses—is different from the after-the-fact disclosure a court would require when a plaintiff challenges a finalized regulation.

49 See Environmental Data and Governance Initiative, "New Digital."

50 Lewis, *Fifth Risk*, 93.

51 For example, the Sunlight Foundation's Web Integrity Project works on ensuring that important information is not lost or suppressed when government websites are updated.

52 See, e.g., Doremus, "Scientific," 1643–44.

CHAPTER 9. NURTURING AND PROTECTING THE BUREAUCRACY

1 Wagner, "Isn't Easy," 1107 (2020).

2 See, e.g., Sklansky, "Private Police," 1206. For examples of individuals pursuing profits as part of their government work, see Parillo, *Against*. Thanks to Jon Michaels for that reference.

3 See Fisher and Shapiro, *Administrative Competence*, 106.

4 See generally Ingraham, *Foundation*, 20–23.

5 See ibid., 20–21. Moreover, scholars have observed that a spoils system helped assure that the bureaucracy was politically accountable to the executive. See, e.g., Fisher and Shapiro, *Administrative Competence*, 131.

6 See Ingraham, *Foundation*, 22 (noting examples of poor regulatory performance during and immediately after the Civil War).

7 See US Census Bureau, *Statistical Abstract 1960*, 392.

8 See DiIulio, *Bring Back*, 15.

9 Ibid.

10 See Aberbach and Rockman, "Clashing Beliefs" (bureaucrats' political preferences); Nathan, *Administrative Presidency*, 28–42 (shadow bureaucracy).

11 See, e.g., Michaels, *Constitutional Coup*, 92–93.

12 See, e.g., Banks and Lewis, "Federalism Disserved," 142 (arguing that deregulatory
   goals drove the Reagan administration's federalism program).

13 See Breton and Wintrobe, "Equilibrium Size," 196 (describing an influential theo-
   rist of bureaucratic behavior as basing his analysis on these assumptions about
   bureaucrats).

14 See Kosar, *Privatization*, 18.

15 See Light, *Government Ill Executed*, 190.

16 US Bureau of the Budget, "Circular A-76," 1.

17 Verkuil, *Valuing*, 19.

18 For space and focus reasons, this book's discussion of the federal government's
   use of private for-profit contractors omits mention of the related phenomena
   of the federal government devolving regulatory responsibilities onto states and
   achieving regulatory results by providing monetary grants to private parties, such
   as social service organizations who in turn provide social welfare services. These
   phenomena are significant. See, e.g., Guttman, "Public Purpose," 875 ("In form,
   the dominant public feature of social spending programs was (and is) federal
   grants-in-aid to state and local agencies and/or nonprofits."). For a discussion of
   both of these phenomena, see DiIulio, *Bring Back*.

19 See, e.g., *Use of Consultants Hearing*, 1 (statement of Sen. Pryor) (stating that EPA
   "relies on contractors to do everything from rule writing to rule enforcement");
   Guttman, "Public Purpose," 875–76 (citing a 1976 source recounting contractors
   evaluating grantee performance).

20 See Osborne and Gaebler, *Reinventing Government* 25–48 (discussing the steering
   and rowing concepts).

21 See Michaels, "War."

22 See Light, *Government Ill Executed*, 200.

23 To be sure, that statement also rested on the undeniable fact that *some* government regulatory programs, most notably the Clinton healthcare initiative, had
   failed to be enacted, and that others, most notably the federal welfare program,
   were being downsized and devolved to the states. Nevertheless, in other fields
   the Clinton administration retained (popular) government programs and even
   expanded them. But, as the quote suggests, President Clinton sought to combine
   those programs' continuation with equally popular restrictions on the size of the
   formal federal workforce.

24 See Light, *Government Ill Executed*, 197.

25 See ibid., 196–201. Hard data on the number of contractors are difficult to come
   by before the 1980s, and one prominent scholar of the bureaucracy has sought to
   estimate the number of federal contractors starting only in 1990. See ibid., 192–
   196.

26 See DiIulio, *Bring Back*, 83 (concluding that there are "too few federal bureaucrats chasing too many [outsourced] proxies and handling too many dollars"); Verkuil, *Valuing*, 65–66 (identifying this phenomenon as the culprit for bureaucratic failures).

27 See Verkuil, *Valuing*, 87–88.

28 See ibid., 85.

29 Outsourcing raises other issues as well. The introduction of an outside contractor into the agency's structure can exacerbate problems with effective control over how the contracted-for work is being carried out. For example, a post-mortem on the botched 2013 rollout of the federal healthcare website cited confusion between the responsibilities of agency officials with power to make changes to the relevant outsourcing contract and the authority of officials who actually monitored the contractor's work. See Health and Human Services Inspector General, "Healthcare.gov," 14.

30 See Verkuil, *Valuing*, 54, 70–72.

31 Ibid., 14–15 ("Not only is hiring [a contractor] easier, but firing is also, since contractors are replaceable if they don't work out.").

32 See Michaels, "War" ("Banishing [the bureaucracy] means jettisoning those willing and legally empowered to speak truth to power").

33 Lewis, *Premonition*, 289 n.*.

34 Tolchin and Tolchin, *Pinstripe Patronage*. See also Michaels, *Constitutional Coup*, 135 (drawing this same analogy).

35 See, e.g., Michaels, "Privatization's Pretensions," 749.

36 See ibid., 720–21.

37 See Sganga and Montoya-Galvez, "Homeland Security."

38 To be sure, the mischief caused by such policy-lock-in-by-contract extends beyond government decisions to contract out for regulatory services. To use Michaels' example, relatively few people would likely classify waste collection as an "inherently government function" of the sort for which Circular A-76 prohibits outsourcing, yet his example of a city's long-term contract with a private waste hauler demonstrates how outsourcing even such non-regulatory functions can nevertheless distort regulatory policy. Still, the potential damage from such outsourcing tactics can be mitigated by prohibiting the outsourcing of core government functions, however one defines them.

39 Verkuil, *Outsourcing*, 4.

40 See Verkuil, *Valuing*, 60–91 (policy disasters); ibid., 54; ibid., 70–72 (perverse incentives); DiIulio, *Bring Back*, 83 (lack of control over "steering"); Michaels, *Constitutional Coup*.

41 See Brown, "Public Laws," 622.

42 See ibid., 623–626.

43 *Use of Consultants Hearing*, 1 (EPA); Gerth, "Contractors' Role" (Department of Energy).

44 Verkuil, *Outsourcing*, 43.

45 Ibid., chs. 4–5. Recall from chapter 4 of this book the note discussing a 1936 case, *Carter v. Carter Coal*, where the Court, striking down a delegation of power to private entities, implied that the problem was a due process violation rather than a violation of the non-delegation doctrine. See chapter 4, note 12.

46 Ibid., 46; see also Michaels, *Constitutional Coup* (explaining the outsourcing issue as a matter of the constitutional separation of powers).

47 Indeed, many observers suspected that slowing the EPA's pace was exactly the point of the Trump EPA's Science Transparency rule, discussed in chapter 8, which would have limited the usability of much privately generated research.

48 For example, a 1962 federal study of the already-prevalent practice of government contracting out for research and development programs nevertheless concluded: "We regard it as axiomatic that policy decisions [related to those programs] must be made by full time Government officials clearly responsible to the President and to the Congress." US Congress, *Report to the President (Bell Report)*, 8.

49 OMB, "Policy Letter," 11–01, § 3(a) and 3(b)(1).

50 Shapiro, "Failure," 1099. After characterizing regulatory expertise in these terms, Professor Shapiro then immediately ascribed it to administrative agencies: "This decision-making expertise is the institutional expertise of agencies; it is the unique wisdom of a regulatory agency." Ibid.

51 See US Congress, *Report to the President (Bell Report)*, 8 (describing the supervision of contractors' work and the evaluation of the results of that work as "the basic functions of management which cannot be transferred to any contractor if we are to have proper accountability for the performance of public functions.").

52 See Davenport and Landler, "Trump Administration."

53 Of course, the prior paragraph revealed that politics, not just expertise, justifies administrative action. But it is an assumption of this book—and, indeed, a generally accepted assumption—that politics alone cannot provide a complete justification for the administrative state. Expertise must also play at least some role. Because outsourcing impairs that expertise, this chapter focuses on how outsourcing can be made consistent with an appropriate role for agency expertise. To put the matter slightly differently, the political inputs into agency action are not threatened by outsourcing because politicians ultimately control the agency process. To be blunt: Politics doesn't need protection from outsourcing. It can take care of itself.

54 See DiIulio, *Bring Back*, 83.

55 See Ingraham, *Foundation*, 116 ("The technical and professional skills needed by a professional engineer, for example, do not necessarily translate into the effective design or management of engineering contracts.").

56 See US Congress, *Report to the President (Bell Report)*, 21 (stating that one of "the [deleterious] effects of the substantial increase in contracting out Federal research and development work on the Government's own ability to carry out research and development work" is that "additional burdens have often been placed on Government research establishments to assist in evaluating the work of increasing

numbers of contractors . . .—without adding to the total staff and thus detracting from the direct research work which appeals to the most competent personnel."); Ingraham, *Foundation*, 116.

57 See Verkuil, *Outsourcing*, 4.

58 Federal Acquisition, *Code of Federal Regulations*, § 7.503(d) and 7.503(d)(4).

59 Ibid.

60 US Congress, *Report to the President (Bell Report)*, 9.

61 Laubacher, "Simplifying," 798.

62 See, e.g., Michaels, *Constitutional Coup*, 92–93.

63 See DiIulio, *Bring Back*, 99.

64 See, e.g., Jahn et al., *Declines*, 1 (discounting the technology explanation); Ingraham, *Foundation*, 115–16 (citing a scholar's conclusion that federal contracting expenditures more than doubled between 1980 and 1990, with most of that increase occurring before 1986).

65 See US Congress, *Report to the President (Bell Report)*, 21–22.

66 See, e.g., Michaels, *Constitutional Coup*, 135; ibid., 135 n.36 (citing additional sources).

67 The 1978 civil service reform law attempted to mitigate this problem by establishing the Senior Executive Service (SES), a corps of high-ranking government officials chosen largely, although not exclusively, from the civil service. The effectiveness of that effort has likely been impaired by the simultaneous explosion in political appointees, such as Schedule C appointments, and the political influence the 1978 law allowed over SES appointments and their management. See Ingraham, *Foundation*, 96–104 (tracing presidents' use of Schedule C appointments from Nixon to Clinton); ibid., 99 (noting the political influence over SES appointments and management).

68 US Congress, Report to the President (*Bell Report*), 21.

69 National Commission, *Urgent Business*, 8.

70 Jahn et al., *Declines*, 2.

71 See, e.g., Light, *Government Ill Executed*, 215–17 (retirement predictions made in 2008); see also Partnership, *Longest* (recounting the increased number of civil servants who began searches for other employment during the 2018–2019 government shutdown).

72 National Commission, *Urgent Business*, 31.

73 5 U.S.C. § 2301(b)(3).

74 See, e.g., National Academy, *No Time*, 21–23; National Commission, *Urgent Business*, 10.

75 See, e.g., National Academy, *No Time*, 19.

76 See, e.g., ibid., 23.

77 See, e.g., National Commission, *Urgent Business*, 9 (noting this phenomenon and its impact on the "equal pay" principle).

78 See, e.g., Partnership, *Time*.

79 See, e.g., Sanders et al., *Building*.

CHAPTER 10. REBUILDING TRUST

1 See generally Michaels, *Constitutional Coup*.

2 See Robinson et al., *Understanding*, 39–40.

3 See Rogowski, "Administrative Presidency," 45–46 (concluding that the author's study "provides evidence that citizens' views of the administrative state are linked, at least in part, to administrative officials' expertise. The experimental results indicate that survey respondents expressed significantly lower levels of confidence in bureaucratic institutions when bureaucrats were described as having lower levels of policy expertise. . . . I found no evidence, however, that Americans' views of bureaucratic institutions were linked either to the personnel capacity of those agencies or the ideological views of the personnel who worked within them.").

4 See ibid., 47 (suggesting this reading but cautioning that more research is necessary).

5 See Michaels, *Constitutional Coup*, 92–93.

6 See, e.g., Stephanopoulos, "Political Powerlessness," 1531 ("[T]he mechanism that typically is thought to protect minorities is, in a word, pluralism. If innumerable groups endlessly are forming and breaking alliances as they jockey for advantage, then each group sometimes will find itself in the majority. No group will be a perennial loser if the winning coalition is reshuffled on each issue."); Sunstein, "Interest Groups," 31–35 (presenting and comparing the republican and pluralist perspectives).

7 See Sunstein, "Interest Groups," 47–48 (referring to "Madisonian republicanism" as a structure "which occupies an intermediate position between interest-group pluralism and traditional republicanism").

8 See Karst, "Religion," 714.

9 See generally Staszewski, "Political Reasons"; Sant' Ambrogio and Staszewski, *Public Engagement*, 14 ("Political theorists note that democratic accountability . . . requires government officials to render a justifiable account of what they are doing on behalf of the public based on the republican idea that the business of government is public business.") (internal quotation and bracket omitted); Seidenfeld, "Civic Republican," 1544 (arguing that such judicial review can further civic republican values).

   Regulatory scholars who value presidential control over the bureaucracy go further, and argue that the president, as the one elected official with a national political constituency, is best suited to promoting the broad national interest. Others disagree. Compare Calabresi, "Normative Arguments" with Shane, *Madison's Nightmare*, 178–85. We can leave this disagreement to the side, except to note that chapter 5 identified serious problems with overbroad presidential control over the bureaucracy.

10 For a sense of how these conceptions could merge, see Sunstein, "Interest Groups," 46–47 ("The framers thus created political checks designed to ensure that representatives would not stray too far from the desires of their constituents.

The result was a hybrid conception of representation, in which legislators were neither to respond blindly to constituent pressures nor to undertake their deliberations in a vacuum.").

11 See, e.g., Seidenfeld, "Civic Republican," 1541–62 (discussing republican theories of administrative law); Seifter, "Second-Order," 1320–22 (summarizing pluralist theories of administrative law).

12 In a 2015 survey of Americans' attitudes toward 17 agencies, the "Don't Know" figure did not exceed 17% for any agency. See Pew, *Beyond Distrust*, 58. See also Robinson et al., *Understanding*, 41–43 (concluding that it is plausible to reach conclusions about persons' trust in agencies at the individual agency level).

13 Davis, *Treatise*, § 6.15.

14 See Herz, *Using Social Media*, 6–7; ibid., 7 n. 20; Robinson et al., *Understanding*, 13 (concluding that government accessibility, transparency, and interactivity yield greater public trust).

15 Herz, *Using Social Media*, 2.

16 See generally Wagner and Walker, *Incomprehensible!* (considering the problems caused by incomprehensibly expressed government regulatory actions).

17 Mendelson, "Rulemaking," 1343.

18 See Hitlin et al., "Public Comments."

19 See McCabe, "Internet Providers."

20 See, e.g., Mendelson, "Rulemaking" (discussing this issue).

21 See Sant' Ambrogio and Staszewski, *Public Engagement*, 5, 74.

22 See, e.g., Bull, "Making," 615 ("[W]idespread antipathy toward administrative agencies may also reflect a sense that the public has been foreclosed from making decisions regarding the proper allocation of resources, decisions that are made by relatively insulated bureaucrats.").

23 To be sure, some citizens have significant knowledge about some regulatory issues, either because of their work or background or because they have acquired that knowledge in order to influence regulation. In the 1980s, for example, AIDS activists became quite knowledgeable about drug research and the drug approval process, in order to participate in (and challenge) the FDA's regulatory process. See, e.g., Collins and Evans, *Rethinking Expertise*, 52–53 (discussing AIDS activists).

24 Herz, *Using Social Media*.

25 Sant' Ambrogio and Staszewski, *Public Engagement*, 69–72.

26 See ibid., 73–74.

27 US Department of Transportation, "Smoking."

28 Champer, "Comment."

29 See Consumer Advocates, "Comment."

30 Stoll, "Effective."

31 Farina et al., "Knowledge," 1187.

32 Sant' Ambrogio and Staszewski, *Public Engagement*, 20 (discussing these issues).

33 See ibid., 97 ("[S]ocial media outreach may increase public awareness of rulemaking beyond sophisticated stakeholders but it will not do much to overcome the 'incentive' and 'capacity' barriers that prevent most people from submitting public comments, let alone meaningful public comments.").

34 See Sant' Ambrogio and Staszewski, *Public Engagement*, 7.

35 See ibid., 159–62.

36 See generally McCoy, "Public Engagement," 3–9.

37 See Wood et al., "Potential Regulatory Challenges," 1492–98.

38 Indeed, depending on how one defines the term, such broader outreach has a long history. For example, a Peabody Award citation for the 1965 television documentary *The National Driver's Test* states that the government used individual test results voluntarily submitted by Americans to develop auto safety rules. See Peabody, "National Driver's Test."

39 See, e.g., Bingham, "Collaborative Governance," 278 (listing "citizens juries" and "the 21st Century Town Meeting" as analogous models for decision-making).

40 See Futrell, "Technical Adversarialism," 461–62.

41 See, e.g., Nou, "Regulating," 621.

42 See, e.g., ibid., 621–22.

43 In *Federalist 10*, Madison wrote that the effect of elections was "to refine and enlarge the public views, by passing them through the medium of a chosen body of citizens, whose wisdom may best discern the true interest of their country, and whose patriotism and love of justice will be least likely to sacrifice it to temporary or partial considerations." He then went on to ask "whether small or extensive republics are more favorable to the election of proper guardians of the public weal," and concluded that "it is clearly decided in favor of the latter." See also Kramer, "Madison's Audience," 630 n.85 ("Even before the break with England, observers had frequently remarked that the absence of a nobility skewed the balance of social forces in colonial government, and to many colonists this seemed to explain the persistent tensions that marked colonial politics. . . . But just because America had neither king nor nobles did not mean that it lacked social orders. Few Revolutionaries doubted that there existed in the community a social and intellectual elite distinguished by its abilities and discernment. This 'natural aristocracy' was distinct from the body of the people—more likely to be learned, more likely to possess wisdom, foresight, and patience. As such, it could counter and restrain the intemperate passions of the people, bringing prudence and stability to government more effectively even than England's corrupt hereditary House of Lords.").

44 See Dahl, "James Madison," 444 (discussing the effect of the rise of parties on Madison's theory); Kramer, "Madison's Audience," 630 n.85 (discussing the difficulty of structuring offices in the way Madison had intended).

45 See Kloppenberg, "To Promote," 383–84 ("[John] Adams, Madison, and [James] Wilson stood on the side of popular government rather than rule by elites. Their goal was Rousseau's goal, to find a way to advance the public interest over the

self-interest of the few. . . . The Constitution is, above all, concerned with the search for the common good. It establishes a government 'to promote the general Welfare.'") (paragraph break omitted).

46 This book is nowhere near the first writing to either find or call for an administrative system that echoes Madison's republican concerns. Among many others, see Sunstein, "Interest Groups"; Seidenfeld, "Civic Republican."

47 See, e.g., Dorf and Sandel, "Constitution," 438 (observing that one response to the anti-democratic character of reliance on administrative agencies holds "that delegation to administrative agencies . . . is democratically legitimate because, under the Administrative Procedure Act (APA), those agencies are accountable to the citizens affected in ways analogous to the way the legislature is accountable to its constituents"); ibid., 438 n.565 (citing sources making that same point).

48 This sequence of increasingly distant accountability concludes with the legislation agencies must implement because often that legislation is worded sufficiently broadly that it becomes hard to speak of a direct connection between the popular preferences that motivated the statute's enactment and the agency's implementing action. For example, climate change was simply not a topic of public discussion when the Clean Air Act was enacted, yet the EPA's thus-far halting steps to confront it have rested on the authority that statute provides the agency.

49 Two scholars have characterized Madison as not a "strong democrat." Liebman and Garrett, "Madisonian Equal Protection," 857. Another has argued that, after 1787, Madison's thinking evolved in a more democratic direction. See generally Dahl, "James Madison." This debate need not detain us.

50 Some legally binding regulations, for example, procedural regulations and those for which the agency demonstrates good cause not to submit to the rulemaking process, are exempt from public participation rights. See 5 U.S.C. § 553.

51 See, e.g., Freedman, "Crisis," 1058 (discussing the risk that "excessive reliance on experts" created "the democratic dilemma of accommodating a 'neutral' expertise with political responsiveness," a risk that "[t]hose who framed the modern administrative process believed . . . could be controlled" by, among other things, "the use of effective and fair procedures in the application of the experts' knowledge"); Dorf and Sandel, "Constitution," 438 (noting the argument that the APA's procedures make administrative agencies accountable to citizens in ways analogous to legislatures' accountability).

52 See Wood et al., "Potential Regulatory Challenges," 1492–98 (recounting how NHTSA sought out drivers' knowledge about their understanding of auto safety features).

53 See McCoy, "Public Engagement," 3–9 (discussing the CFPB's consideration of the public's preferences regarding mortgage disclosure forms).

54 See, e.g., Nou, "Regulating" (proposing a process by which citizen juries can influence heavily value-inflected decisions such as the quantification of values that are not otherwise easily quantifiable).

55 Some states have citizen-lawmaking procedures such as initiatives and referenda, which do not exist at the federal level.

56 The qualifier is necessary because a state may, if it wishes, require an elector to vote for the candidate of the party that selected her, and fine her if she does not. *Chiafalo v. Washington*, 140 S.Ct. 2316 (2020).

CONCLUSION

1 Konyndyk, "Lessons."

2 See Golden, *What Motivates*, 121–22.

3 Compare *South Bay United Pentecostal Church v. Newsom*, 140 S.Ct. 1613, 1613 (2020) (Roberts, C.J., concurring) (recognizing broad government latitude "to act in areas fraught with medical and scientific uncertainties") with *Roman Catholic Diocese of Brooklyn v. Cuomo*, 141 S.Ct. 63 (2020) (refusing to defer to state authorities' determinations of the riskiness of particular types of gatherings).

BIBLIOGRAPHY

Aberbach, Joel D., and Bert A. Rockman. "Clashing Beliefs Within the Executive Branch: The Nixon Administration Bureaucracy." *American Political Science Review* 70, no. 2 (1976): 456–68.

Administrative Conference of the U.S. *Administrative Conference Recommendation 2012-5, Improving Coordination of Related Agency Responsibilities.* (June 15, 2012).

American Anthropological Association, et al., Letter to the Honorable Andrew Wheeler, May 18, 2020. www.aaas.org/.

American Water Works Association. "Survey Shows High Confidence in U.S. Tap Water, Lower Satisfaction Among Black, Hispanic Respondents." www.awwa.org/.

Andreen, William. "Success and Backlash: The Remarkable (Continuing) Story of the Clean Water Act." *George Washington Journal of Energy and Environmental Law* 4, no. 1 (2013): 25–36.

Anthony, Robert A. "Interpretive Rules, Policy Statements, Guidances, Manuals, and the Like: Should Federal Agencies Use Them to Bind the Public?" *Duke Law Journal* 41, no. 6 (1992): 1311–84.

Araiza, William D. "In Praise of a Skeletal APA: *Norton v. Southern Utah Wilderness Alliance*, Judicial Remedies for Agency Inaction, and the Questionable Value of Amending the APA." *Administrative Law Review* 56, no. 4 (2004): 979–1002.

Baldwin, Robert. "Regulation: After Command-and-Control." In Keith Hawkins, ed., *The Human Face of Law: Essays in Honor of Donald Harris.* New York: Oxford University Press, 1997.

Banks, William C., and Kirk M. Lewis. "Federalism Disserved: The Drive for Deregulation." *Maryland Law Review* 45, no. 1 (1986): 141–78.

Barker, David, and Kathleen Knight. "Political Talk Radio and Public Opinion." *Public Opinion Quarterly* 64, no. 2 (2000): 149–70.

Barmore, Cynthia. "*Auer* in Action: Deference after *Talk America*." *Ohio State Law Journal* 76, no. 4 (2015): 813–46.

Berman, Emily, and Jacob Carter. "Policy Analysis: Scientific Integrity in Federal Policymaking Under Past and Present Administrations." *Journal of Science Policy & Governance* 13, no. 1 (2018).

Berry, Jeffrey, and Sarah Sobieraj. "Understanding the Rise of Talk Radio." *PS: Political Science and Politics* 44, no. 4 (2011): 762–67.

Bingham, Lisa Blomgren. "Collaborative Governance: Emerging Legal Practices and the Incomplete Legal Framework for Public and Stakeholder Voice." *Journal of Dispute Resolution* 2009, no. 2 (2009): 269–326.

Blumstein, James F. "Regulatory Review by the Executive Office of the President: An Overview and Policy Analysis of Current Issues." *Duke Law Journal* 51, no. 3 (2001): 851–99.

Breger, Marshall, and Gary Edles. *Independent Agencies in the United States: Law, Structure, and Politics.* New York: Oxford University Press, 2015.

Bressman, Lisa Schultz, and Michael P. Vandenbergh. "Inside the Administrative State: A Critical Look at the Practice of Presidential Control." *Michigan Law Review* 105, no. 1 (2006): 47–99.

Breton, Albert, and Ronald Wintrobe. "The Equilibrium Size of a Budget-maximizing Bureau: A Note on Niskanen's Theory of Bureaucracy." *Journal of Political Economy* 83, no. 1 (1975): 195–207.

Brown, Kimberly N. "Public Laws and Private Lawmakers." *Washington University Law Review* 93, no. 3 (2016): 615–80.

Bruns, Axel. *Are Filter Bubbles Real?* Cambridge: Polity Press, 2019.

Bull, Reeve T. "Making the Administrative State 'Safe for Democracy': A Theoretical and Practical Analysis of Citizen Participation in Agency Decisionmaking." *Administrative Law Review* 65, no. 3 (2013): 611–64.

Bureau of National Affairs. "Office of Management and Budget Plays Critical Part in Environmental Policymaking, Faces Little External Review." *Environmental Reporter* 7 (1976): 693–97.

Calabresi, Steven G. "Some Normative Arguments for the Unitary Executive." *Arkansas Law Review* 48, no. 1 (1995): 23–104.

Calabresi, Steven G., and Christopher S. Yoo. *The Unitary Executive: Presidential Power from Washington to Bush.* New Haven, CT: Yale University Press, 2012.

Chafetz, Josh. "Gridlock?" *Harvard Law Review Forum* 130 (2016): 51–59.

Champer, James E. "Comment." In U.S. Department of Transportation, *Rulemaking Docket: Smoking of Electronic Cigarettes on Aircraft.* (November 14, 2011). www.regulations.gov.

Clarke, Conor. "The Uneasy Case Against *Auer* and *Seminole Rock*." *Yale Law & Policy Review* 33, no. 1 (2014): 175–95.

Clinton, Joshua, David Lewis, and Jennifer Selin. "Influencing the Bureaucracy: The Irony of Congressional Oversight." *American Journal of Political Science* 58, no. 2 (2014): 387–401.

Clinton, William J. "Remarks to the Community in Salem, New Hampshire." In *Public Papers of the Presidents of the United States: William J. Clinton (1996, Book I).* Washington, DC: US Government Publishing Office, 1996.

Coglianese, Cary. "Weak Democracy, Strong Information: The Role of Information Technology in the Rulemaking Process." In Viktor Mayer-Schönberger and David Lazer, eds. *Governance and Information Technology: From Electronic Government to Information Government.* Cambridge, MA: MIT Press, 2007.

Coglianese, Cary, and Daniel E. Walters. "Agenda-Setting in the Regulatory State: Theory and Evidence." *Administrative Law Review* 68, no. 1 (2016): 93–118.

Collins, Harry, and Robert Evans. *Rethinking Expertise.* Chicago: University of Chicago Press, 2007.

Comptroller General of the United States. *Recent Government-Wide Hiring Freezes Prove Ineffective in Managing Federal Employment*. Washington, DC: US General Accounting Office, March 10, 1982.

Consumer Advocates for Smoke-Free Alternatives Association and the Competitive Enterprise Institute. "Comment." In US Department of Transportation, *Rulemaking Docket: Smoking of Electronic Cigarettes on Aircraft*. (November 14, 2011). www.regulations.gov.

Criddle, Evan J. "*Chevron*'s Consensus." *Boston University Law Review* 88, no. 5 (2008): 1271–1325.

Criddle, Evan J. "Fiduciary Administration: Rethinking Popular Representation in Agency Rulemaking." *Texas Law Review* 88, no. 3 (February 2010): 441–504.

Dahl, Robert A. "James Madison: Republican or Democrat?" *Perspectives on Politics* 3, no. 3 (2005): 439–48.

Davenport, Coral. "Trump's Environmental Rollbacks Find Opposition Within: Staff Scientists." *New York Times* (March 31, 2020), A-19.

Davenport, Coral, and Mark Landler. "Trump Administration Hardens Its Attack on Climate Science." *New York Times* (May 27, 2019). www.nytimes.com/.

Davis, Kenneth C. *Administrative Law Treatise*. St. Paul, MN: West Publishing, 1971.

Dawes, Charles. Quoted in John J. Patrick, Richard M. Pious, and Donald A. Ritchie, eds., *The Oxford Guide to the United States Government*. Oxford: Oxford University Press, 2001.

Dearen, Jason, and Mike Stobbe. "Trump Administration Buries Detailed CDC Advice on Reopening." *Associated Press* (May 7, 2020). https://apnews.com/.

de Beaumont Foundation. "Changing the COVID Conversation" Focus Group (2021). https://debeaumont.org/.

DeMuth, Christopher, and Douglas Ginsburg. "Rationalism in Regulation." *Michigan Law Review* 108, no. 6 (2010): 877–912.

Desikan, Anita. "150 Attacks on Science and Counting: Trump Administration's Anti-Science Actions Hurt People and Communities Nationwide." *Union of Concerned Scientists* (August 3, 2020). https://blog.ucsusa.org/.

DiIulio, John, Jr. *Bring Back the Bureaucrats*. West Conshohocken, PA: Templeton Press, 2014.

Doremus, Holly. "Scientific and Political Integrity in Environmental Policy." *Texas Law Review* 86, no. 7 (2008): 1601–54.

Dorf, Michael C., and Charles F. Sabel. "A Constitution of Democratic Experimentalism." *Columbia Law Review* 98, no. 2 (1998): 267–473.

Douthat, Ross. "When You Can't Just 'Trust the Science.'" *New York Times* (December 20, 2020), SR-9.

Dreyfus, Hubert, and Stuart Dreyfus. *Mind Over Machine: The Power of Human Intuition and Expertise in the Era of the Computer*. Oxford: Basil Blackwell, 1986.

Driesen, David. "Distributing the Costs of Environmental, Health, and Safety Protection: The Feasibility Principle, Cost-Benefit Analysis, and Regulatory

Reform." *Boston College Environmental Affairs Law Review*, 32, no. 1 (2005): 1–95.

Driesen, David. "Is Cost-Benefit Analysis Neutral?" *University of Colorado Law Review* 77, no. 2 (2006): 335–406.

Emerson, Blake, and Jon Michaels. "Abandoning Presidential Administration: A Civic Governance Agenda to Promote Democratic Equality and Guard against Creeping Authoritarianism." *UCLA Law Review Discourse* 68 (2020–2021): 418–47.

Environmental Data and Governance Initiative. "The New Digital Landscape: How the Trump Administration Has Undermined Federal Web Infrastructures for Climate Information." (July 2019). https://envirodatagov.org/.

Erikson, Robert, and Christopher Wlezien. "Forecasting US Presidential Elections Using Economic and Noneconomic Fundamentals." *Political Science and Politics* 47, no. 2 (2014): 313–16.

Eyal, Gil. *The Crisis of Expertise*. Cambridge: Polity, 2019.

Farber, Daniel, and Paul Hemmersbaugh. "The Shadow of the Future: Discount Rates, Later Generations, and the Environment." *Vanderbilt Law Review* 46, no. 2 (1993): 267–304.

Farina, Cynthia R. "The 'Chief Executive' and the Quiet Constitutional Revolution." *Administrative Law Review* 49, no. 1 (1997): 179–86.

Farina, Cynthia, et al. "Knowledge in the People: Rethinking 'Value' in Public Rulemaking Participation." *Wake Forest Law Review* 47, no. 5 (2012): 1185–1241.

Federal Acquisition Regulations System. *US Code of Federal Regulations*, title 48, no. 2 (2002): 118–20.

Fisher, Elizabeth, and Sidney Shapiro. *Administrative Competence: Reimagining Administrative Law*. Cambridge: Cambridge University Press, 2020.

Fisk, Catherine L., and Erwin Chemerinsky. "Political Speech and Association Rights after *Knox v. SEIU, Local 1000*." *Cornell Law Review* 98, no. 5 (2013): 1023–92.

Francis, Kathryn. *Statutory Inspectors General in the Federal Government: A Primer*. Washington, DC: Congressional Research Service, January 3, 2019.

Freedman, James O. "Crisis and Legitimacy in the Administrative Process." *Stanford Law Review* 27, no. 4 (1975): 1041–76.

Friedman, Lisa. "EPA Cancels Talk on Climate Change by Agency Scientists." *New York Times* (October 22, 2017). www.nytimes.com/.

Futrell, Robert. "Technical Adversarialism and Participatory Collaboration in the U.S. Chemical Weapon Disposal Program." *Science, Technology, and Human Values* 28, no. 4 (2003): 451–82.

Garand, James C., Catherine T. Parkhurst, and Rusanne Jourdan Seoud. "Bureaucrats, Policy Attitudes, and Political Behavior: Extension of the Bureau Voting Model of Government Growth." *Journal of Public Administration Research and Theory: J-PART* 1, no. 2 (1991): 177–212.

Garland, Merrick B. "Deregulation and Judicial Review." *Harvard Law Review* 98, no. 3 (1985): 505–91.

Garrett, R. Sam, James A. Thurber, A. Lee Fritschler, and David H. Rosenbloom. "Assessing the Impact of Bureaucracy Bashing by Electoral Campaigns." *Public Administration Review* 66, no. 2 (2006): 228–40.

Gerstein, Josh. "Trump Appointee Arrested in Connection with Capitol Riot." *Politico* (March 4, 2021). www.politico.com/.

Gerth, Jeff. "Contractors' Role at Energy Dept. Called Pervasive." *New York Times* (November 6, 1989), A-21.

Gilroy, John, and Robert Shapiro. "The Polls: Environmental Protection." *Public Opinion Quarterly* 50, no. 2 (1986): 270–79.

Glicksman, Robert L. "Shuttered Government." *Arizona Law Review* 62, no. 3 (2020): 573–636.

Golden, Marissa Martino. *What Motivates Bureaucrats? Politics and Administration During the Reagan Years.* New York: Columbia University Press, 2000.

Goldman, Gretchen T., Jacob M. Carter, Yun Wang, and Janice M. Larson. "Perceived Losses of Scientific Integrity Under the Trump Administration: A Survey of Federal Scientists." *PLoS ONE* 15, no. 4 (2020). https://doi.org/10.1371/journal.pone.0231929.

Gotsch, Kara, and Vinay Basti. "Capitalizing on Mass Incarceration: U.S. Growth in Private Prisons." *Sentencing Project* (August 2, 2018). www.sentencingproject.org/.

Guttman, Daniel. "Public Purpose and Private Service: The Twentieth Century Culture of Contracting Out and the Evolving Law of Diffused Sovereignty." *Administrative Law Review* 52, no. 3 (2000): 859–926.

Halberstam, David. *The Best and the Brightest.* New York: Random House, 1969.

Hansen, James. "Political Interference with Government Climate Change Science." Columbia University (March 19, 2007). www.columbia.edu.

Herz, Michael E. "Using Social Media in Rulemaking: Possibilities and Barriers." Washington, DC: Administrative Conference of the United States, 2013.

Hiatt, Fred. "For Biden, 44 Confirmations Down, Only 1,156 to Go." *Washington Post* (May 2, 2021). www.washingtonpost.com.

Hirschman, Albert. *Exit, Voice, and Loyalty: Responses to Decline in Firms, Organizations and States.* Cambridge, MA: Harvard University Press, 1970.

Hitlin, Paul, Kenneth Olmstead, and Skye Toor. "Public Comments to the Federal Communications Commission About Net Neutrality Contain Many Inaccuracies and Duplicates." *Pew Research Center* (August 17, 2020). www.pewresearch.org/.

Hollis-Brusky, Amanda. "Helping Ideas Have Consequences: Political and Intellectual Investment in the Unitary Executive Theory, 1981–2000." *Denver University Law Review* 89, no. 1 (2011): 197–244.

Hsu, Spencer S., and Carrie Johnson. "White House Refuses to Release Documents on Air-Quality Policy." *Washington Post* (June 21, 2008). www.washingtonpost.com/.

Hubbell, Larry. "Ronald Reagan as Presidential Symbol Maker: The Federal Bureaucrat as Loafer, Incompetent Buffoon, Good Ole Boy, and Tyrant." *American Review of Public Administration* 21, no. 3 (1991): 237–53.

Ingraham, Patricia Wallace. *The Foundation of Merit: Public Service in American De-mocracy*. Baltimore, MD: Johns Hopkins University Press, 1995.

Institute for Policy Integrity. *Roundup: Trump-Era Agency Policy in the Courts*. https://policyintegrity.org/.

Iuliano, Jason, and Keith Whittington. "The Non-Delegation Doctrine: Alive and Well." *Notre Dame Law Review* 93, no. 2 (2017): 619–45.

Jaffe, Susan. "Media Reports Reveal Political Interference at the US CDC." *The Lancet* 396 (September 26, 2020): 875.

Jahn, Molly, et al. *Are Declines in U.S. Federal Workforce Capabilities Putting our Gov-ernment at Risk of Failing?* (Senior Executives Association, 2019).

Kagan, Elena. "Presidential Administration." *Harvard Law Review* 114, no. 8 (2001): 2245–2385.

Karst, Kenneth L. "Religion, Sex, and Politics: Cultural Counterrevolution in Constitu-tional Perspective." *UC Davis Law Review* 24, no. 3 (1991): 677–734.

Katzen, Sally. "OIRA at Thirty: Reflections and Recommendations." *Administrative Law Review* 63, special edition (2011): 103–12.

Kendall, Mary, Letter to the Honorable Raul Grijalva, June 7, 2018. www.document-cloud.org/.

Kennedy, Joshua B. ""Do This! Do That!" And Nothing Will Happen': Executive Or-ders and Bureaucratic Responsiveness." *American Politics Research* 43, no. 1 (2015): 59–82. https://doi.org/10.1177/1532673X14534062.

Kilgore, Ed. "Starving the Beast." *Blueprint* (June 30, 2003). https://web.archive.org.

Kim, S. E. "The Role of Trust in the Modern Administrative State: An Integrative Model." *Administration & Society* 37, no. 5 (2005): 611–35.

Kloppenberg, James T. "To Promote the General Welfare: Why Madison Matters." *Supreme Court Review* 2019 (2019): 355–84.

Konyndyk, Jeremy. "Lessons Ignored: John Bolton's Bogus Defense of 'Streamlining' Away Our Bio-Readiness." *Just Security* (March 16, 2020). www.justsecurity.org.

Kosar, Kevin. *Privatization and the Federal Government: An Introduction*. Washington, DC: Congressional Research Service, 2007.

Kramer, Larry D. "Madison's Audience." *Harvard Law Review* 112, no. 3 (1999): 611–79.

Krotoszynski, Ronald. "'History Belongs to the Winners': The Bazelon/Leventhal De-bate and the Continuing Relevance of the Process/Substance Dichotomy in Judicial Review of Agency Action." *Administrative Law Review* 58, no. 4 (2006): 995–1015.

Kum, Dezimey. "Fueled by a History of Mistreatment, Black Americans Distrust the New COVID-19 Vaccines." *Time* (December 28, 2020). https://time.com/.

Laubacher, Thomas J. "Simplifying Inherently Governmental Functions: Creating a Principled Approach from Its *Ad Hoc* Beginnings." *Public Contract Law Journal* 46, no. 4 (2017): 791–832.

Layzer, Judith A. *Open for Business: Conservatives' Opposition to Environmental Regula-tion*. Cambridge, MA: MIT Press, 2012.

Levinson, Daryl. "Foreword: Looking for Power in Public Law." *Harvard Law Review* 130, no. 1 (2016): 31–143.

Lewis, David E. "Testing Pendleton's Premise: Do Political Appointees Make Worse Bureaucrats?" *Journal of Politics* 69, no. 4 (2007): 1073–88.

Lewis, Michael. *The Fifth Risk*. New York: W.W. Norton, 2018.

Lewis, Michael. *The Premonition*. New York: W.W. Norton, 2021.

Lieb, Ethan. "Also, No." *Tulsa Law Review* 53, no. 2 (2018): 267–77.

Liebman, James S., and Brandon L. Garrett. "Madisonian Equal Protection." *Columbia Law Review* 104, no. 4 (2004): 837–974.

Light, Paul C. *A Government Ill Executed: The Decline of the Federal Service and How to Reverse It*. Cambridge, MA: Harvard University Press, 2008.

Lippman, Walter. *The Phantom Public*. New York: Macmillan, 1927.

Livermore, Michael A., and Richard L. Revesz. *Reviving Rationality: Saving Cost-Benefit Analysis for the Sake of the Environment and Our Health*. New York: Oxford University Press, 2020.

Locke, John. "The Second Treatise of Government." In Peter Laslett, ed., *Two Treatises of Government*. Cambridge: Cambridge University Press, 1988.

Lowi, Theodore. *The End of Liberalism*. New York: W. W. Norton, 1969.

Luneberg, William. "Civic Republicanism, The First Amendment, and Executive Branch Policymaking." *Administrative Law Review* 43, no. 3 (1991): 367–410.

Madison, James. "Federalist No. 10." In George W. Carey and James McClellan, eds., *The Federalist*. Indianapolis, IN: Liberty Fund, 2001.

Magill, M. Elizabeth. "The Revolution that Wasn't." *Northwestern University Law Review* 99, no. 1 (2004): 47–76.

Magill, M. Elizabeth. "Agency Choice of Policymaking Form." *University of Chicago Law Review* 71, no. 4 (2004): 1383–447.

Mashaw, Jerry L.. "Prodelegation: Why Administrators Should Make Political Decisions." *Journal of Law, Economics, and Organization* 1, no. 1 (1985): 81–100.

Mashaw, Jerry L. "Recovering American Administrative Law: Federalist Foundations, 1787–1801." *Yale Law Journal* 115, no. 6 (2006): 1256–344.

Mashaw, Jerry L.. *Reasoned Administration and Democratic Legitimacy: How Administrative Law Supports Democratic Government*. Cambridge: Cambridge University Press, 2018.

Mashaw, Jerry L., and David Harfst. "Regulation and Legal Culture: The Case of Motor Vehicle Safety." *Yale Journal on Regulation* 4, no. 2 (1987): 257–316.

Mashaw, Jerry L., and David Harfst. "From Command and Control to Collaboration and Deference: The Transformation of Auto Safety Regulation." *Yale Journal on Regulation* 34, no. 1 (2017): 167–278.

May, Randolph. "Defining Deference Down: Independent Agencies and *Chevron* Deference." *Administrative Law Review* 58, no. 2 (2006): 429–53.

McCabe, David. "Internet Providers Funded Effort Behind Fake Net Neutrality Comments, New York Says." *New York Times* (May 6, 2021). www.nytimes.com/.

McCoy, Patricia A. "Public Engagement in Rulemaking: The Consumer Financial Protection Bureau's New Approach." *Brooklyn Journal of Corporate, Financial & Commercial Law* 7, no. 1 (2012): 1–24.

McGarity, Thomas. "The Internal Structure of EPA Rulemaking." *Law and Contemporary Problems* 54, no. 4 (1991): 57–111.

McGarity, Thomas. *Reinventing Rationality: The Role of Regulatory Analysis in the Federal Bureaucracy.* Cambridge: Cambridge University Press, 1991.

McGarity, Thomas. "Some Thoughts on 'Deossifying' the Rulemaking Process." *Duke Law Journal* 41, no. 6 (1992): 1385–1462.

McGarity, Thomas O., and Wendy E. Wagner. "Deregulation Using Stealth 'Science' Strategies." *Duke Law Journal* 68, no. 8 (2019): 1719–804.

Meazell, Emily Hammond. "Presidential Control, Expertise, and the Deference Dilemma." *Duke Law Journal* 61, no. 8 (2012): 1763–1810.

Mendelson, Nina A. "Rulemaking, Democracy, and Torrents of E-Mail." *George Washington Law Review* 79, no. 5 (2011): 1343–80.

Merriam-Webster. "Information Age." In Merriam-Webster.com dictionary. www.merriam-webster.com/dictionary/Information%20Age.

Meyer, Robinson. "We Knew They Had Cooked the Books." *The Atlantic* (February 12, 2020). www.theatlantic.com/.

Michaels, Jon D. "Privatization's Pretensions." *University of Chicago Law Review* 77, no. 2 (2010): 717–80.

Michaels, Jon D. *Constitutional Coup: Privatization's Threat to the American Republic.* Cambridge, MA: Harvard University Press, 2017.

Michaels, Jon D. "The War on Federal Employees." *American Prospect* (December 11, 2017). https://prospect.org/.

Miller, James, III. "The Early Days of Reagan Regulatory Relief and Suggestions for OIRA's Future." *Administrative Law Review* 63, special edition (2011): 93–101.

Milward, H. Brinton. "Implications of Contracting Out: New Roles for the Hollow State." In Patricia W. Ingraham and Barbara S. Romzak & Associates, *New Paradigms for Government.* San Francisco: Jossey-Bass, 1994.

Mintz, Morton. "Energy Aide's Controversial Findings Lead to Downfall in Bureaucracy." *Washington Post* (June 4, 1977). www.washingtonpost.com/.

Mortenson, Julian, and Nicholas Bagley. "Delegation at the Founding." *Columbia Law Review* 121, no. 2 (2021): 277–367.

Mounk, Yascha. "The Undemocratic Dilemma." *Journal of Democracy* 29, no. 2 (2018): 98–112.

Nagareda, Richard A. "*Ex Parte* Contacts and Institutional Roles: Lessons from the OMB Experience." *University of Chicago Law Review* 55, no. 2 (1988): 591–628.

Nathan, Richard P. *The Administrative Presidency.* New York: Wiley, 1983.

National Academy of Public Administration. *Presidential Management of Rulemaking in Regulatory Agencies* (1987).

National Academy of Public Administration. *No Time to Wait: Building a Public Service for the 21st Century* (2017).

National Commission on the Public Service. *Urgent Business for America: Revitalizing the Federal Government for the 21st Century*. Washington, DC: Brookings Institution (January 2003). www.brookings.edu.

Nelkin, Dorothy. "The Political Impact of Technical Expertise." *Social Study of Science* 5, no. 1 (1975): 35–54.

Nichols, Tom. *The Death of Expertise: The Campaign Against Established Knowledge and Why It Matters*. New York: Oxford University Press, 2017.

Niskanen, William. *Bureaucracy and Representative Government*. London: Routledge, 1971.

Nou, Jennifer. "Regulating the Rulemakers: A Proposal for Deliberative Cost-Benefit Analysis." *Yale Law & Policy Review* 26, no. 2 (2008): 601–44.

Nourse, Victoria, and Jane Schachter. "The Politics of Legislative Drafting: A Congressional Case Study." *NYU Law Review* 77, no. 3 (2002): 575–624.

Novak, William J. *The People's Welfare: Law and Regulation in Nineteenth-Century America*. Chapel Hill: University of North Carolina Press, 2000.

O'Connell, Anne Joseph. "Vacant Offices: Delays in Staffing Top Agency Positions." *Southern California Law Review* 82, no. 5 (July 2009): 913–1000.

O'Connell, Anne Joseph. "Actings." *Columbia Law Review*, 120, no. 3 (2020): 613–728.

Office of Legal Counsel, US Department of Justice. "Proposed Exec. Order Entitled 'Fed. Regulation.'" 5 *Opinions of the Office of Legal Counsel* 59 (1981).

Office of Management and Budget, Policy Letter 11–01. *Federal Register* 76, no. 176 (September 12, 2011): 56227–62.

Osborne, David, and Ted Gaebler. *Reinventing Government: How the Entrepreneurial Spirit Is Transforming the Public Sector*. London: Penguin, 1992.

Parillo, Nicholas. *Against the Profit Motive: The Salary Revolution in American Government 1780–1940*. New Haven, CT: Yale University Press, 2013.

Pariser, Eli. *The Filter Bubble: What the Internet Is Hiding From You*. London: Penguin, 2011.

Partnership for Public Service. *A Time for Talent: Improving Federal Recruiting and Hiring*. (August 2020). https://ourpublicservice.org/.

Partnership for Public Service. *Longest Federal Government Shutdown in History Created the Risk of a Federal Brain Drain*. (August 2020). https://ourpublicservice.org/.

Pasachoff, Eloise. "The President's Budget as a Source of Agency Policy Control." *Yale Law Journal* 125, no. 8 (2016): 2182–2290.

Peabody Awards. "The National Driver's Test." www.peabodyawards.com/.

Percival, Robert V. "Checks Without Balance: Executive Office Oversight of the Environmental Protection Agency." *Law and Contemporary Problems* 54, no. 4 (1991): 127–204.

Percival, Robert V. "Who's in Charge? Does the President Have Directive Authority over Agency Regulatory Decisions?" *Fordham Law Review* 79, no. 6 (2011): 2487–2540.

Perlstein, Rick. *Reaganland: American's Right Turn, 1976–1980.* New York: Simon & Schuster, 2020.

Pew Research Center. *Beyond Distrust: How Americans View Their Government.* (November 23, 2015). www.pewresearch.org.

Pew Research Center. *Public Trust in Government 1958–2019.* (April 11, 2019). www.pewresearch.org/.

Piaker, Zach. "Help Wanted: 4,000 Presidential Appointees." *Partnership for Public Service.* (March 16, 2016). https://web.archive.org.

Pierce, Richard J., Jr. "Two Problems in Administrative Law: Political Polarity on the District of Columbia Circuit and Judicial Deterrence of Agency Rulemaking." *Duke Law Journal* 1988, no. 2/3 (1988): 300–28.

Pierce, Richard J., Jr.. "Judicial Review of Agency Actions in a Period of Diminishing Agency Resources." *Administrative Law Review* 49, no. 1 (1997): 61–94.

Pierce, Richard J., Jr., and Sidney A. Shapiro. "Political and Judicial Review of Agency Action." *Texas Law Review* 59, no. 7 (1981): 1175–1222.

Pildes, Richard, and Cass Sunstein. "Reinventing the Regulatory State." *University of Chicago Law Review* 62, no. 1 (1995): 1–130.

Polsby, Nelson W. "Presidential Cabinet Making: Lessons for the Political System." *Political Science Quarterly* 93, no. 1 (1978): 15–25.

Posner, Eric A., and Adrian Vermeule. "Interring the Nondelegation Doctrine." *University of Chicago Law Review* 69, no. 4 (2002): 1721–62.

Reagan, Ronald. "Speech to Hilldale College." *American Rhetoric* (November 10, 1977). www.americanrhetoric.com/.

Reagan, Ronald. *Inaugural Address.* Presidential Inauguration, Washington, DC, January 20, 1981.

Reagan, Ronald. *Speaking My Mind: Selected Speeches.* New York: Simon & Schuster, 1992.

Reilly-Diakun, Jori. "Addressing Blurred Lines: Institutional Design Solutions to Transgressions Across the Science-Policy Boundary." *Texas Environmental Law Journal* 49, no. 2 (2019): 199–230.

Revkin, Andrew C. "Cheney's Office Said to Edit Draft Testimony on Warming." *New York Times* (July 9, 2008): A-12.

Robinson, Scott, James Stoutenborough, and Arnold Vedlitz. *Understanding Trust in Government: Environmental Sustainability, Fracking, and Public Opinion in American Politics.* New York: Routledge, 2017.

Rogowski, John. "The Administrative Presidency and Public Trust in Bureaucracy." *Journal of Political Institutions and Political Economy* 1, no. 1 (2020): 27–51.

Rosenberg, Eli. "The CDC Softened a Report on Meatpacking Safety during the Pandemic. Democrats Say They Want to Know Why." *Washington Post* (September 30, 2020). www.washingtonpost.com/.

Rosenberg, Gerald. *The Hollow Hope: Can Courts Bring About Social Change?* Chicago: University of Chicago Press, 1991.

Rosenberg, Morton. "Congress's Prerogative over Agencies and Agency Decisionmakers: The Rise and Demise of the Reagan Administration's Theory of the Unitary Executive." *George Washington Law Review* 57, no. 3 (January 1989): 627–703.

Rosenwald, Brian. "Mount Rushmore: The Rise of Talk Radio and Its Impact on Politics and Public Policy." Doctoral Dissertation, University of Virginia (2015).

Rubenstein, David. "Supremacy, Inc." *UCLA Law Review* 67, no. 5 (November 2020): 1130–1203.

Rudalevige, Andrew. "Executive Orders and Presidential Unilateralism." *Presidential Studies Quarterly* 42, no. 1 (2012): 138–60.

Saad, Lydia. "U.S. Readiness to Get COVID-19 Vaccine Steadies at 65%." Gallup (January 21, 2021). https://news.gallup.com/.

Saadoun, Sarah. "The Coal Mine Next Door." *Human Rights Watch*. (December 10, 2018). www.hrw.org.

Sabin Center for Climate Change Law. "10 Year Research Project Cancelled by DOE." https://climate.law.columbia.edu/.

Saiger, Aaron J. "Obama's 'Czars' for Domestic Policy and the Law of the White House Staff." *Fordham Law Review* 79, no. 6 (May 2011): 2577–2616.

Sanders, Ronald, ed. *Building a 21st Century SES: Ensuring Leadership Excellence in Our Federal Government*. Washington, DC: National Academy of Public Administration, 2017.

Sant'Ambrogio, Michael, and Glen Staszewski. *Public Engagement with Agency Rulemaking*. Washington, DC: Administrative Conference of the United States, 2018.

Sassone, Peter, and William Schaffer. *Cost-Benefit Analysis: A Handbook*. San Diego: Academic, 1978.

Scalia, Antonin. "The Legislative Veto: A False Remedy for System Overload." *American Enterprise Institute* (December 6, 1979). www.aei.org.

Schlafly, Phyllis. *A Choice Not an Echo*. Alton, IL: Pere Marquette Press, 1964.

Schmidt, Christopher. *The Sit-Ins: Protest and Legal Change in the Civil Rights Era*. Chicago: University of Chicago Press, 2018.

Schmitt, Mark. "The Legend of the Powell Memo." *American Prospect* (April 27, 2005). https://prospect.org/.

Schoenbrod, David. *Power Without Responsibility: How Congress Abuses the People Through Delegation*. New Haven, CT: Yale University Press, 1993.

Seidenfeld, Mark. "A Civic Republican Justification for the Bureaucratic State." *Harvard Law Review* 105, no. 7 (1992): 1511–76.

Seidenfeld, Mark. "The Long Shadow of Judicial Review." *Journal of Land Use & Environmental Law* 32, no. 2 (2017): 579–98.

Seifter, Miriam. "Second-Order Participation in Administrative Law." *UCLA Law Review* 63, no. 5 (2016): 1300–1365.

Sganga, Nicole, and Camilo Montoya-Galvez. "Homeland Security Officials Scrap Trump-Era Union Deal That Could Have Stalled Biden's Immigration Policies." CBS News (February 16, 2021). www.cbsnews.com/.

Shane, Peter M. *Madison's Nightmare: How Executive Power Threatens American Democracy*. Chicago: University of Chicago Press, 2009.

Shane, Peter M. "*Chevron* Deference, The Rule of Law, and Presidential Influence in the Administrative State." *Fordham Law Review* 83, no. 2 (2014): 679–702.

Shapiro, Sidney A. "OMB and the Politicization of Risk Assessment." *Environmental Law* 37, no. 4 (2007): 1083–106.

Shapiro, Sidney A. "The Failure to Understand Expertise in Administrative Law: The Problem and the Consequences." *Wake Forest Law Review* 50, no. 5 (2015): 1097–1154.

Shapiro, Sidney A., and Christopher Schroeder. "Beyond Cost-Benefit Analysis: A Pragmatic Reorientation." *Harvard Environmental Law Review* 32, no. 2 (2008): 433–502.

Shapiro, Sidney A., Rena Steinzor, and Matthew Shudtz. "Regulatory Dysfunction: How Insufficient Resources, Outdated Laws, and Political Interference Cripple the 'Protector Agencies.'" *Center for Progressive Reform White Paper No. 906* (August 2009). http://progressivereform.net/.

Shapiro, Sidney A., and Ronald F. Wright. "The Future of the Administrative Presidency: Turning Administrative Law Inside-Out." *University of Miami Law Review* 65, no. 2 (2011): 577–620.

Sitaraman, Ganesh. "Foreign Hard Look Review." *Administrative Law Review* 66, no. 3 (2014): 489–563.

Sklansky, David A. "The Private Police." *UCLA Law Review* 46, no. 4 (April 1999): 1165–1288.

Smith, Hedrick. *The Power Game: How Washington Works*. New York: Random House, 1988.

Staszewski, Glen. "Political Reasons, Deliberative Democracy, and Administrative Law." *Iowa Law Review* 97, no. 3 (2012): 849–912.

Steinzor, Rena. "The Case for Abolishing Centralized White House Regulatory Review." *Michigan Journal of Environmental & Administrative Law* 1 (2012): 209–86.

Stephanopoulos, Nicholas O. "Political Powerlessness." *New York University Law Review* 90, no. 5 (November 2015): 1527–1608.

Stewart, Richard B. "The Reformation of American Administrative Law." *Harvard Law Review* 88, no. 8 (1975): 1667–1813.

Stewart, Richard B. "*Vermont Yankee* and the Evolution of Administrative Procedure." *Harvard Law Review* 91, no. 8 (1978): 1805–22.

Stewart, Richard B. "Beyond Delegation Doctrine." *American University Law Review* 36, no. 2 (1987): 323–43.

Stiff, Robert. "A Battle Best Not Waged." *St. Petersburg Evening Independent* (May 12, 1980). https://news.google.com/.

Stine, Jeffrey. "Environmental Policy During the Carter Presidency." In Gary Fink and Hugh Graham, *The Carter Presidency: Policy Choices in the Post New Deal Era*. Lawrence: University Press of Kansas, 1998.

Stoll, Richard. "Effective Written Comments in Informal Rulemaking." *Administrative Law and Regulatory News* 32, no. 4 (2007): 15–17.

Sunlight Foundation. *Web Integrity Project*. https://sunlightfoundation.com/.

Sunstein, Cass R. "Interest Groups in American Public Law." *Stanford Law Review* 38, no. 1 (1985): 29–87.

Sunstein, Cass R. *Going to Extremes: How Like Minds Unite and Divide*. New York: Oxford University Press, 2011.

Sunstein, Cass R. "There Are Two 'Major Questions' Doctrines." (November 4, 2020). https://papers.ssrn.com/.

Thomas, Craig W. "Maintaining and Restoring Public Trust in Government Agencies and Their Employees." *Administration & Society* 30, no. 2 (May 1998): 166–93.

Thompson, Jonathan. "The First Sagebrush Rebellion: What Sparked It and How It Ended." *High Country News* (January 14, 2016). www.hcn.org/.

Tolchin, Martin, and Susan Tolchin. *Pinstripe Patronage: Political Favoritism From the Clubhouse to the White House and Beyond*. London: Routledge, 2010.

Trager, Rebecca. "US Funder Ends Coronavirus Research with Wuhan Lab Amid Political Pressure." *Chemistry World* (May 5, 2020). www.chemistryworld.com/.

Union of Concerned Scientists. "Federal Climate Scientists Survey Essay Responses." www.ucsusa.org/.

US Bureau of the Budget. "Circular Number A-76, Policies for Acquiring Commercial or Industrial Products and Services for Government Use." (1966).

US Census Bureau. Statistical Abstract of the United States: 1960. Washington, DC: US Government Printing Office, 1960.

US Congress. Senate. Committee on Government Services. *Report to the President on Government Contracting for Research and Development*. 87th Cong., 2nd sess., 1962. S. Doc. 94. ("Bell Report").

US Department of Health and Human Services, Office of Inspector General. *Health-care.gov: CMS Management of the Federal Marketplace* (February 2016).

US Department of Interior, Office of Inspector General. *Investigative Report on Allegations Against Julie MacDonald, Deputy Assistant Secretary, Fish, Wildlife, and Parks*. www.doioig.gov/.

US Department of Justice, Office of the Inspector General and Office of Professional Responsibility. *An Investigation into the Removal of Nine U.S. Attorneys in 2006*. (2008). www.justice.gov.

US Department of Justice, Office of Legal Counsel. "Memorandum, Proposed Executive Order Entitled 'Federal Regulation (Feb. 13, 1981)." *In Role of OMB in Regulation: Hearing Before Subcommittee on Oversight & Investigation of H. Comm. on Energy & Commerce, 97th Cong*. Washington, DC: Government Printing Office, 1981.

US Department of State. *Foreign Affairs Manual*. https://fam.state.gov/.

US Department of Transportation. "Smoking of Electronic Cigarettes on Aircraft." *Federal Register* 76, no. 179 (2011): 57008–012.

US Environmental Protection Agency. *Scientific Integrity Policy* (n.d.).

US Environmental Protection Agency. "Strengthening Transparency in Pivotal Science Underlying Significant Regulatory Actions and Influential Scientific Information." *Federal Register* 86, no. 3 (January 6, 2021): 469–93.

US Environmental Protection Agency, Office of Inspector General. *EPA Does Not Always Adhere to Its Established Action Development Process for Rulemaking.* (March 31, 2021). www.epa.gov/.

US President. Executive Order. "Improving Government Regulations, Executive Order 12,044 of March 23, 1978." *Federal Register* 43, no. 58 (March 24, 1978): 12661–665.

US President. Executive Order. "Federal Regulation, Executive Order 12,291 of February 17, 1981." *Federal Register* 46, no. 33 (February 18, 1981): 13193–198.

US President. Executive Order. "Regulatory Planning, Executive Order 12,498 of January 5, 1985." *Federal Register* 50, no. 5 (January 8, 1985): 1036–38.

US President. Executive Order. "Regulatory Planning and Review, Executive Order 12,866 of September 30, 1993." *Federal Register* 58, no. 190 (October 4, 1993): 51735–44.

US President. Executive Order. "Improving Regulation and Regulatory Review, Executive Order 13,563 of January 18, 2011." *Federal Register* 76, no. 14 (January 21, 2011): 3821–23.

US President. Executive Order. "Reducing Regulation and Controlling Regulatory Costs, Executive Order 13,771 of January 30, 2017." *Federal Register* 82, no. 22 (February 3, 2017): 9339–41.

US President. Memorandum. "Restoring Trust in Government Through Scientific Integrity and Evidence-Based Policymaking of January 27, 2021." *Federal Register* 86, no. 26 (February 10, 2021): 8845–51.

Use of Consultants and Contractors by the Envtl. Protection Agency and the Dep't of Energy: Hearing Before the Subcomm. on Fed. Serv., Post Office, and Civil Serv. of the Senate Comm. on Governmental Affairs, 101st Cong. 1 (1989).

Van Schooten, Daniel, and Nick Schwellenbach. "Stifling Dissent: How the Federal Government's Channels for Challenging Policies from Within Fall Short." *Project on Government Oversight* (July 31, 2020). www.pogo.org/.

Verkuil, Paul R. *Outsourcing Sovereignty: Why Privatization of Government Functions Threatens Democracy and What We Can Do about It.* Cambridge: Cambridge University Press, 2007.

Verkuil, Paul R. *Valuing Bureaucracy: The Case for Professional Government.* Cambridge: Cambridge University Press, 2017.

Vermeule, Adrian. "Conventions of Agency Independence." *Columbia Law Review* 113, no. 5 (2013): 1163–1238.

Vermeule, Adrian. *Law's Abnegation: From Law's Empire to the Administrative State.* Cambridge, MA: Harvard University Press, 2016.

Virelli, Louis. "Deconstructing Arbitrary and Capricious Review." *North Carolina Law Review* 92, no. 3 (2014): 721–86.

Volokh, Alexander. "The New Private-Regulation Skepticism: Due Process, Non-Delegation, and Antitrust Challenges." *Harvard Journal of Law and Public Policy* 37, no. 3: (2014): 931–1007.

Wagner, Wendy E. "The Science Charade in Toxic Risk Regulation." *Columbia Law Review* 95, no. 7 (1995): 1613–1723.

Wagner, Wendy E. "Science in Regulation: A Study of Agency Decision Making Approaches." Washington, DC: Administrative Conference of the US, February 18, 2013.

Wagner, Wendy E. "A Place for Agency Expertise: Reconciling Agency Expertise with Presidential Power." *Columbia Law Review* 115, no. 7 (2015): 2019–69.

Wagner, Wendy E. "It Isn't Easy Being a Bureaucratic Expert: Celebrating the EPA's Innovations." *Case Western Reserve Law Review* 70, no. 4 (Summer 2020): 1093–1120.

Wagner, Wendy E., and Will Walker. *Incomprehensible!: A Study of How Our Legal System Encourages Incomprehensibility, Why It Matters, and What We Can Do About It.* Cambridge: Cambridge University Press, 2019.

Walters, Daniel. "Litigation-Fostered Bureaucratic Autonomy: Administrative Law Against Political Control." *Journal of Law and Politics* 28, no. 2 (2013): 129–84.

Watts, Kathryn A. "Controlling Presidential Control." *Michigan Law Review* 114, no. 5 (2016): 683–745.

Webb, Romany, Lauren Kurtz, and Susan Rosenthal. "When Politics Trump Science: The Erosion of Science-Based Regulation." *Environmental Law Reporter* 50, no. 9 (2020): 10708–13.

Weiland, Noah. "How the C.D.C. Lost Its Voice Under Trump." *New York Times* (December 17, 2020), A-8.

Weiland, Noah, et al. "Political Appointees Meddled in CDC's Virus Literature." *New York Times* (September 13, 2020), A-4.

Werner, Erica. "White House Asserts Executive Privilege in EPA Dispute." *USA Today* (June 20, 2008). www.usatoday.com/.

Wheaton, Sara. "Obama to Ask His Political Appointees to Clear Way for Clinton." *Politico* (November 5, 2016). www.politico.com/.

White House, Office of the Press Secretary. "Memorandum for the Heads of Executive Departments and Agencies." March 9, 2009. https://obamawhitehouse.archives.gov/.

White House, Office of the Press Secretary. "Press Release: Obama Administration Finalizes Historic 54.5 MPG Fuel Efficiency Standards." August 28, 2012. https://obamawhitehouse.archives.gov/.

Williams, Walter. *Mismanaging America: The Rise of the Anti-Analytic Presidency.* Lawrence: University Press of Kansas, 1990.

Wilson, Woodrow. "The Study of Administration." *Political Science Quarterly* 2, no. 2 (June 1887): 197–222.

Wood, Stephen P., Jesse Chang, Thomas Healy, and John Wood. "The Potential Regulatory Challenges of Increasingly Autonomous Motor Vehicles." *Santa Clara Law Review* 52, no. 4 (2012): 1423–1502.

Wurman, Ilan. "Delegation at the Founding." *Yale Law Journal* 130, no. 6 (2021): 1490–1556.

Yackee, Susan Webb, and David Lowery. "Understanding Public Support for the U.S. Federal Bureaucracy: A Macro Politics View." *Public Management Review* 7, no. 4 (2005): 515–36.

INDEX

ACA. *See* Affordable Care Act

accessibility: limitations of, 215; in pluralism, 211; in rulemaking, 212–13. *See also* participation

accountability, 253n79, 274n48; of agencies, 261n41; in civil service, 205; in democracy, 137, 209, 226–27, 228–29; Madison on, 226–27, 229; political accountability justification regulatory action, 41–42

ACUS. *See* Administrative Conference of the United States

administrative agencies, 3–4, 15–16; accountability of, 261n41; agenda-setting, 253n68; autonomy of, 91–92, 242n60; binding of, 191; boundary-setting by, 216; bureaucrats in, 116–18; capture of, 139; citizen communication with, 211, 212; Congress delegation to, 91; congressional delegation to, 91; congressional oversight of, 177; contractors used by, 191; cost-benefit mandate impacting, 96–97; decision-making in, 81, 128–29; dissent channels at, 133; expertise of, 228–29; growth of, 113; hard look review and operation of, 158; heads of, 161; information development in, 123–28, 165–69; internal procedures, 150; judicial review for, 156–58, 260n35; leadership of, 170; leeway of, in choosing between rulemaking and adjudication, 158; legitimacy of, 197, 211, 228–29; outward-facing procedures, 150; personnel protection at, 131–34; politics-

expertise interface management of, 128–31; presidential administration and, 103–8; public trust in, 212–15; roles of, 10–11, 256n43; scientific staff at, 182; self-censorship at, 168; social media use by, 216; websites of, 179–80. *See also* independent agencies

Administrative Conference of the United States (ACUS), 102; on participation, 220–21; on rulemaking, 213, 216

administrative law, 8, 210

administrative presidency, 115

Administrative Procedure Act (APA), 39, 45, 75, 210, 242n53, 274n47; comment process, 219; judicial review under, 139–40, 148; rulemaking provisions, 140–41, 156, 212; statutory law and, 137

administrative record, 27, 95, 147, 149, 150–51, 156–58, 180, 191, 257n54, 260n28

Advance Notice of Proposed Rulemaking (ANPRM), 219–20

Affordable Care Act (ACA), 261n37; Roberts on, 79–80

Afghanistan, 188–89

Age of Uncertainty, The (TV), 25

AIDS, 272n23

ancillary functions, outsourcing of, 193

animal testing, 126

ANPRM. *See* Advance Notice of Proposed Rulemaking

antidemocratic dilemma, 68

anti-elitism, 63

anti-regulation movement, 24–25; political impact of, 25–26; pre-Reagan, 26–28 antitrust laws, 82

APA. *See* Administrative Procedure Act

Arab Oil Embargo, 23

Article II, Constitution, 32, 39, 43, 90, 94, 101

Atwater, Lee, 254n98

at-will firing, 108–9

audits, 212

Auer v. Robbins, 60

Barrett, Amy Coney, 247n14

Bazelon, David, 141–42

Bell Report, 200, 202, 203

Biden, Joe, 62, 68, 69, 169, 172, 204; on climate change, 103

bipartisan agreement, 86

Bituminous Coal Conservation Act, 46n12

blue pencil editing, 172–76

Brown v. Board of Education, 158

bureaucracy, 5; under Clinton, 57; defining, 226; democracy and, 227–28; goals of, 116–18; Golden on, 118–21; growth of, 113; history of, 183–85; needs of, 200–201; politicization of, 13; public trust in, 21, 58–60, 244n41; under Reagan, 117–21, 186–87; rebuilding, 201–4; reorganization of, 232; science and, 167–68; sources of perceived incompetence of, 239n22; success of, 3; White House influence on, 271n9. *See also* civil service

bureaucrat bashing, 31; public trust and, 58–60; studies on, 59

bureaucrats: in agencies, 116–18; citizen communication with, 211; decision-making of, 122–23; goals of, 116–18; incentives for, 121–23; role of, 121–22, 198; self-interest of, 121–22

Bush, George H. W., 113; regulatory review under, 49

Bush, George W., 13, 55, 114, 202; Hurricane Katrina and, 106; on peer review, 264n21; political appointees under, 124;

presidential administration under, 51–53; rulemaking under, 243n14

cabinet members: filling strategies, 240n23; under Nixon, 99–100. *See also* political appointees

Carter, Jimmy, 12, 25, 27, 36, 38, 113, 167; deregulation under, 186

Carter v. Carter Coal, 242n52

CBA. *See* cost-benefit analysis

Centers for Disease Control and Prevention (CDC), 64, 166, 206; in COVID-19 pandemic, 168, 173; Morbidity and Mortality Weekly Report, 173

CFPB. *See* Consumer Financial Protection Bureau

Chamber of Commerce, US, 24

Chevron USA v. Natural Resources Defense Council, 40–42, 44, 47, 60, 62, 85; deference, 78–79, 81, 152–53, 242n45, 242n48, 242n49, 247n21, 261n39; statutory interpretation in, 152–53

Circular A-76, OMB, 187–88, 192, 195, 197, 268n38; on sovereign functions, 199

citizen-juries, 223–25, 227

civil rights, 22, 86; Republican Party on, 238n2

Civil Rights Act of 1964, 86

Civil Rights Division (CRD), 118, 120. *See also* Department of Justice

civil service, 180; accountability in, 205; attacks on, 186–87; authority in, 204–6; career paths in, 202–3; Clinton on, 188, 192; DiIulio on, 202; expertise in, 198–99, 204–5; federal government, 202, 205; history of, 183–85; job protection in, 190; modern, 183–85; Nixon on, 186; outsourcing of, 189–92; Reagan on, 31; reforming, 204–6; salaries in, 205; Trump on, 204; White House influence over staff, 112–15; workforce quality in, 202–3; working conditions in, 203–4

Civil Service Reform Law, 1978, 113

Clean Air Act, 3, 26, 86, 103, 274n48; EPA and, 93, 137, 159; hard look review and, 159

Clean Power Plan, 193

Clean Water Act, 3

clear statement rules, 83

climate change, 86, 174, 196; Biden on, 103; DOE on, 170; DOI on, 167; EPA on, 167; research on, 170; suppression of information about, 180; Trump on, 124

Clinton, Bill, 13, 68; bureaucracy under, 57; on CBA, 95–96; on civil service, 188, 192; independent agencies under, 109; National Performance Review under, 201; OIRA under, 95; presidential administration under, 48–51, 56–57; regulatory review under, 49–50, 95; Reinventing Government initiative, 188; rulemaking directives, 104; social welfare under, 267n23; on unemployment insurance, 104

Cold War, 188

Collins, Harry, 6–7

command and control regulation, 238n11

community of practice, 218–19

Community Review Teams, 224

comprehensive analytical rationality, 9

confirmation bias, 62–63

Congress, 14, 73; agencies overseen by, 177; congressional supremacy, 140; constitutional oversight responsibilities of, 127; delegation to administrative agencies, 91; disclosure of information to, 177; failures of, 85–87; federal law and, 94; independent agencies influenced by, 109; information distortion and oversight of, 174; non-delegation doctrine and, 74–78; oversight by, 249n7; regulatory review by, 127; statutory authority of, 43–44

Constitution, US: Article II, 32, 39, 43, 90, 94, 101; Fifth Amendment, 39, 257n3; First Amendment, 64, 264n23

constitutional jurisprudence: under Rehnquist, 60; under Roberts, 61–62

Consumer Financial Protection Bureau (CFPB), 222, 224

contractors, 189–90; agency use of, 191; at EPA, 193; federal government use of, 114, 189, 192, 241n34, 267n18; outsourcing, 114; suggested reduction of reliance on, 202–3; Trump administration use of, 191; Verkuil on, 194

contributory expertise, 7

coronavirus pandemic. See COVID-19 pandemic

cost-benefit analysis (CBA), 33–34, 54; Clinton on, 95–96; of OIRA, 93; regulatory review distorted by, 95–96

cost-benefit mandate, 37, 49; agencies impacted by, 96–97

Council on Economic Advisors, 108

Council on Economic Quality, 103

COVID-19 pandemic, 3–5, 17–18, 55, 177, 190, 207, 231–32; CDC in, 168, 173; Delta variant, 233; information during, 179; Trump and, 124, 173, 231; vaccine, 12, 64

CRD. See Civil Rights Division

criminal law, 183, 187

DC Circuit, 141, 150, 159

decision-making, 142–43, 200; in agencies, 81, 128–29; of bureaucrats, 122–23; information in, 165, 168; politics in, 175–76

Deep State, 55

deference: to agencies' own regulations, 60, 62; Chevron, 78–79, 81, 242n45, 242n48, 242n49, 247n21, 261n39; expertise and, 244n48; of judicial review, 139; political accountability and, 41–42; Roberts on, 79–80; Supreme Court on, 242n45 democracy: accountability in, 137, 209, 226–27, 228; bureaucracy and, 227–28; expertise and, 12; legitimacy in, 208–9; non-delegation doctrine and, 209; participation in, 227; public trust and, 207

Democratic Party, 25; New Democrats, 56–57, 188

dental programs, 189

Department of Agriculture, 36, 180. *See also* Food and Nutrition Service

Department of Energy (DOE), 193; on climate change, 170; under Trump, 117; use of contractors, 193

Department of Health and Human Services, 173

Department of Homeland Security (DHS), 106, 191, 206

Department of Interior (DOI), 36; on climate change, 167; information at, 166–67; Inspector General investigation, 134; National Academy of Sciences and, 170. *See also* Fish and Wildlife Service; National Park Service; US Geological Survey

Department of Justice, 94. *See also* Civil Rights Division

Department of Labor, 104

Department of Transportation (DOT), 217, 221. *See also* National Highway Transportation and Safety Administration

Department of Veterans Affairs, 4

deregulation: under Carter, 186; under Clinton, 56; expertise and, 239n5; under Nixon, 35–37; under Reagan, 30–31, 42–47, 118–21, 186, 209. *See also* anti-regulation movement

desegregation, 158

Desert One, 1

DHS. *See* Department of Homeland Security

DiIulio, John, 192, 198, 205; on civil servants, 202

discretion, 220

dissent channels, at agencies, 133

DOE. *See* Department of Energy

DOI. *See* Department of Interior

Doremus, Holly, 257n54

DOT. *See* Department of Transportation

Douthat, Ross, 12

Dreyfus, Hubert, 7–8

Dreyfus, Stuart, 7–8

due process, 136

Due Process Clause, Fifth Amendment, 39, 257n3

Eisenhower, Dwight, 22, 167

electoral outcomes, 209, 248n2

electronic cigarettes, 217

Environmental Impact Statement, 224

environmental law, 32–33

Environmental Protection Agency (EPA), 5, 9, 32, 33–34, 36, 42, 118, 166, 249n13; authority to regulate air pollution, 93, 137; chemical risk assessment database of, 174–75; Clean Air Act and, 93, 137, 159; on climate change, 167; contractors at, 193; expertise at, 130, 157–58; under Gorsuch, 119; hit lists at, 130–32; information at, 166–67; McGarity on, 123, 129; NHTSA and, 176–77; under Obama, 173, 193; OIRA and, 174; on particulate matter pollution, 157, 169; on private data, 264n17; rulemaking, 129; Science Advisory Board, 173; Science Transparency Rule, 170–72, 269n47; under Trump, 170, 176, 269n47

environmental regulation, support for, 238n8

EPA. *See* Environmental Protection Agency

epistemic bubbles, 64–69; expertise and, 68; Internet and, 66–67; on social media, 216; talk radio and, 65–67

Equal Rights Amendment, 239n1

Evans, Robert, 6–7

Executive Order 12,291, 32, 35, 37, 40, 49, 93, 94, 240n14

Executive Order 12,866, 49

expertise, 16; of agencies, 228; American attitudes on, 14; in civil service, 198–99, 204–5; contributory, 7; credibility of, 174; decline of, 2; deference and, 244n48; defining, 5–10; democracy and, 12; deregulation and, 239n5; at EPA, 130, 157–58; epistemic bubbles and, 68; in-house, 198; interactional, 7, 237n13; iterative processes of, 176; judicial review reinforcing, 146–49; 264n19; outsourcing of, 195, 196; political appointees and, 231–32; politics and, 12, 128–31, 157; public participation and, 227; public trust in, 62–64, 207–8; quasi-instinctual, 7; rationality and, 160; regulatory, 8–10, 91, 129–30, 196; role of, 122; science and, 6, 182; sovereign functions and, 194–200; technical, 254n88; Wagner on, 182; White House administration and, 110–12; White House influence and, 112

expert participation in regulation, importance of, 130, 198

external advisory boards, 178

Eyal, Gil, 7–8, 63

FAA. *See* Federal Aviation Administration

Facebook, 64, 222

factions, 225–26

Fairness Doctrine, 65

FCC. *See* Federal Communications Commission

FDA. *See* Food and Drug Administration

feasibility principle, 250n28

Federal Aviation Administration (FAA), 208

Federal Communications Commission (FCC), 40, 42, 65, 76, 109; on rulemaking, 214

Federal Emergency Management Agency (FEMA), 106, 208

federal government: civil servants used by, 202, 205; contractors used by, 114, 189, 192, 241n34, 267n18; expenditures, 185; public trust in, 21; Reagan on, 59; reinvention of, 56–57; size of, 56–57; social problems addressed by, 78; websites, 180. *See also* sovereign functions

federalism, 225–26

Federal Register, 194–95, 212, 215

Federal Reserve Board, 40, 109

FEMA. *See* Federal Emergency Management Agency

Fifth Amendment, Constitution, 39, 257n3

Fifth Risk, The (Lewis), 117

Firing Line (TV), 66

First Amendment, Constitution, 64, 264n23

Fish and Wildlife Service (FWS), 134, 166. *See also* Department of Interior

Flint, Michigan, 4

FNS. *See* Food and Nutrition Service

focus groups, 220, 245n59; NHTSA use of, 222–23

FOIA. *See* Freedom of Information Act

Food and Drug Administration (FDA), 36, 166, 272n23

Food and Nutrition Service (FNS), 118, 124. *See also* Department of Agriculture

Ford, Gerald, 23–24, 26

Fox News, 66–67

fracking, 173

Freedom of Information Act (FOIA), 265n39

free market advocates, 187

Free to Choose (TV), 25

Friedman, Milton, 25

FWS. *See* Fish and Wildlife Service

Galbraith, John Kenneth, 25

Garfield, James, 185

Garland, Merrick, 150
Golden, Marissa, 31, 100, 124, 127, 130, 149, 161, 265n32; on bureaucracy, 118–21
Goldwater, Barry, 22; campaign of, 29
Gorsuch, Anne, 232; EPA under, 119
Great Depression, 185
Great Society, 22, 24, 185
greenhouse gases, regulation of, 77–78
gridlock, congressional, 111–12

Hamilton, Alexander, 111
Hansen, James, 172, 174
hard look review, 141–46, 148–49; agency operation and, 158; Clean Air Act and, 159; defense of, 145–46; defining, 141; rulemaking ossification from, 144; *State Farm* and, 143–46
Hirschman, Albert, 119
hit lists, at EPA, 130–32
Hubble Telescope, 6
Hurricane Katrina, 207; Bush, G. W., and, 106
hydraulic fracking, 173

IGs. *See* Inspectors General
independent agencies, 32, 45, 49, 60; under Clinton, 109; congressional influence on, 109; constitutionality of, 40, 42; defining, 240n14; informal norms regarding, 109; under Reagan, 109; reconceptualizing, 109–10; regulatory expertise of, 91; unitary executive theory and, 43; White House influence and, 108–10
industrialization, 63
Inflation Impact Statements, 26
information, 135; agency development of, 123–28, 165–69; alteration of, 172–76; blue pencil editing of, 172–76; climate change and suppression of, 180; during COVID-19 pandemic, 179; in decision-making, 165, 168; development of, 169–72; disclosure of, to

Congress, 177; disclosure of, to public, 177–79, 266n48; dissemination of, 122; distortion of, 172–76; at DOI, 166–67; at EPA, 166–67; integrity of, 180–81; McGarity on processing of, 125–26; as power, 169; role of, 180–81; science and development of, 126, 196; suppression of, 176–80; Wagner on processing of, 125–26
Inspectors General (IGs), 133–34, 257n54
intelligible principle, 61, 75–77
interactional expertise, 7, 237n13
interest groups, 223–24
Internal Revenue Service (IRS), 4. 80
Internet, 52; epistemic bubbles and, 66–67; participation and, 214; rulemaking and, 213–14
interpretive authority, Congress and, 80–85
Interstate Commerce Act, 185
Interstate Commerce Commission, 253n74
Iraq War, 188–89
iron triangle, 99
IRS. *See* Internal Revenue Service
Italian Communist Party, 23

Jackson, Andrew, 184, 190
Johnson, Lyndon B., 2, 22, 29, 167, 185
judicial doctrine, under Reagan, 39–42
judicial review, 260n26; agency records for, 156–58, 260n35; under APA, 139–40, 148; benchmarks for, 154; deference of, 139; different styles of, 139–41; expertise-reinforcing, 146–49, 264n19; goals of, 136–39; hard look, 141–46; implementation of, 154–56; politics and, 147, 155; pre-decisional documents as important for, 156–57; science in, 154–55; stringency of, 139–40. *See also* hard look review; procedural review
Judulang v. Holder, 261n39; statutory interpretation and, 152–53

Kagan, Elena, 49, 52, 92, 103–4; on partisanship, 111–12; on presidential administration, 111–12; on regulatory review, 104–5; on technical expertise, 254n88
Kavanaugh, Brett, 247n14
Kennedy, John F., 2, 21–22, 113
King v. Burwell, 79–81, 261n37
Korean War, 185

legal briefs, 218
legal doctrine, under Reagan, 39–42
legitimacy: of agencies, 197, 211, 228–29; in democracy, 208–9
Leventhal, Harold, 142
Lewis, Michael, 117, 190, 231
LGBT rights, 86
libertarianism, 24
Light, Paul, 239n20, 254n100
Limbaugh, Rush, 65–66
Lippman, Walter, 63, 67, 69
listening sessions, 220
lobbyists, 193; growth of, 238n7
Lowi, Theodore, 75
Luntz, Frank, 64

Madison, James, 210, 223–24, 273n43; on accountability, 226–27, 229; on factions, 225–26; on federalism, 225–26
Madisonian structure, 225–28, 229
majority, tyranny of, 210
major questions doctrine, 78–81; drawbacks of, 87; non-delegation doctrine and, 84, 87; stronger version of, 82–85
managers, tasks as distinct from regulating, 198
mass commenting, 213–14
mass media, politicization and, 64–65
McGarity, Thomas, 9–10; on EPA, 123, 129; on information processing, 125–26; on regulatory review, 125
McLaughlin Group, The (TV), 66

Medicaid, 189–90
Meet the Press (TV), 66
methane, 137
Michaels, Jon, 38, 251n32, 268n38; on OIRA, 98
minimal reasonableness, 261n42
Mobil Oil Corporation, 238n7
Morrison v. Olson, 43
mortgages, 222
Motor Vehicle Manufacturers Association v. State Farm Mutual Insurance Company, 45–46, 53, 85, 154–55, 160, 259n19; hard look review of, 143–46; NHTSA in, 120–21, 149; procedural review in, 150–51
Mounk, Yasha, 68
MSNBC, 66–67

NASA, 172, 206
National Academy of Sciences, DOI and, 170
National Bureau of Standards (NBS), 167
National Driver's Test, The, 273n38
National Highway Transportation and Safety Administration (NHTSA), 45, 91, 118–19, 143–44, 256n24; EPA and, 176–77; focus groups used by, 222–23; in *State Farm* case, 120–21, 149. *See also* Department of Transportation
National Industrial Recovery Act (NIRA), striking down of, 76
National Labor Relations Board (NLRB), 109
National Oceanic and Atmospheric Administration (NOAA), 6, 166
National Park Service (NPS), 4, 166. *See also* Department of Interior
National Performance Review, 201
National Security Council, 232
natural gas regulation, 96
NBS. *See* National Bureau of Standards
net neutrality, 214, 224

New Deal, 13, 22, 24, 30, 47, 48, 56, 185

New Democrats, 56–57, 188

New York Times, 238n7

NHTSA. *See* National Highway Transportation and Safety Administration

Nimitz, USS, 1

1984 (Orwell), 179

NIRA. *See* National Industrial Recovery Act

Nixon, Richard, 2, 26; cabinet members under, 99–100; on civil service, 186; deregulation under, 35–37; PSAC eliminated by, 167

NLRB. *See* National Labor Relations Board

NOAA. *See* National Oceanic and Atmospheric Administration

non-delegation doctrine, 44–45, 61; Congress and, 74–78; democracy and, 209; drawbacks of, 87; enforcement of, 77–78; major questions doctrine and, 84, 87; statutory interpretation and, 105

non-discrimination, 86

norms, 127; in independent agencies, 109

Notice of Proposed Rulemaking (NPRM), 219

NPS. *See* National Park Service

Obama, Barack, 13, 54, 167, 222; EPA under, 173, 193; natural gas regulation under, 96; presidential administration under, 51–53

Occupational Safety and Health Administration (OSHA), 6, 27, 30, 31, 33, 68, 94–95, 175; OIRA and, 97; workplace exposure standards, 251n32

Office of Information and Regulatory Affairs (OIRA), 32–33, 49, 128, 209, 251n32; CBA of, 93; under Clinton, 95; constitutionality of, 101; defenses of, 93–94; EPA and, 174; Michaels on, 98; OSHA and, 97; policy costs of its regulatory review, 100–101; under

Reagan, 93–95, 98, 101–2; regulatory review, 92–101; role of, 101–3; White House influence and, 92–103. *See also* Office of Management and Budget

Office of Management and Budget (OMB), 32, 52, 54; Circular A-76, 187–88, 192, 195, 197, 199, 268n38; in regulatory review, 102; White House influence on, 252n58. *See also* Office of Information and Regulatory Affairs

oil industry, 238n7

OIRA. *See* Office of Information and Regulatory Affairs

OMB. *See* Office of Management and Budget

Orwell, George, 180

OSHA. *See* Occupational Safety and Health Administration

outsourcing, 59, 182, 206, 268n29; of ancillary functions, 193; of civil service, 189–92; contractors, 114; scope of, 192–94; of sovereign functions, 194–95, 199

outsourcing, effects of, 189–92

outsourcing, of expertise, 195, 196

outsourcing, under Reagan, 37–38

Outsourcing Sovereignty (Verkuil), 194

particulate matter pollution, 169; EPA on, 157

partisanship: bipartisan agreement, 86; gridlock, 111–12; Kagan on, 111–12

patronage system, 184

peer review, 157; Bush, G. W., on, 264n21

Pendleton Act, 185, 205

Pentagon Papers, 24

personnel, protection of, at agencies, 131–34

Pew Research Center, 4, 24

pinstripe patronage, 190

Plan B contraceptive, 52

plebiscites, 220

pluralism, 271n6; accessibility in, 211; defining, 210; power in, 210; in regulatory law, 210–11

polarization, 3

police force, 184

political accountability: as component of public trust in government, 208–9; justification for *Chevron* deference, 41–42

political appointees: under Bush, G. W., 124; contractors used by, 114; experts' relations with, 231–32; leadership of, 114; numbers of, 113; performance of, 203; under Reagan, 113–14, 254n100; reliance on, 205; Schedule C, 113, 254n98, 270n67; under Trump, 124; Verkuil on, 114; Volker on, 114–15; White House influence over, 99–100, 112–15. *See also* cabinet members

political vetting, 89; under Reagan, 35–37

politicization: of bureaucracy, 13; of regulations, 42

politics: in decision-making, 175–76; expertise and, 12, 128–31, 157; judicial review and, 147, 155; science and, 126–27, 155, 167–68, 170–71

Postal Service, 4

Powell, Lewis, 24–25

Premonition, The (Lewis), 231–32

presidential administration, 89, 92, 263n56; agency action and, 103–8; under Bush, G. W., 51–53; under Clinton, 48–51, 56–57; goals of, 90; Kagan on, 111–12; under Obama, 51–53; regulatory review and, 48–51; rulemaking and, 243n14; under Trump, 53–56; Wilson on, 90. *See also* White House influence; White House review

President's Science Advisory Committee (PSAC): Johnson vetting potential members of, 167; Nixon eliminating, 167

prison population, 241n31

privatization, 47; under Reagan, 37–38; in Texas, 189–90. *See also* outsourcing

procedural fairness justification for administrative autonomy, 249n11

procedural requirements in regulatory process, 127, 137–38, 239n22

procedural review, 146; quasi-procedural review, 151, 161; in *State Farm* case, 150–51; in *Vermont Yankee* case, 150–51

Program Assessment Rating Tool, 14

Progressive Era, 92

Proposition 13, 25

PSAC. *See* President's Science Advisory Committee

the public: disclosure of information to, 177–79, 266n48; government interaction with, 179

public affairs officials within agencies, 180

public interest, 211

public participation in regulation, 233; ACUS on, 220–21; of citizen-juries, 223–25, 227; in democracy, 227; expertise and, 227; formats for, 221–22; Internet and, 214; regulations.gov and, 212–17; technology and, 222–23; vehicles for, 220–21

public trust, 2, 3, 17; in agencies, 212–15; in bureaucracy, 21, 58–60, 244n41; bureaucrat bashing and, 58–60; components of, 208–11; democracy and, 207; in expertise, 62–64, 207–8; in federal government, 21; Watergate and, 239n20

quasi-instinctual expertise, 7

quasi-procedural review, 151, 161

racial equality, 238n2

RARG. *See* Regulatory Analysis Review Group

rationality, 239n22; comprehensive analytical, 9; expertise-based, 160

Reagan, Ronald, 12–15, 25, 38, 59, 68, 255n23; anti-regulation movement before, 26–28; bureaucracy under, 117–21, 186–87; deregulation under, 30–31, 42–47, 118–21, 186, 209; election of, 27–30; on federal government, 59; independent agencies under, 109; legal and judicial doctrine under, 39–42; OIRA under, 93–95, 98, 101–2; outsourcing under, 37–38; political appointees of, 113–14, 254n100; political vetting under, 35–37; privatization under, 37–38; regulatory review under, 31–35, 48–49, 104

reasoned decision, 142

Reform of Regulation Act, 27

regulation: command and control, 238n11; defining, 91; environmental, 238n8; of greenhouse gases, 77–78; invisibility of, 208; natural gas, 96; participation in, 216; politicization of, 42; promulgation of, 11, 53, 104, 239n22; under Trump, 53–54. See also deregulation

regulations.gov, 212–17

Regulatory Analysis Review Group (RARG), 26–27

regulatory czars, 53

regulatory expertise, 8–10, 129–30; of independent agencies, 91; scientific knowledge and, 196

regulatory failures, 4–5

regulatory law: pluralism in, 210–11; republicanism in, 210–11

regulatory rationality, 9–10

regulatory review: under Bush, G. H. W., 49; CBA distorted by, 95–96; under Clinton, 49–50, 95; of Congress, 127–28; Kagan on, 104–5; McGarity on, 125; of OIRA, 92–101; OMB in, 102; presidential administration and, 48–51; under Reagan, 31–35, 48–49, 104. See also Office of Information and Regulatory Affairs; White House review

Rehnquist, William, 46; constitutional jurisprudence under, 60; death of, 61

Reinventing Government initiative, 188

representatives, communication with, 211

republicanism, 227–28; defining, 210; deliberation in, 210–11; power in, 210; in regulatory law, 210–11

Republican National Committee (RNC), 37

Republican Party, 22, 51; on civil rights, 238n2

RNC. See Republican National Committee

Roberts, John: on ACA, 79–80; on regulatory law, 61

Roosevelt, Franklin, 12–13, 22, 139

Rose Garden, 50–51, 103

Ruckelshaus, William, 120

rulemaking, 239n22; accessibility in, 212–13; ACUS on, 213, 216; APA procedures for, 140–41, 156, 212; under Bush, G. W., 243n14; under Clinton, 104; community of practice in, 218–19; deliberation in, 219–20; DOT, 217; EPA, 129; FCC on, 214; finding information about, 212; hard look review and, 144; incentivization of citizen engagement with, 215; informal, 260n28, 263n56; Internet and, 213–14; presidential administration and, 243n14; process broadening, 219–22; public understanding of, 218–19; scientific knowledge and, 221

Sagebrush Rebellion, 25

Scalia, Antonin, 42, 245n53

Schedule C positions, 113, 254n98, 270n67

Schlafly, Phyllis, 239n1

Schoenbrod, David, 75

science: bureaucracy and, 167–68; defining, 5–6; expertise and, 6, 182; information development and, 126, 196; integrity policies, 167; in judicial review, 154–55; politics and, 126–27, 155, 167–68, 170–71; regulatory expertise and, 196; rulemaking and knowledge of, 221. *See also* information

Science Advisory Board, EPA, 173

Science Advisory Committee. *See* President's Science Advisory Committee

Science Transparency Rule, EPA, 269n47; justification for, 170–71; striking down of, 171–72

scientific modeling, 124; assumptions in, 196

scientific staff, at agencies, 182

seat belts, 259n18

Sebelius, Kathleen, 52

SEC. *See* Securities and Exchange Commission

Second Oil Shock (1979), 23, 58

Second Volker Commission, 205

Securities and Exchange Commission (SEC), 6, 11, 53, 76–77, 91

self-censorship, at agencies, 168

self-interest, of bureaucrats, 121–22

Senior Executive Service (SES), 113; reforming, 206

separation of powers, 192

September 11, 2001 attacks, 24

SES. *See* Senior Executive Service

Sexual Offender Registration and Notification Act (SORNA), 77

Shapiro, Sidney, 8–10

shell games, 80, 85

socialization model, 255n7

social media, 52, 64, 67, 273n33; agency use of, 216; epistemic bubbles on, 216

Social Security Administration, 212

social welfare, under Clinton, 267n23

soot pollution, 157, 169

SORNA. *See* Sexual Offender Registration and Notification Act

sovereign functions: Circular A-76 on, 199; defining, 192–93, 199–200; ex-

pertise and, 194–200; outsourcing of, 194–95, 199; Verkuil on, 194–95

Soviet Union, 37

spoils system, 184, 190, 266n5

standing doctrine, 139

statutory grants of regulatory authority, 84–85

statutory interpretation, 80–82, 93–94; in *Chevron* case, 152–53; *Judulang v. Holder* and, 152–53; non-delegation doctrine and, 105

statutory law, APA and, 137

Stevens, John Paul, 41, 81

Sunlight Foundation, 266n51

Supreme Court, US, 40, 43, 62, 64, 86, 140; on deference, 242n45

talk radio, epistemic bubbles and, 65–67

taxation, 183, 187; audits, 212; tax credits, 80–81

technical expertise, 254n88

technical feasibility, 96–97

Telecommunications Act, 65

tenure, 205

Texas, privatization in, 189

Thomas, Lee, 120

Trump, Donald, 13–14, 17–18, 64, 196; on civil servants, 204; on climate change, 124; contractors used by, 191; COVID-19 and, 124, 173, 231; DOE under, 117; EPA under, 170, 176, 269n47; executive orders under, 53–54; lies of, 55; on natural gas regulations, 96; political appointees under, 124; presidential administration under, 53–56; regulations under, 53–54

trust. *See* public trust

Twitter, 64, 222

tyranny of the majority, 210

Ukraine, 55

unemployment insurance, under Clinton, 104

unitary executive theory, 40, 47, 241n38; independent agencies and, 43
United Kingdom, 37
United States Steel, 37
US Geological Survey (USGS), 124, 166, 196, 264n32. *See also* Department of Interior

Verkuil, Paul, 4, 38, 205; on contractors, 194; on political appointees, 114; on sovereign functions, 194–95
Vermeule, Adrian, 259n19
Vermont Yankee Nuclear Power Corp. v. Natural Resources Defense Council, 140, 145–46, 156, 159; procedural review in, 150–51
Vietnam War, 2, 23, 185
Vindman, Alexander, 54–55
Volker, Paul, 205; on political appointees, 114–15
Volker Report, 114–15, 203–4
voting, 209

Wagner, Wendy: on expertise, 182; on information processing, 125–26
Wald, Patricia, 159
Wallace, George, 22
Wall Street, 11

Washington Post, 114
Watergate, 24; public trust and, 239n20
websites, of agencies, 179–80
whistleblowers, protection of, 132–33
White, Byron, 151
White House administration, 103–8; expertise and, 110–12
White House influence, 228–29, 231; balancing with agency autonomy, 90–92; on bureaucracy, 271n9; over civil service staff, 112–15; criticisms of, 106–7; defining, 89–90; expertise and, 112; federal law and, 94; inappropriate, 89–90; independent agencies and, 108–10; informal, 105, 110–11; OIRA and, 92–103; on OMB, 252n58; over political appointees, 99–100, 112–15; studies on effects of, 253n83
White House review of regulatory action, 15, 28, 35, 44, 95; criticism of, 96; defense of, 99
Wilson, Woodrow, 92; on presidential administration, 90
Wolverines, 231–32
World War II, 23, 185

Xerox, 189

ABOUT THE AUTHOR

WILLIAM D. ARAIZA is the Stanley A. August Professor of Law at Brooklyn Law School. He teaches and writes in the areas of constitutional law, First Amendment law, and administrative law. Professor Araiza earned a BA from Columbia University, an MS from Georgetown University, and a JD from Yale University. After law school he clerked for Judge William Norris of the US Court of Appeals for the Ninth Circuit, and for Justice David Souter of the US Supreme Court.

www.ingramcontent.com/pod-product-compliance
Lightning Source LLC
Chambersburg PA
CBHW031535260326
41914CB00032B/1820/J